Creating
Connections

Creating Connections

Museums and the Public Understanding of Current Research

DAVID CHITTENDEN, GRAHAM FARMELO,
AND BRUCE V. LEWENSTEIN

A Division of
ROWMAN & LITTLEFIELD PUBLISHERS, INC.
Walnut Creek • *Lanham* • *New York* • *Toronto* • *Oxford*

AltaMira Press
A division of Rowman & Littlefield Publishers, Inc.
1630 North Main Street, #367
Walnut Creek, CA 94596
www.altamirapress.com

Rowman & Littlefield Publishers, Inc.
A wholly owned subsidary of The Rowman & Littlefield Publishing Group, Inc.
4501 Forbes Boulevard, Suite 200
Lanham, MD 20706

PO Box 317
Oxford
OX2 9RU, UK

British Library Cataloguing in Publication Information Available

Library of Congress Cataloging-in-Publication Data

Chittenden, David, 1944–
    Creating connections : museums and the public understanding of current research /
David Chittenden, Graham Farmelo, and Bruce V. Lewenstein.
        p. cm.
Includes bibliographical references and index.
    ISBN 0-7591-0475-1 (cloth : alk. paper)—ISBN 0-7591-0476-X (pbk. : alk. paper)
    1. Museums—Social aspects. 2. Museum exhibits—Social aspects. 3. Science—Social
aspects. 4. Research—Public opinion. 5. Communication and culture. 6. Cultural
property—Protection. 7. Museums—Historiography. 8. Museums—Philosophy.
I. Farmelo, Graham. II. Lewenstein, Bruce V. III. Title.
    AM7.C48 2004
    069—dc22
                                2003020351

Printed in the United States of America

∞™ The paper used in this publication meets the minimum requirements of American
National Standard for Information Sciences—Permanence of Paper for Printed Library
Materials, ANSI/NISO Z39.48–1992.

Contents

Foreword

Bill Nye

It may be that deep down we are all researchers. Don't we all have an interest in the world around us, in the nature of nature? Look around the room where you're sitting or where you picked up this book: everything you see was produced or shaped by people—even your houseplants and especially your dog. Every time we throw a mass-produced ball, a light switch, or trash into a bin to be carried away by trucks, we are taking advantage of technology brought to us ultimately by research. If you've had a vaccination, taken antibiotics, or had an infected appendix removed, you have benefited from research. Not all of us have the inclination to pursue a career in science or research, but science and research affect us all daily as we consider buying organic produce, getting another vaccination, or driving a particular kind of car.

This fundamentally human need to find out about the world led to the creation of this book. Think about it: there are so many people with so much to learn that we are long past the point where it is individually possible to know everything. We are in an era where we need special people to tell the rest of us what's going on in science. For me, there's nothing more important or exciting than the creation of these kinds of translations, from the world of research to all of us—and sometimes back again. Museums are an especially cool place for these translations because they combine real objects and hands-on opportunities with spaces for doing research. To bring together ideas from all kinds of translators—scientists, journalists, television producers, *and* museum staff—the Science Museum of Minnesota, supported by the National Science Foundation, organized a conference titled "Museums, Media, and Public Understanding of Research" in the fall of 2002.

The importance of this kind of work is hard to exaggerate. We're living in a remarkable time. We can feed heretofore unimaginable numbers of people, we can send missions to Mars, and we can save and extend lives that only a century ago would have been doomed. Yet the more technology we develop, the more is at stake. There are new epidemics each year, our crops are less diverse and almost certainly more susceptible to devastation, we have tens of thousands of tons of nuclear material and waste stored in essentially temporary facilities around the world, and it looks like we've altered the climate of our whole planet, pretty much by accident. Understanding all of this is more than important: it's vital.

People lived for millions of years without an alphabet and for perhaps 30,000 more years without making a phone call. But in just the past few centuries, people have discovered astonishing things about the cosmos and the operation of everything from physics to genes. It's not just that we're learning new things, we're learning new things at an ever-increasing rate. There is so much that we *could* know that it would be very difficult indeed to have as thorough an understanding of the body of human knowledge today as, say, Leonardo da Vinci had of the body of human knowledge in his time. It would take *more* than a lifetime. That's why educating the public about science and research is so important: we all need to know of new discoveries just to be literate citizens.

As you look through this volume, you will get a glimpse of the processes involved in producing exhibits, museum programs, television shows, and journalism that can lead to a scientifically literate populace. These authors have something to tell us. They want us to know what they've learned about informing the public and to appreciate how important and exciting it is. Of course, for me there is nothing more exciting than science. Every minute of every day, something new that affects us all is discovered. As Carl Sagan once pointed out in his charming, matter-of-fact style, "When you're in love, you want to tell the world."

I know I do. I spent several years developing a kids' television show about science called *Bill Nye, the Science Guy*. We aimed our show at ten-year-olds, fourth graders in the United States. It seemed at that time (in the early 1990s) that ten is about as old as you can be to develop that lifelong passion for science. But it turns out a decade later that about half our viewers are grown-ups, adults with an interest in elementary science. In the United States, people watch a lot of television, some as much as eight hours a day (yikes!). In that time, they watch a great deal of science programming. I always assumed they watch science mostly because it is on and, perhaps, because it is more interesting than much of what else our hundreds of channels have to offer. In my occasional trips abroad, however, I have learned that people all over the world love science and research, with and without televisions, and are fascinated by such things as magnetism, digestion, and lightning. We humans can't get enough.

So how do we go about getting information about new scientific developments—about research!—out to the public? You can start with this book. At least half of what each of us knows about science and the research associated with it was learned informally, outside the classroom. The work that these authors do through museum exhibits, video production, newspapers, and magazines acknowledges and exploits this informal-learning model. It is, as the saying goes, all good.

Creating Connections: Museums and the Public Understanding of Current Research contains nearly two dozen careful analyses of how to let people know what goes on up in the ivory towers and down in the tinkerers' basements. While you're reading, please note: these writers aren't just dabbling; they are from all over the world, and they're passionate about their ideas. Perhaps we can even forgive them for the fervent language that riddles their prose with acronyms: the public understanding of science (PUS), the public understanding of research (PUR), and the public understanding of science and technology (PUST), among a host of others. (There may be more disturbing acronyms than these three, but I can't think of any.) Don't let the letters fool you. These authors are committed to helping the public improve and expand its understanding of the world. Since there are so many of us, it makes sense that there are a lot of ideas about how to best do that. Fundamentally, they want us all to know how to go about doing nothing less than *Changing the World*. Please, read on.

NOTE

Bill Nye trained and worked as an engineer before creating "Bill Nye, the Science Guy" as a stand-up comedian's character. His children's show, *Bill Nye, the Science Guy*, appeared on both public and private broadcast networks in the United States. His new show, *The Eyes of Nye*, began in late 2003.

Acknowledgments

The book you are holding is an outgrowth and expansion of the conference "Museums, Media, and the Public Understanding of Research" held in St. Paul, Minnesota, in September 2002. When my colleagues and I at the Science Museum of Minnesota were planning the meeting, we knew it would be a very special gathering, one that should not end up as a scattered collection of memories. So we are delighted that so many of the meeting's participants—and others besides—have come together to produce this collection of essays and articles, which we believe capture the spirit of and discussion around current initiatives to promote the public understanding of research.

There are many people to thank for making this book happen. First, we are grateful to Dr. Hyman Field, senior adviser for public understanding of research at the National Science Foundation, who provided unfailingly valuable guidance to the development of the conference as well as supporting the production of the book.

We are indebted to our superb copy editor Deborah Schoenholz, whose cheerful candor strengthened the book and whose gentle prodding kept us on schedule. Special thanks as well to Sylvia Crannell, who provided consistently insightful editorial comments and support. We appreciated the constructive comments on the authors' original manuscripts from reviewers appointed by

AltaMira Press and, of course, the continuous encouragement and support from Susan Walters, our editor at AltaMira.

I am also grateful to my two coeditors, Graham Farmelo and Bruce Lewenstein, who provided a consistently high level of creative and intellectual input to the development and production of this book. Thank you, my friends.

Finally, let me provide assurance that the opinions and recommendations in this book are not necessarily representative of the National Science Foundation. It is a pleasure to thank the Foundation for their generosity in supporting the conference and this book and for their impeccable integrity in making no attempt to influence its editorial content.

David Chittenden

This project was supported, in part,
by the

National Science Foundation

Opinions expressed are those of the authors
and not necessarily those of the Foundation

Introduction

Only Connect: Linking the Public with Current Scientific Research

Graham Farmelo

Holden Caulfield, patron saint of teenagers, loved New York's American Museum of Natural History. In *The Catcher in the Rye*, he tells us that the museum appealed to him as a boy simply because it always remained the same. Whenever he returned, "Everything always stayed right where it was," so that when he returned "nobody'd be different. The only thing that would be different would be *you*" (Salinger 1958, 124).

The young Holden would not be enamored of the museum today. Like most of the world's great natural history museums—notably the ones in London, Washington, D.C., and Paris—New York's is continually refreshed with new exhibits and programs that bring the latest science to visitors in ways that are attractive to them. No longer can the leading natural history museums be fairly described as "dead zoos," places where visitors are virtually obliged to file past crowded ranks of cases stuffed full of poorly labeled specimens that mean little or nothing to anyone apart from experts. While most visitors can never see enough dinosaur remains, there is a limit to how many rocks and stuffed animals most people will enjoy in a single visit.

One of the ways that these natural history museums are seeking to keep themselves fresh for visitors is to bring to the fore research that had previously been hidden in the background. According to today's visitor-centered perspective, it is vital to link behind-the-scenes research activities to the visitor's experience,

BOX 1

WELLCOME WING AT LONDON'S SCIENCE MUSEUM

When the Wellcome Wing opened to visitors in July 2000, it announced its ambition to be the world's leading center for presenting contemporary science and technology to the public. The $75 million Wing features exhibits on four floors and has a complementary Web site, which also presents hot science news stories. On the Wing's ground floor is Antenna, a program area with exhibits devoted to contemporary themes and with small displays on science news (one of these changes every week). Above is the *Who Am I?* exhibit on the theme of genetics and brain science, presented through a visitor-centered exploration of personal identity. On the third floor is *Digitopolis,* an exhibit on modern electronic digital technology and the impact it makes on visitors' lives. Finally, the top floor features *In Future*, an interactive exhibition that invites visitors to reflect on the impact that foreseeable technological developments (such as implantable computer chips, taking vacations in outer space, and men having babies) might have on their lives. The Wing, funded in major part by the Wellcome Trust and the U.K. National Lottery, also features several pieces of contemporary art in its exhibits. In November 2003, the Museum opened a new building, known as the Wellcome–Wolfson Building, which houses a new center for contemporary science programs that targets exclusively adults. Called the Dana Centre (www.danacentre.org.uk), it is one of the most wired spaces of its kind in Europe, featuring a large café/bar, a TV studio, a host of meeting rooms. The Museum intends the Dana Centre to be a lively focus for innovative PUR programming, especially for young adults who would not normally go near a science-related event.

Photo courtesy of Science Museum, London

whether in live demonstrations, in regularly updated electronic displays, or just in well-informed labels that reflect the latest thinking on the items on display. We are witnessing the slow death of the hackneyed image of fusty curators and scholars who condescend to foray to meet the unwashed public once in a blue moon. Can anyone imagine those hip, down-to-earth scientists in the *Jurassic Park* movies being reluctant to share their dinosaur findings with the rest of us?

There are signs that this trend in natural history museums toward making current scientific research a powerful and attractive programming theme is taking hold more widely in the international community of science museums and science centers.[1] Indeed, this is all part of a wider trend toward using research in science and technology as a content generator in the media.[2] For decades, the public has been able to glean high-quality, comprehensive information about contemporary research from sequences on radio and television as well as from reports and features in newspapers and magazines. It is easy to overlook how much science is featured in this way; editors know that it would be absurd to feature science as undiluted as many scientists would like but that the public does have an appetite for science that has a potentially strong impact on their lives, on their imaginations, or both. Look, for example, at the prominence given on prime-time news to health issues such as robotic surgery and the possible dangers of hormone-replacement therapy. Likewise, there is no shortage of coverage of the latest startling images from the Hubble Telescope of the spectacular stellar formations in the early stages of the development of the universe.

With the advent of the World Wide Web—itself a spin-off from fundamental research (Caillau and Gillies 2000)—it has never been easier for the public to find out about the latest developments in science. For people who want to know more about the background, there is now an abundance of popular science books that bring both the history and contemporary practice of the subject to wide audiences. The great success of Stephen Hawking's multimillion-selling *A Brief of History of Time* and of Dava Sobel's *Longitude*, along with the remarkable sales of books by Jared Diamond and Steven Pinker, attest to the renaissance in popular science publishing and to the sheer range of topics covered (Lewenstein 2002). It is also a safe bet that any widely acclaimed research breakthrough will be followed within a few years by one of the leading researchers eager to give us more background, often in collaboration with a science writer: witness the book on the first cloned mammal, Dolly the sheep, written by Colin Tudge in collaboration with the pioneering scientists Ian Wilmut and Keith Campbell.

Scientific research has also recently become a popular stimulant for the imagination of artists. Over the past 15 years, many leading artists who have used the raw materials of scientific research to craft new work—the author John Updike, the poet Lavinia Greenlaw, the playwright Stephen Poliakoff, and the visual artist Cornelia Parker—have produced first-rate pieces that have brought fresh and thoughtful insights on research to new audiences. Scientists have also begun to take seriously the artist's perspective: witness NASA's imaginative appointment of the leading New York artist Laurie Anderson as its artist in residence. Over in the United Kingdom, it is no coincidence that the leading science journal magazine *Nature* has featured a regular column by the Oxford University art historian Martin Kemp since 1997.[3]

With science changing so rapidly and with so many quick-response media ready to cover news at a moment's notice, it is commonly argued that museums are not best placed to present current scientific research. The argument goes that they should concentrate on what they arguably do best: programs about well-established science, including unique historical artifacts and lots of hands-on exhibits (a.k.a. interactives). Moreover, the speed required to keep up with rapidly changing science runs counter to the tradition of careful scholarship and definitive statement associated with the museum as a cultural institution whose primary assets are their authoritativeness and stability.

Yet over the past decade, museum visitors have demonstrated an appetite for contemporary science programming in natural history museums and other types of science museums. It is plain that we are now in an era in which these institutions are becoming less focused on the past, more responsive to the present, and more willing to look to the future. As the writer C. P. Snow remarked, "Scientists have the future in their bones" (Snow 1962, 63).

The first international conference solely dedicated to the challenge of presenting contemporary science in museums and science centers was held only comparatively recently, in 1996. The announcement of the conference "Here and Now," organized by London's Science Museum, was greeted with puzzlement by some leading members of the museum community: why would we need an entire conference to address such a marginal issue? On the other hand, many scientists were surprised that contemporary science should be a new issue in the museum community. After all, practicing scientists are interested only in new science—the rest is for the archives. "Here and Now" featured presentations from many leaders in the international museum

BOX 2

LA CITÉ DES SCIENCES ET DE L'INDUSTRIE

Europe's largest science center, La Cité in Paris, presents what is undoubtedly one of the world's leading programs of exhibits and events on themes in contemporary science and technology. Shortly after it opened in 1986, this center became the first in the world to have an interactive exhibit area solely devoted to science and technology news when they presented Sciences Actualités. This area was later refurbished and then reopened in spring of 2002 as a space occupying 6,000 square feet focusing on two themes: current science news and the science news communication process. Every year, 3.5 million people visit the center in Paris and another 500,000 visit related exhibitions in cities around France. In addition, La Cité's Forum des Sciences program has presented complementary exhibits and public events on themes including medical ethics, cancer, mad cow disease, and climate change. Each of these events has attracted large audiences (normally between 50 and 200 people) and most were organized in partnership with the media, notably newspapers, radio, and television. After learning from these experiences, La Cité has set up Le Collêge, an interdisciplinary team (including scientists, journalists, philosophers, organizers) that will promote public discussion of life sciences, information technology, and the environment, beginning with an annual resource budget of 300,000 euros. The intention is to make many of these deliberations fully available on La Cité's website, once identified by U.N. Secretary-General Kofi Annan as one of the best Web sites (www.cite–sciences.fr) in the world.

Photo courtesy of CSI/Michel Lamourex

community as well as from other media, notably television, radio, and the Internet. From the proceedings, one clear message emerged: if science museums really want to present current science, they have no choice but to collaborate much more effectively with other institutions that are "content-rich" in contemporary science. In other words, if museums really want to cover new developments in scientific research, they will have to forswear their traditional insularity and conservatism—an undertaking often claimed but more often honored in the breach than the observance.

Within three years of "Here and Now," the Nobel Museum and the Swedish Academy's Center for History of Science organized another meeting on the same theme in Stockholm. These proceedings featured many thoughtful contributions, notably on the value of historical approaches and of presenting original objects, all of which gave food for thought to planners of the proposed Nobel Museum in the city (Lindqvist 2000).

Soon after the proceedings of the Swedish conference had been published, it was plain that current science programs were starting to flourish. Several projects, ranging from multimillion-dollar buildings to smaller events, were springing up in museums in Europe and North America (a selection including three large-scale projects and three comparatively small ones are described in the boxes that accompany this chapter). At last, museums were beginning to catch up with other media in the field of PUR (public understanding of research), and there were some encouraging collaborations between museums and other media, notably one in which the journal *Nature* first provided early warning of top news stories to the Science Museum in London (a collaboration that followed in the wake of "Here and Now").

About this time, the U.S. National Science Foundation's Hyman Field suggested that the time was ripe for a successor to the conference. He noted,

> Most informal science educators have not focused on how best to further the public understanding of what research is being conducted, who is doing it, why it is being done, and what the possible impacts may be. I wanted a working conference that would be an opportunity for leading museum professionals, scientific researchers, science journalists, television producers, web developers, and others to develop new strategies for informing the public about research, to learn from each other's preliminary experiences in this area, and to establish collaborations that will facilitate providing the public with timely, ongoing information about current research. (Field 2003)

The interdisciplinary meeting that Field envisaged was subsequently held at the Science Museum of Minnesota in St. Paul in September 2002. The contents of this volume are based on the presentations and discussions during the proceedings. Most of the presentations are represented here (usually in extended form), and we have included other articles to give the collection additional richness and context.[4]

From the outset, the theme of the conference was declared as the public understanding of research, or PUR, an admittedly weak acronym (except for those who speak ancient Greek, in which the word *pur* means "fire"[5]). This term does not actually convey the core theme of the conference, which is the public understanding of *current* scientific research—research that is under way, has just been published, or has been in the public eye for the past few years.[6] Such an emphasis on currency precluded detailed discussions about the value of communicating the nature and consequences of scientific research by considering projects that are already largely complete and that therefore can be evaluated by historians with the benefit of hindsight. No one can reasonably deny, for example, that a study of the epoch-making discovery of the structure of DNA in 1953 is more likely to yield clearer lessons about the nature of research than a study of the enormously exciting but messy and still-incomplete process of the recent discovery of RNAi some 50 years later.

Nonetheless, the principal reason why the organizers of the PUR meeting chose to minimize historical perspective was that this approach, while undeniably invaluable, has already been widely studied and debated. As numerous other books and conference proceedings attest, this approach has formed the basis of most museological thinking in science since the first science museums were founded (Finn 1990; Porter 1990; Shapiro 1990). In this meeting and in this volume, we wanted to look at the comparatively new issue of how to engage the public with current research themes and with freshly minted research. Moreover, we wanted to focus on empirical rather than theoretical issues.

Because the museum field of the public understanding of current research is so new—one might even say nascent—even its aims and terms of discourse are not yet clear, still less agreed on by its practitioners. No discussions can be concluded without someone expressing concerns about whether the rather blunt term *understanding* is the best word to use in this context or whether it would be preferable to talk in terms of engagement, appreciation, and/or awareness. Might these less ambitious aims be more appropriate to describe

BOX 3

CURRENT SCIENCE & TECHNOLOGY (CS&T) CENTER

The Current Science & Technology (CS&T) Center in Boston's Museum of Science caters to family, teenage, and adult audiences. The program focuses on newsworthy science and technology through a continually changing menu of presentations, live links to research expeditions, guest researcher talks, science theater, exhibits, multimedia, and a Web site, www.mos.org/cst. Each day, the Center's staff develop and deliver multimedia-enhanced live presentations on the CS&T stage, centrally located in the main exhibit hall, encouraging audience questions and discussion. Subjects range from stem-cell research and astrobiology to biotech and nanotech. CS&T was established with funds donated by corporate and foundation sponsors and operates with museum revenue and through education outreach partnership grants with research organizations. The Museum of Science intends to build on the project, notably by developing a museumwide initiative in technology and engineering.

Tania Ruiz presents an update on the space shuttle Columbia investigation. The CS&T Center engages teen and adult audiences in the stories of today's scientists, explorers, and engineers and the impact of their work on our lives and communities. Through live events, exhibits, and multimedia, CS&T staff interpret new research findings and evolving technologies in clear and compelling language. The Center experiments with a variety of formats and venues to illuminate the processes of research and innovation and to foster discussion on the goals and outcomes.

Photo courtesy of Museum of Science, Boston

what we might realistically achieve? Likewise, there is the perennial issue of what "the public" refers to: is it everyone in a society or just a subset such as those who are not practicing scientists or those who are potential visitors, whether adult or children?

Whichever definition one chooses, the question of practicability soon arises. Is there any realistic possibility in today's industrialized societies of linking the recondite, fast-paced world of scientific research with any but a tiny minority of the public (Shamos 1995)? Although there is a paucity of data on public knowledge of science and on public attitudes toward it, valuable information concerning the public in Europe and the United States indicates that, broadly speaking, most citizens have a good opinion of the contribution that scientific research has made to their lives and that a sizable proportion of adults (about one person in five) is interested in finding out more about scientific developments, although there is some skepticism about the reliability of information from some sources.[7] Given that museums are generally a trusted source of information, these data suggest that there is potentially an audience for PUR projects in museums.

But what would we want our audiences to know about research in science? The most popular answer is that there is a crying need for people to have a better appreciation of the process of research—its underlying procedures, its competitiveness, its aspiration to objectivity along with its undoubted reliance on subjective judgment, the provisional nature of published results, and so on. In practice, these elements tend to take second place to the factual and human-interest angles—what scientists have found out and why most people should give a damn. Finally, there is the superficially tedious matter of how scientific research is governed. For most of the time, most people don't care at all about this, but occasionally research leads to avenues that the public (or at least their representatives in government) want to be regulated, such as research into stem cells and nuclear weapons. How much effort should be put into providing information about the institutional and political forces that shape science?

The question of *how* the public should engage with researchers is one of the most pressing issues in the PUR field. Apart from continuing debates about how formal consultations should be organized, there is now new interest in the style of informal public events that bring together scientists and the public, notably in museums. In Europe and especially in the United Kingdom, the climate of opinion is that there is an urgent need to move from a "monologue" model of communication, with scientists lecturing the public on what it should know, to a "dialogue" model, in which scientists meet the public in forums that are evenhanded, giving nonspecialists much more time to air their concerns and share them with the "experts." This change has been motivated by what is widely seen as the failure of the comparatively authoritarian monologue style of communication to win public trust during the two most contentious debates of the 1990s: genetically modified foods and mad cow disease. As yet, this move toward dialogue models of communication is not as strong in North America, and it will be interesting to see whether the European trend spreads across the Atlantic. Chapter 4 in this volume by Albert and Edna Einsiedel addresses some of these issues, as does the box in this chapter about the activities of La Cité des Sciences et de l'Industrie in Paris.

Although current research is a new topic on the agenda of science museums, the field of the public understanding of research is as old as research itself. To put this collection of essays in historical perspective, section 1 of this volume, "On the History and Challenges of Public Understanding of Research," begins with a review of the development of the field by leading historian of science Larry Stewart. He describes the origins of modern science in Renaissance Florence through the present via Francis Bacon, whose views on scientific inquiry set the agenda for museum programs. Bacon's belief that scientific progress is best ensured by close attention to the results of observations and experiments is reflected in the classic museological agenda of communicating science through dense displays of artifacts and hands-on exhibits. The very idea of providing public understanding of research in museums is foreseen by Bacon in his unfinished book *Atlantis*, which describes how the science of his day could be made available to a wider public in the imaginary House of Solomon (Gregory 1989).

The Cabinets of Curiosities of the Italian Renaissance are often identified as precursors of today's museums. Just how far museums of science have come since those beginnings is clear from chapter 2, where John Durant sets out his stirring vision of the challenge and opportunity of presenting research to the public. Durant, chief executive of the Bristol Science Center in England and the United Kingdom's first professor of the public understanding of science, characterizes scientific research as "unfinished science"—science that has yet to be digested and put in the textbooks along with other "finished science"

(Shapin 1992). Durant believes that if museums can successfully tackle the challenge of presenting contemporary research, "it may also help transform our culture in ways that will provide untold benefits both to science itself and to the wider society."

Section 2, "Public Understanding of Research: The Big Opportunities and Issues," addresses the opportunities and issues involved in making contemporary PUR programs happen in museums. First, it is important to be clear about what we mean by PUR and whether it differs from other initiatives involving science and the public, such as the public understanding of science, science and society, and so on. In chapter 3, Bruce Lewenstein, associate professor of science communication at Cornell University, and Rick Bonney, education director of the Cornell Laboratory of Ornithology, examine the nomenclature of the field and conclude that no definition is as important as being clear about the goals and outcomes intended by the public programs. In this volume, we have chosen to focus almost entirely on current research.

The question of how museums can become the focus of public consultation about contemporary science issues is explored in chapter 4 by Albert and Edna Einsiedel. They imaginatively suggest that museums might play the same role in their communities as the Agora did in ancient Athens—as the cauldron of public debate. The Einsiedels describe how some museums have extended their function (at least as it's usually perceived) to become forums for their visitors by expanding their programs to include workshops, consensus conferences, and other inquiry-based learning activities. By using new communication technologies, notably the video conferencing and the Internet, museums can readily involve participants—experts and laypeople—from all over the world in ways that Socrates could scarcely have dreamed of.

Whatever the shape of the science museums of the future, it is a fair bet that they will be increasingly focused on their visitors' needs, wants, attitudes, and behaviors. In chapter 6, Heather Mayfield, deputy head of London's Science Museum, considers PUR programs from the public's point of view, arguing that every museum should strive to be clear not only about who its programs are for, but also about what they are seeking to achieve. Is the primary aim to inspire our visitors with new science? Are we seeking to give them a voice in public debate? Or, are we simply trying to bring researchers out of their laboratories to show that they are human? Muddled priorities lead inexorably to poor programming. Mayfield's arguments lead her to conclude that much

BOX 4

HEUREKA!, THE FINNISH SCIENCE CENTER, VANTAA, FINLAND

www.heurek.fi/portal/englanti

OPEN QUESTIONS: What Does Science Not Yet Know?

Heureka is one of Europe's leading science centers. It began as a small, enthusiastic project group within the Finnish scientific community. Its first milestones in content development became pilot exhibitions in which the future science center's working practices were devised. The internationally famous, futuristic Heureka building eventually gave its name to the entire center.

Heureka is known not only for its core exhibits, but for the traveling exhibits that it presents all over the world (until now 23 countries and 4 continents). Many of these exhibits feature material on contemporary science and technology, such as communication technology, paper technology, and biosciences.

The goal of Open Questions, Heureka's present traveling interactive exhibit, is to let visitors experience current research through such topics as *The Universe*, *Life,* and *Thought*. Targeted at secondary and high school students as well as international adult audiences, this 5,000-square-foot space strives for relevance by incorporating information on political, social, and ethical views about scientific issues, including Bionet virtual exhibits about state-of-the-art life sciences where visitors can vote on ethical questions to stimulate debate and compare legal issues across Europe.

The director of Heureka, Dr. Per-Edvin Persson, is now leading a strategic plan to expand the Center to include a new giant screen theater and a science laboratory building, where state-of-the-art laboratory equipment will be made available to different educational groups. The building will host the Adult Education Center of the University of Helsinki, and on the Heureka campus a conglomerate of other cultural institutions will be built over the next ten to twelve years.

more needs to be done to understand the needs, wants, and prior knowledge of the intended audiences before we can be confident that we are presenting research in ways that are both palatable and effective. Mayfield concludes that the most urgent priority is to carry out more high-quality audience research and that it is vital that the information be widely shared.

Currently, there is a dearth of high-quality evaluation in museum PUR programs. Too often, program producers take it on themselves to pass judgment on their own work, partly through lack of resources and expertise and partly because a thumbs-down evaluation on a single project could be seen as a death knell to an entire program, especially if a damaging report got into the hands of influential skeptics (of which there is no shortage in most museums). As Mayfield says, this urgently needs to be put right; just as every scientific research project is evaluated, so every PUR project deserves the same treatment, so that the planners—and their funders—can learn from their successes and failures. The key questions that potential PUR practitioners should answer before they evaluate any of their programs are set out and pondered in chapter 5 by two leading evaluators: Martin Storksdieck and John Falk of the Institute for Learning Innovation. For them, the key questions are, What are appropriate and realistic outcomes for PUR efforts in museums, and what are the implications of these decisions on assessment?

One example of an evaluation program that provided invaluable information to museum developers is the subject of chapter 7 by Xerxes Mazda of the Science Museum in London. He describes how evaluation data constituted one of the principal planning tools used by the team that developed the Wellcome Wing, an extension of the London Science Museum devoted entirely to contemporary science. Mazda, a member of the Wellcome Wing team, describes how he and his colleagues probed visitors' perceptions of controversial topics, such as Internet censorship and the treatment of depression with drugs. He was especially interested in encouraging visitors to give their views on these and other subjects so that the exhibit space could be a place of dialogue between scientists and the public. The conclusions, although derived from audiences in London, have much to teach anyone interested in obtaining visitors' views on issues raised by current research.

In chapter 8, geologist Chris Paola from the University of Minnesota gives us valuable insights into PUR from the point of view of a scientist who wants to talk about his work with a lay audience. He suggests how some of the obstacles might be overcome and points out the benefits for researchers of presenting something of the importance and excitement of their work to the public. Too often, researchers realize this only when it's too late. It's worth remembering the spectacle (in the early 1990s) of the demise of the giant atom smasher, the Superconducting Super Collider, with distraught particle physicists seeing their flagship project unceremoniously sunk by lawmakers unconvinced that the public would get value for money spent on the planned research.

One of the reasons for that disaster was that the lawmakers had little appreciation of the value of research that does not have easily identifiable economic benefits. Many researchers understand that this lack of understanding can be overcome only if they reach out to the community and make their case. There are pitifully few examples of researchers having devoted quality time to working closely with educators on projects that give students outside higher education a sense of what is involved in doing research. There are, however, some reasons for optimism. In chapter 9, Peter Bruns and Mark Hertle of the Howard Hughes Medical Institute describe some examples of researcher–educator collaborations that have had pleasing results. One of their most inspiring examples is a remarkable partnership in Birmingham, Alabama, between the city's public school system, the McWane Science Center and the University of Alabama Medical College. Together, colleagues from these institutions set up an imaginative program of student-centered activities on modules that focus on DNA fingerprinting, sickle cell anemia, protein structure, and protein–protein interactions.

Whatever the PUR program in a museum, it is virtually certain that collaboration will be involved. In chapter 10, Larry Bell, senior vice president of research, development, and production, at the Boston Museum of Science, sets out the definitive case for collaboration as the principal tool of the PUR programmer and gives abundant examples of how his own museum is putting its visitors (in real space as well as cyberspace) in touch with the latest developments in science via collaborations with other institutions. Admittedly, Boston is especially well placed to set up win–win arrangements with other media and academic institutions—it is not for nothing that the city likes to call itself "the hub"—but other museums can also benefit from the Boston Museum's experience and his reflections on the nature of collaboration.

As Bell and his colleagues have found, most first-rate PUR programs are based on cultivating good relations with researchers. This is not always easy;

most researchers don't want to spend time on activities that deflect them from their main aim of doing the best possible research. To spend time with the public is usually a low priority for the very best researchers when they are in their prime or looking for tenure (or both), not least because such "outreach" programs gain them little or no credit in the academic rat race. Indeed, it was not so long ago that any attempt to popularize research would invite the proverbial "peer sneer"; thankfully, those days seem to be drawing to an end.

Paola's enthusiasm for PUR, Bruns and Hartel's examples of initiatives taken by researchers and educators, and the welter of imaginative projects described by Bell should not blind us to the fundamental point that PUR programming is still very much a minority pursuit in today's science centers. For the great majority of them, the top priority is to present exhibits and events that give the satisfying mix of entertainment and education, the raison d'être of these centers since 1969, when Frank Oppenheimer set up the first one, the Exploratorium in San Francisco. The sheer labor intensiveness of programs that focus on contemporary scientific research make PUR a luxury for science centers, all of them in a permanent state of financial precariousness. This is one reason why it is such a challenge to launch PUR ventures in most science centers, especially when they are required to compete with the more overtly populist and potentially money-spinning ventures, such as traveling exhibitions and large-format movies. The institutional challenges that face those of us who seek to set up PUR programs in museums are discussed in chapter 11 by Laura Martin, Rob Semper, and Sally Duensing of the Exploratorium, an institution that continues its pioneering spirit today, not least in its PUR programs.

Although PUR in museums is still in its infancy, many innovative and exciting programs have been developed over the past few years. In section 3, "Some Emerging Strategies and Approaches," eight prime examples from the United States, Europe, and Australia are discussed in detail in order to highlight the challenges they had to overcome and the lessons their developers would like to share.

All the projects seek, in one way or another, to improve the science literacy of its target audience. Alan Leshner, chief executive of the American Association for the Advancement of Science, has eloquently stressed the need for public education about what constitutes genuinely scientific evidence; in his

BOX 5

CALIFORNIA ACADEMY OF SCIENCES, SAN FRANCISCO

ScienceNOW

The ScienceNOW kiosk at California Academy of Science interprets headline news in the natural sciences as well as current research or expedition activities of scientists at the academy. A live animal or plant that's seasonal or in the news is always on display. Effort is made to integrate features with current exhibits at the Academy whenever possible (e.g., *Headline Science* feature on hominid skull discovery in Africa concomitant to *SKULLS* exhibit), or with public program themes such as a focus on research currently taking place in Brazil during Latin American Heritage Month. Every week, one of the four components is changed. Thus, each month, an entirely new set of items is on display.

The ScienceNOW kiosk features four sections:

- *Headline Science*—a significant news story related to the natural sciences

- *Where in the World?*—focus on research sites visited by Academy scientists

- *Academy Research*—recent achievements and discoveries by Academy scientists

- *Wild Live*—a featured animal or plant, aquatic or terrestrial

ScienceNOW was inaugurated in October 2000, after seven months of planning. The kiosk has a live animal tank and three vitrines and is designed for four text/graphic panels, one of which changes each week (full rotation monthly). The vitrines are equipped with fiber optic lighting for small specimens. Objects from the collections and photographs from the Academy's Manzanita (photo archive) project are often used to illustrate news. A computer station with touch screen at the kiosk provides access to the Academy Web site for ScienceNOW, including archives of all features since October 2000. Key links are provided so people can pursue further learning. The ScienceNOW archives are all available via the Web site at www.sciencenow.org.au/.

keynote speech to the meeting, he memorably pointed out that "in science, evidence is not the plural of anecdote." In chapter 12, Rick Bonney, director of education at the Cornell Laboratory of Ornithology, describes several projects that seek to improve scientific literacy, including the remarkable series of citizen-science projects in his own unit at Cornell. These projects have their origins in 1929, when amateur bird-watchers' findings were used to construct a comprehensive database in New York State's Cayuga Lake basin. Today, the program continues to flourish, yoking together the rigors of life-science research methodology to the passion and industry of tens of thousands of amateur ornithologists.

It is vital that these projects learn from one another, a conclusion also reached in chapter 13 by David Ucko, for many years the leader of a science museum and now president of Museums + More in Washington, D.C., who reviews the strategies for producing research-related content. He points out the value of user-friendly and easily updated digital displays. But more important, he stresses the crucial need for museums to set up synergistic collaborations with research institutions and other media. In a conclusion that reflects the feeling of many of the meeting's participants, Ucko points out how important it is to "establish connections and communications that break down barriers between organizations and institutions involving scientists, media, educators, and others involved in PUR activities."

A very different project—the setting up of the Current Science & Technology Center in the Boston Museum of Science in 2001—is the subject of chapter 14 by its leader, Carol Lynn Alpert. This was the first major project in the United States to bring visitors daily presentations of items of science news on topics as diverse as nanotechnology, astrobiology, and biotechnology. Alpert describes how she and her colleagues planned and implemented the program, overcoming the challenges they met en route.

The Boston Center is seeking to become a place where local research institutions can present their work to its visitors, enabling these institutions to take their research to a guaranteed audience. There are, however, examples where research institutions set up their own in-house exhibits and do the job on their own. In chapter 15, Christine Cansfield-Smith describes one such example at the Discovery Center in the Commonwealth Scientific and

Industrial Research Organization (CSIRO) in Canberra, Australia. Cansfield-Smith explains why Australia's leading research agency decided to set up its own in-house science center and how it presents the work of CSIRO's scientists to the public. She also takes the opportunity to raise some perceptive questions about the ability of typical science centers to adequately present current research.

The example presented in chapter 16 is very different. It concerns a large exhibition about the science of archaeology based on the excavation at Çatalhöyük in central Turkey. The exhibit's leader, Don Pohlman of the Science Museum of Minnesota, describes candidly how the exhibit team sought to use the subject matter to illustrate themes about contemporary research but without the benefit of any original artifacts to display. Pohlman describes several illuminating and sometimes painful lessons for PUR that he learned from his work in this exhibit.

Finally in this section, by way of presenting another sharply contrasting example, we turn the spotlight on an internationally significant project in which a leading natural history museum has built an extension specifically to enhance the public's access to its research.

In most museums of this type, visitors are almost completely unaware of the research program going on behind the scenes. There have been many attempts to rectify this, but undoubtedly one of the boldest initiatives in this PUR field was the opening of the Darwin Center at London's Natural History Museum in the early fall of 2002. The Darwin Center is a new building entirely dedicated to opening up to its visitors the research being pursued by its 300 scientists on its collection of 70 million specimens of animals, plants, rocks, minerals, and fossils. In chapter 17, the museum's director, Sir Neil Chalmers, sets out the strategic thinking behind the planning of the Darwin Center and describes how he and his colleagues addressed the challenges. He describes how the project was funded, how sensitive conservation issues were tackled, how research staff were encouraged to become involved in the project, and how the vision of making backroom research public was brought to fruition. The result is a building that has in one fell swoop changed the museum's relationship with its visitors, using its research to effect that change.

Successful as many of these museum projects undoubtedly are, they cannot match the impact of most research coverage on television, in newspapers, on the radio, and on the Internet. By their very nature, these media can reach larger audiences and can respond much more quickly than museums to new developments. Thus, museums that are interested in PUR projects have much to gain by examining comparable initiatives in other media, which is why we have included section 4, "What Museums Can Learn from Media Public Understanding of Research Initiatives."

In chapter 18, Rick Borchelt of the Whitehead Institute candidly summarizes some of the findings of the review he carried out in 2002 for NASA of best practices in public communication of science and technology in research organizations. He points out in the opening of his chapter that the effectiveness of this communication is especially important for many technological research organizations now that the Cold War is over, so that there is no readily identifiable "bad guy" whom we must outdo. Borchelt finds much to praise but also some instructive examples of poor practice and some revealing consequences of customized public communication projects, such as the new cottage industry of freelance communications firms that help scientists spend their budgets on reaching the public.

In chapter 19, the respected U.K. science journalist Tim Radford reminds us that the public will tolerate science news in small doses and with plenty of sugar. There is little or no appetite for the strong meat of hard concepts and subtle argumentation that many scientists naively seem to believe is essential to a presentation of their work. Radford has been science editor of the U.K. quality broadsheet *The Guardian* since 1980, working in a very competitive environment in which he has to "sell" his stories every day to news editors who know that if dull material finds its way into the paper too often, readers will stop buying the paper and advertisers will take their business elsewhere. Despite these constraints, Radford has established an enviable reputation for making even the most obscure stories accessible to lay readers by ruthlessly focusing on what will make the stories appealing to even the most hurried reader.

In chapter 20, Cornelia Dean, science editor of the *New York Times*, which has long provided its readers with the most extensive and authoritative coverage of any newspaper in the United States, explains that what makes the newspaper's science reporting so remarkable is not so much its articles on hot news and about the latest must-have electronic gadgets but rather its willingness to devote space to relatively recondite stories, such as progress in the proof of a famous mathematical conjecture or the nature of the dark energy in the universe. A platform as prominent and prestigious as this leads inexorably to there being enormous pressure on the staff in matters of editorial content and style. An exciting article praising a research group's latest project can substantially increase their chances of getting a million-dollar grant, a well-timed feature could propel a book up the Amazon.com sales ranking, and an unfavorable piece on a new drug could cause sales to plummet, along with the stocks of the pharmaceutical company that produces it. Dean tells us something of how the newspaper avoids pitfalls like these and how she and her colleagues work with researchers to produce the award-winning coverage that its readers—of the morning paper and the Web version—enjoy almost every day of the year.

Important though newspapers are, television remains the most popular source of news and information in most industrialized countries, certainly in the United States. For many years there, *Nova* has been the flagship of public television's science coverage, with its weekly, hour-long features, many of which are coproduced with other television production agencies, notably the British Broadcasting Corporation. In chapter 21, Nancy Linde of the *Nova* team gives us an insider's view of the production values that underpin the programs, stressing the overwhelming importance of a compelling narrative. Without it, viewers will exercise their right to zap the program and turn over to the latest reality television crowd pleaser. Linde also outlines plans for a magazine information program, *Leading Edge*, to be broadcast quarterly, focusing on current and emerging research. Unlike *Nova*, *Leading Edge* intends to use on-air correspondents and a series anchorperson.

It is important not to forget radio. In chapter 22, Marc Airhart describes how the brief but effective *Earth and Sky* programs bring the voices of science researchers to 3.6 million listeners in the United States via some 650 radio stations. The shows do not present science news; rather, they feature researchers in the midst of projects that might lead to big breakthroughs in future months or years. This is an intriguing approach; most PUR projects concentrate on research that has been completed and peer reviewed, ready for glossy packaging. Perhaps like the Darwin Center described in chapter 17, museums can learn from the *Earth and Sky* programs by enabling visitors to have a peek into "work in progress" in local research laboratories.

Apart from occasional sequences in their news bulletins, commercial television networks feature little scientific research. Yet the organization ScienCentral has found ingenious ways of defying the trend, securing places for science among the local newscasts of the commercial networks and thereby reaching millions of Americans, many of whom rarely watch public television. In chapter 23, Eliene Augenbraun, president and chief executive officer of ScienCentral, describes two projects that bring science to a wider television audience. The first, "Nova News Minutes," exposes a new audience to *Nova* by repackaging the documentary material into two-minute news pieces appropriate for ABC local newscasts. The second project, "Science Stories," follows five significant fields in science and technology, reporting on developments as they happen for broadcast on NBC and ABC local newscasts. Both ventures use a new distribution system for science content that ScienCentral has pioneered. The broadcast pieces are supplemented with more in-depth information on the Web.

The enthusiasm of our expert contributors should not blind us to the fact that many are skeptical of the emerging PUR agenda. In a skeptical afterword, Don Pohlman shares some of his concerns about the trends that seem to be emerging in modern science museums. Among his anxieties, Pohlman is concerned about the prominence given to resource-hungry projects, such as those in London and Boston, that seek to bring hot science news to visitors, to some extent in competition with quick-response media, such as television, radio, and the Internet. Perhaps Pohlman is right to argue that it is too soon in the development of PUR in museums to accept any one of the paradigms on offer. We are, to borrow from the thinking of Francis Bacon, in the fact-gathering stage of our subject; only later can we have the experience to put forward grand, overarching principles that we can all acknowledge. In other words, perhaps today is the time for bottom-up initiatives, and top-down thinking is for tomorrow.

However the field of PUR in museums develops, it is certain that the St. Paul conference will long be remembered by all its participants. To help preserve some of these happy memories, conference leader David Chittenden, vice president for education at the Science Museum of Minnesota, reminisces about the meeting and some of the conclusions resulting from it in the closing appendix.

BOX 6

DOLAN DNA LEARNING CENTER

www.dnalc.org

The Genes We Share

The Dolan DNA Learning Center (DNALC) is world renowned for its genetic resources and protocols. Its on-site audiences tend to be self-selecting: they visit for gene-related laboratory programs, or because they have a particular interest in DNA. Using program opportunities to test concepts and prototype elements of the exhibition, visitors to the DNALC tend to expect that they will learn something about DNA, find out about current research, and see things they haven't seen before. However, even with a self-selecting audience, an exhibition about the human genome presents challenges in making complex and changing elements relevant to the visitor. To engage visitors who had different levels of understanding, The Genes We Share was made a kiosk-heavy, image-rich exhibition with interactives and objects used whenever possible. Summative evaluation using surveys and interviews was conducted in early 2003.

The Genes We Share is a 3-D exhibition that engages visitors in explorations that complement the programmed gene-based activities at the Dolan DNA Learning Center. It enables visitors with limited access to the Internet to explore some of the DNALC's extensive genetics Web resources and provides a suitable venue for the 2003 celebrations of both the fiftieth anniversary of the discovery of DNA's structure and the completion of the Human Genome Project. Major components are

We Share/We Differ/Comparing Characteristics—physical and behavioral similarities and differences between individuals;

Gene Genealogy—comparisons between populations, following human migrations using mitochondrial DNA (includes using J. D. Watson's DNA to trace ancestry);

Our Genome—structure of the genome and stories about locations within it;

Our Common Origins—DNA evidence and the fossil record (includes the first reconstruction of an adult Neanderthal skeleton from four different fossil finds compared with human and chimp skeletons);

DNA Discovery—history of DNA, DNA structure, and the genetic code (includes an adaptation of the first DNA model that continues over the ceiling "into" a working DNA sequencer); and

Genes and Health—genetic disorders, gene testing, and therapy, medicines that "make the most of our differences."

The great Harvard University sociologist of science Talcott Parsons argued that "science is intimately integrated with the whole social structure and cultural tradition. They mutually support each other—only in certain types of society can science flourish, and conversely without a continuous and healthy development and application of science, such a society cannot function properly" (Parsons 1982, 102).

He wrote those words in 1951, when science rode high in public esteem, not least because of the work of the physicist and Manhattan Project leader J. Robert Oppenheimer, just a few years before his brother Frank opened the Exploratorium in San Francisco, the first science center. Since that opening, science museums—a term that subsequently had to be modified to include science centers—have matured, although their role has remained confined largely to that of communicating with their visitors about the principles of science and its history.[8] Now, as one might glean from this collection of chapters and the meeting on which they are based, it may be time for the community of science museums to take a new direction by taking fresh inspiration from current research. Perhaps this would enable them better to contribute to Parsons's vision of a mutually supportive relationship between science and society.

As the chapters in this volume demonstrate, there is a long way to go before museums could make such a profound change. New partnerships would have to be set up with research organizations and with researchers who have a talent for science communication; new collaborations with other, more intrinsically flexible media would be needed; new, more audience-centered ways of communicating would have to be developed; new ways would have to be found of engaging audiences in scientific controversy; and so on. And, make no mistake, museums would have to ensure that their PUR programs were perceived not as loss leaders, as they usually are at present, but as part of an offering to visitors that is genuinely attractive and sustainable.

It is commonplace to note that science, museums, and democracy all have their roots in ancient Greece (Bronowski and Mazlish 1960). Could it be that, as Albert and Edna Einsiedel hint in chapter 4, all three could have a new relationship in modern life? There are certainly powerful reasons for such a change. First, in Western society there is a manifest and widely lamented lack of trust in politicians and in governance. Second, we live in a time when there is widespread mistrust of some scientists, especially those working for governments and industrial corporations. Finally, science museums are short of fresh ideas; the lazy and condescending display policies of yesteryear are long defunct, and the days of the decontextualized, utterly predictable collection of hands-on exhibits also seem to be numbered. A new approach to science programming in museums is urgently needed.

Perhaps science museums could be the new Agora, as the Einsiedels suggest. It's a vision that would have set even the imagination of Socrates afire. Even if we set aside prejudices about what science museums should be about and how they should do their job, there is still a pressing need for these museums to reinvent themselves, as many of their leaders agree.[9] Somehow, museums need to become even more attractive not only to their staple visitor cohorts of schoolchildren and families but also to teenagers and new groups, such as the burgeoning numbers of senior citizens. Will science museums ever become places where both Bart Simpson and Holden Caulfield would feel comfortable?

Although Holden loved New York's American Museum of Natural History when he was a young boy, as a teenager he "wouldn't have gone inside for a million bucks" (Salinger 1958, 128). Stasis no longer appealed to him, just as it doesn't for most of today's visitors. Like all other media, science museums will die unless they change continually and respond to societies' needs. Might current science be the engine of this change?

NOTES

1. Here I make the distinction between science centers (whose displays primarily feature hands-on exhibits) and science museums (whose displays feature mainly real artifacts). For the rest of the volume, we are quite relaxed about this distinction, which seems to be gradually fading away.

2. I mean the phrase "science and technology" to include all the sciences, including medicine as well as industry. In the rest of this chapter, I take the liberty of shortening the phrase to simply "science." Likewise, in the rest of the volume, we use "science" as a one-word signifier, if only to avoid the clumsy articulation of a broader meaning.

3. A sumptuously presented collection of some of Martin Kemp's "Nature" columns are featured in *Visualizations: The "Nature" Book of Art and Science* (2000).

4. The conference is fully documented on its Web site at http://pie.smm.org/pur.

5. In Donna Tart's *The Secret History* (1992), the narrator writes, "Pur: that one word contains for me the secret, the bright, terrible clarity of Ancient Greek" (224). On the same page, Tart writes of "the *pur* that roared from the towers of Illion or leapt and screamed on that desolate, windy beach, from the funeral pyre of Patroklos."

6. During discussions at the meeting, several conference participants argued that it was unwise to focus on "public understanding of *current* research" rather than to consider the more general topic of the "public understanding of research."

7. For a review of U.S. data, see Miller (2003). For U.K. data and references to complementary data, see Wellcome Trust (2000).

8. It is worth repeating and stressing here that I am taking "science" to be shorthand for "science and technology" because most science museums are much more concerned with technology than with science.

9. A flavor of the debate can be obtained from two articles in the journal *The Public Understanding of Science* (Bradburne 1998) and Persson's (2000) reply in the journal.

REFERENCES

Bradburne, J. 1998. Dinosaurs and white elephants: The science center in the twenty-first century. *Public Understanding of Science* 7, no. 3: 237–54.

Bronowski, J., and B. Mazlish. 1960. *The Western intellectual tradition.* London: Harper and Brothers.

Caillau, R., and J. Gillies. 2000. *How the Web was born.* Oxford: Oxford University Press.

Field, H. 2003. E-mail to author, February 24.

Finn, B. S., ed. 1990. The museum of science and technology. In *The museum: A reference guide.*

Gregory, R. 1989. Turning minds on to science by hands-on exploration: The nature and potential of the hands-on medium. *Sharing Science.* London: Nuffield Foundation, 1–9.

Kemp, M. 2000. *Visualizations: The "Nature" book of art and science.* Oxford: Oxford University Press.

Lewenstein, B. 2002. How science books drive public discussion. In *Communicating the future: Best practices for communication of science and technology to the public,* edited by G. Porter. Gaithersburg, Md.: National Institute of Standards and Technology, 69–76 (available at www.nist.gov/bestpractices).

Lindqvist, S., ed. 2000. Museums and modern science. Nobel Symposium no. 112. Stockholm: Science History Publications/USA, Watson Publishing International.

Miller, J. D. 2003. Public understanding of and attitudes toward scientific research: What we know and what we need to know. Excerpts from a report to the National Science Foundation. *Public Understanding of Science* 12, no. 4.

Parsons, T. [1951] 1982. *The social system*. Reprint, New York: Macmillan.

Persson, P. E. 2000. Science centers are thriving and going strong! Reply to Dinosaurs and white elephants: The science center in the twenty-first century. *Public Understanding of Science* 9, no. 4: 449–60.

Porter, C. M. 1990. The natural history museum. In *The museum: A reference guide*, ed. M.S.

Salinger, J. D. 1958. *The catcher in the rye*. London: Penguin.

Shamos, M. 1995. *The myth of scientific literacy*. Piscataway, N.J.: Rutgers University Press.

Shapin, S. 1992. Why the public ought to understand science-in-the-making. *Public Understanding of Science* 1, no. 1: 27–30.

Shapiro, M. S., ed. 1990. *The museum: A reference guide*. Westport, Conn.: Greenwood Press, 1–31, 59–85.

Snow, C. P. 1962. *A postscript to science and government*. London: Macmillan.

Tart, D. 1992. *The secret history*. New York: Penguin.

Wellcome Trust. 2000. Science and the public: A review of science communication and public attitudes to science in Britain (available at www.wellcome.ac.uk/en/images/sciencepublic_3391.pdf).

Section 1

ON THE HISTORY AND CHALLENGES OF PUBLIC UNDERSTANDING OF RESEARCH

Attempts to create a public understanding of current scientific research are almost as old as science itself. First, a distinguished historian of science takes a look at how the subject has evolved from the perspective of museums and science centers. Then a chief executive of one of the United Kingdom's new science centers gives a personal perspective on the opportunities and challenges for museums and science centers that are brave—and wise—enough to seek to bring current research to their visitors.

1

La buona e non mascherata filosofia, or the Exhibitionists

Larry Stewart

If scientific research can matter in a democracy, it is by engaging a public in debates that affect a public. Surely no one aware of the intense controversies surrounding bovine spongiform encephalopathy (BSE) or severe acute respiratory syndrome (SARS) can possibly leave understanding to fate when fate might take a turn in upsetting government policy or public safety. Suddenly, science is more than a measure of success; it has also become the foundation by which societies and economies survive. This even politicians have been forced to accept. Such a realization is dependent on the long trajectory that, at least since the seventeenth century, has elevated science to a matter of broad public concern. Crises contain the seeds of comprehension.

In 1622, when Prince Fredrico Cesi, Galileo's protector and patron in a Rome then riddled with intrigue, wrote about a nature that was good and not "faked," he raised the specter of the natural world commonly misinterpreted and misunderstood (Freedberg 2002, 28).[1] Yet the cultivation of nature and its hidden laws was the purpose of Cesi and his small band of sometimes disreputable followers in the short-lived Accademia dei Lincei that evaporated on Cesi's early death in 1630. Faced with the profound variety of nature, the rules and relations that governed its parts were not readily revealed. Cesi's attempt to bring together a small cadre of philosophers represented not the conquest of nature's bounty but a challenge to its overwhelming and confusing diversity. The "lynx-eyed" became a model for scientific societies ever since. While anticlerical, it was also a priesthood of the anointed, kept exclusive, that would face the puzzle of nature's order and be defeated. A strategy was conceived for collecting and contemplation, in bringing together the material world with a human comprehension, of bringing the mind to bear on a universe that, in the seventeenth century, seemed without boundary and contained variety seemingly without limit. Collections became museums, social boundaries eased by access, public contemplation transformed by private insight. But the hurdles were many.

The discoveries of nature were too important to be left to philosophers. This would, nonetheless, prove a much-contested view. Even a universe once focused on the creation of the world was turned upside down, or at least turned around, when Copernicus suggested that the world does move through the heavens. But Copernicus hedged his bets, insisting that "mathematics is for mathematicians," hoping, presumably, to avoid the conflict with scripture he and his disciples saw coming. Of course, there were always those like Cesi's friend Galileo who would later open the floodgates by publishing in the vernacular for a literate audience and trying to slip one by the authorities in the Church. Galileo's longtime friend Maffeo Barberini, elected to the papacy, was not amused in the slightest by such a challenge to authority. The Inquisition was not about to be convinced by the musings of a wayward astronomer who believed that inquiry comprises a multitude of truths. Sentencing Galileo, in a convent built on the ruins of an ancient temple to Minerva, the goddess of Wisdom, was only one of the many ironies in a tale that would dissect scientific questions before a wider public (Finocchiaro 1989, 87–118). But what the audience philosophers sought to reach would be overwhelmed by the conflict of authority and expertise and by the great breadth of the universe of which this world suddenly seemed a small part.[2]

A kaleidoscope nature must then have been a riot of this thing and that thing, without names sometimes, without apparent arrangement or taxonomy, a jumble of drawers and jars or just put away in corners, no sense of vegetable, mineral, or even animal, nothing made of sense that made mad the senses. In early-modern Europe, the vast treasure house of nature broke open and spilled out into the rooms of gentlemen and princes anxious to show their learning or their purse. But who would actually see what fewer still could comprehend? Was this yet another tale of boundaries crumbling in the early-modern world, like those that once kept readers of scripture policed by priests? Or was this just a tale of nature's plenty, a profusion of goods and curiosities, as though some visiting salesman had left behind his samples?

The purpose of this chapter is to explore the manner by which a wide public has become engaged in the scientific universe. We will celebrate the great philosophers not simply by their discoveries, but by their public recognition. Early-modern natural philosophers were no longer monks in cloisters making solitary commentaries on long-forgotten manuscripts as signs of Christian devotion. Indeed, the emergence of the immense force of modern science involved the conquest of nature under the intensity of a widening public gaze. By the seventeenth century, it was the great achievement of the Elizabethan chancellor Francis Bacon to recognize the importance of useful knowledge, justifying the exploration of nature's laws in the interests of the emerging nation-state.[3] But Bacon, in a tradition of authoritarian counselors ever since, was no champion of the curious who simply saw nature as one vast entertainment. This tension between knowledge and audience would be worked out only in the century of experiment and industrialism that followed the Enlightenment of the eighteenth-century North Atlantic world. From Europe to the Americas, public understanding became crucial as scientific and industrial civilization gained the power to transform the natural world and defined the culture of the West.

TESTING THE BOUNDARIES OF NATURE

Nature would not permit the exclusions philosophers and priests proposed. The colonization of the natural world by those made wealthy led to the creation of Cabinets of Curiosities for men of means. It was some time before curiosities were merely commodities, as much as with cochineal, Captain Bligh's breadfruit, or the Jesuit's bark. Yet with the collections of rarities, of strange sights made manifest, the sites of science rapidly expanded. Understanding nature, despite suspicions, was no sorcery at all even if there remained a reluctance to admit the vulgar and the unschooled into the deepest secrets of nature. Every oddity inevitably meant, in an effort to sustain social stability, an attempt to ground curious objects in some framework—often scriptural—long established. Hence, according to the *Daily Courant* of May 25, 1713, when a whale was marooned near Greenwich in 1713, its skeleton was put on display for the curious and for those who wanted to see the evidence of Jonah's tale. Even the "Little Black Man," no more than three feet tall, who was exhibited near Charing Cross from 1704 to 1712 represented more than a freak show for occasional philosophers. Novelties attracted audiences, then as now. Likewise, as reported by the *Daily Post* on January 23, 1742, the Royal Society of London could become as much an object of interest as the appearance of a "Gigantick Swede" who, on being shown to the Society, "made him a handsome Present, and express'd no less satisfaction at the Sight of this prodigious Person than he did at the numberless Curiosities [gathered] together by that learned Body in their Repository." By the middle of the eighteenth century, there was a broad interest in natural curiosities amid a public audience that would not otherwise have had access to the private cabinets of princes or royal societies. The evolution of cabinets into museums was part of the long trajectory of widening the audience for nature. If cabinets might be policed, this was not readily true of nature's many surprises.

The private world of aristocratic and scholarly collections, with the proper introduction, often offered the possibility of access. Thus, the Jesuit Athanasius Kircher in Rome in the middle of the seventeenth century had made possible the opening of his remarkable cabinet as part of the growing adventure of the gentlemanly grand tour. Similarly, Ulisse Aldrovandi in Bologna and Conrad Gesner in Switzerland had collections of such note that they established books of "friends" who were given entrée (Findlen 1994, 131, 136–37; see also Bedini 1994). Seeking out collections became as much of the sport of the cultivated as seeking additions to a cabinet. In the seventeenth century, John Evelyn knew of shops, as in Paris at "Noahs-Arke," which might supply to collectors "Shells, Ivorys, Purselan, Dried fishes, rare Insects, Birds, Pictures, & a thousand exotic extravagances" (Altick 1978, 13). So too the continental traveler Zacharias Conrad von Uffenbach, in England in 1710, sought out centers of the new science on which emergent English fame in natural philosophy seemed to rest. He was singularly unimpressed even by the Ashmolean, where, on a market day, "all sorts of country-folk, men and women, were up there" (Findlen 1994, 147). Von Uffenbach failed to recognize the signs of the future.

The creation of museum collections transformed public culture. Whether among a continental public or the emergent mercantile and scholarly society of metropolitan London, the essential problem common to collections was that someone, sometime, would want to see them. Thus, access to museums was regulated from the beginning. Gentlemanly curiosity became a sign of cultivation and of friendship linking men of means with men of knowledge, but increasingly nature's bounty was transformed into a usefulness that raised its specter in Baconian dreams. To propose research into natural use was to open the gates to those who would turn objects into goods. The result was problematic. When von Uffenbach visited the Bodleian, he was considerably irritated by "peasants and women-folk, who gaze at the library as a cow might gaze at a new gate with such noise and trampling of feet that others are much disturbed" (Goldgar 2000, 195–212). The public audience became ubiquitous in western Europe, whether crowding around Magna Carta or with the entertained and the studious mixed in hushed tones as under the dome of the old Reading Room of the British Museum.

Museums have been underestimated in the evolution of the enlightened public realm. As in the reading of newspapers in genteel coffeehouses, curiosities in private museums were liberated when payment replaced privilege for unlocking doors. But this did not simply follow the emergence of a commercial culture in the nascent empires of western Europe, although that certainly was a major factor. Access was increasingly justified by the stunning epistemological change tied to observation and experiment that overtook western Europe in the seventeenth century. For example, one of the reasons the Italian traveler Lorenzo Magolotti, of the Accademia del Cimento, was underwhelmed by the English collection of John Tradescant, before its resurrection in the Ashmolean, or even by the Royal Society is that he had only recently left the spectacular hive of activity of Francesco Redi in the laboratory of the Medici palace in Florence (Findlen 1994, 149).

The value of the natural world increasingly meant nature put to use, not merely in mechanics but especially in research, through observation and experiment. For this same reason, Italians who followed Galileo had come to the realization that even the most spectacular drawings and dramatic accounts could never suffice. No one was likely to be convinced by pictures of sunspots or Jovian planets when telescopes might answer better. Even then, seeing was only superficially believing. As with the telescope, the microscope probed further, for appearance was misleading, and only physical examination and chemical experiments would reveal the truth beneath the surface. Evidence of nature could not be confined to those who filled cabinets to their brims or painted pictures as memento mori. Museum and laboratory were mirror images. As Cesi had put it in 1616, before Galileo and the Accademia dei Lincei, invention and investigation mattered most:

> Unfortunately, only a few seek the convenience of this approach, and embark on their studies with weak means and little order. . . . It is hardly surprising that of the few people who study, even fewer—actually, very few indeed—arrive at any noteworthy degree of knowledge. (Freedberg 2002, 376)

THE CULTURE OF OBSERVATION

Usefulness and observation distrusted the surface of things. The consequences of such a doctrine were profound, for they meant that cultural and social elites in the early-modern world could not subdue the sources of knowledge as easily as they might buy paintings by the gross or libraries by the yard (Jordanova 1989, 22–40). If elites could no longer control natural knowledge as they once had galleries and cabinets, the reason was fundamentally the rapid spread of sites where curiosities might be displayed. In the early seventeenth century, perhaps under the influence of Lord Chancellor Bacon, consideration was given to establishing Repositories or Offices of Address, the purpose of which was the collection of useful knowledge and models of machines. Such a proposition also lay behind the Royal Society's failed History of Trades, but the notion continually resurfaced that collections could impart information for those seeking useful application. By the eighteenth century, the linking of utility with progress became essential to an enlightened vision.

The public has long been with us. Exclusivity was diluted by growing numbers of sites where natural and experimental philosophy was revealed, often for a price. Public science was to be redefined by commerce. In Newton's experimental age, and very much despite his reservations of consorting with the vulgar sort, there was an explosion of interest in the world of natural and experimental philosophy. Indeed, Newton's discovery of the universal law of gravity and his remarkable but solitary investigation of the refraction of light in his college rooms in Cambridge were not without controversy or confusion. One of the great ironies is that Newton's immense public reputation in his lifetime happened despite the general reaction among students at the time that he wrote what no one could understand. Neither his magisterial and incomprehensible calculus nor the imperfect prisms that complicated the business of reproducing his experiments could have helped. Yet coffeehouses,

taverns, and theaters became centers of scientific display; of lectures on Newton's principles; of demonstrations of the latest experiments concerning light,
magnetism, and electricity; of astronomical displays to coincide with brilliant
northern lights and predicted comets; and of numerous competing courses
advertised daily in the press. In the growing conviviality of a coffeehouse culture in eighteenth-century Europe, science mixed with politics and trade in a
world very much enhanced by rapidly expanding empires and growing proof
of the fecundity of nature. Take, for example, London's Don Saltero's Coffee
House, described as "London's first public museum" by John Slater, "master of
publicity" where, according to the press,

> Monsters of all sorts here are seen,
> Strange relics in nature as they grew so;
> Some relics of the Sheba Queen,
> And fragments of the famed Bob Crusoe

The politician and pamphleteer Richard Steele, whose own Censorium at
York Buildings on the Strand promoted plays and astronomical displays, once
described in *Mist's Weekly Journal* (1723) the famed Don Saltero's as crippled
by the problem of all museums: "It is the misfortune of persons of great genius, to have their faculties dissipated by attention to too many things at
once," especially as they might contain "the Pope's infallible candle" and
"manna from Canaan, a petrified oyster, a pair of garter snakes from South
Carolina, an Indian ladies' back scratcher, [and] a fifteen-inch-long frog"
(Altick 1978, 17–18). Skepticism raised the bar. It was increasingly clear that
there was an audience keen for credible scientific knowledge.

Science was soon for sale. There had long been a tension regarding those
who had sought access to the collections philosophers and princes. But by the
eighteenth century, the rising clamor and curiosity elevated the distinction
between the intellectually serious and the easily entertained, as by the optical
displays and electrical effects revealed in Paris fairs (Isherwood 1986, 48–50;
see also Fara 2002). Notably brilliant devices, like the singing birds and mechanical chess players of the mechanic Jacques Vaucanson, established a place
in popular culture. By 1742, in London's Haymarket Theatre, French au-
tomata packed in crowds, and the Newtonian lecturer John Theophilus De-
saguliers translated Vaucanson's pamphlets to promote an emerging public

science. However, the difficulty imposed by fraud and fantasy, once the lucrative realm of country showmen, was magnified. How could an uneducated public ever discern a truth unless the depth of nature's laws was increasingly displayed?

The aim of some philosophers was to enlist an audience in the advancement of science and the interests of the state. And in a North Atlantic world increasingly enamored with the power of mechanical contrivances, on the verge of industrial revolution, the participation of a public would have great consequence to those who would invest and to those who believed that the security of states and empires depended on the conquest of nature's laws. For example, the urgent need in maritime nations to solve the problem of longitude while at sea induced the Newtonian lecturer William Whiston to call for the public to witness his experimental mortars, set off over Hampstead, Greenwich, and Gravesend, to assess the delay between the sound and flash of explosions. Whiston, by such means, hoped to assess distance from a precise location, and this even led to the British government's Longitude prize, causing an enormous number of pretenders to seek this particular grail. Baconianism was alive and well and living in London (Stewart 1992, chap. 6).[4]

THE EMPIRE AND THE SENSES

Princes still might seek the impressive, but nations would enlist nature in their empires. At the cusp of empire and industrial revolution, when the Peace of Paris would divide the world, George III purchased from Cardinal Albani the magnificent natural history drawings once owned by Cassiano dal Pozzo in the early seventeenth century (Freedberg 2002, 15–16, 62). At the same time, George III would obtain one of the most stunning cabinets of scientific apparatus in a century enamored with experiment and demonstration. This is was largely a collection of instruments designed explicitly as demonstration devices to reveal scientific principles to the curious (Morton and Wess 1993). It is significant that during the Enlightenment, science and technology became increasingly interwoven, if largely in the minds of public lecturers. But in the burgeoning industrial revolution and rapidly expanding European empires, mechanical achievement provided a powerful argument for the uses of philosophers and their promotion of natural research. By the middle of the century, at the moment of the birth of the British Museum out of the personal collection of the physician Hans Sloane, new societies emerged that attempted to capture the rhetoric of improvement—such as the Society for the Encouragement of Learning and the Society for the Encouragement of Arts, Manufactures and Commerce. Indeed, by 1778 it was asserted that a "Harvest of Learning" in "Arts, Sciences, Manufactures, &c." could be gathered from exhibitions at the British Museum (Goldgar 2000, 198). Thus, the gathering of Eden and the examination of nature's laws were turned to use in the interests of the imperial state (Drayton 2000, 4).

Under George III, princely patronage reasserted itself with the establishment of a physic garden at Kew in 1759. Victorious battles in the Seven Years' War were celebrated by new gardens and structures at Kew. Empire had then extended its reach at the expense of the French on the Slave Coast and at Guadeloupe, while botanical discovery and transfer was enhanced by the Crown's control of war and finance. In the widening competition with other European powers, Kew assumed by the early nineteenth century a crucial role in the new Pax Britannica, so much so that we may "begin to recognize that the world, from the sixteenth century, colonized Britain." In such a view, Kew was the essential—and metropolitan—focus of globalization. By the middle of the nineteenth century, Kew was domesticated by the import and donation of thousands of unsolicited plants from increasing numbers of colonial gardens that had been created as symbols of "wise government" (Drayton 2000, 170–71, 183).

Throughout the eighteenth and nineteenth centuries, conquests thus made both markets and new sites for science, the key transfer being that of nature from the expanding periphery to the European center. The trick, as the German naturalist Johann Reinhold Forster put it in a 1772 English translation of the remarkable voyage of the French explorer Louis de Bougainville, was to

> send a set of men properly acquainted with mathematics, natural history, physic, and other branches of literature, to their vast possessions in the Indies, and every other place where their navigations extend, and enable them to collect all kinds of useful and curious informations; to gather fossils, plants, seeds, and animals, peculiar to these regions; . . . to make observations on the climate and constitution of the various countries; the heat and moisture of the air, the salubrity and noxiousness of the place, the remedies usual in the diseases of hot countries, and various other subjects. (Bougainville 1967, viii–ix)

Imperial policy was a policy of plants as much as conquest, and public gardens took on a form not limited by the pleasures of London's Vauxhall or the Luxembourg in Paris. Notably, this was not merely a matter of consumption of new goods but of the existence in places like the Jardin du Roi or Kew of centers of naming, collecting, and display that solidified the link between natural knowledge, wealth, and the reach of European power (Dettelbach 1996, 258; Miller 1996, 22–23; Schaffer 1996, 336–37).

One of the most crucial characteristics of this amazing expansion of knowledge was the convergence between the interests of state and the passions of the scientific public. This was an age of the rapid development of scientific societies populated by gentlemanly amateurs, along with the promotion of natural research in the Musee d'Histoire Naturelle and the Zoological Society in Regent's Park. Even Kew, it was thought, did not measure up to the Jardin des Plantes, where, the Dutchess of Somerset complained, "[t]hey have a variety of lectures *gratis* & the establishment does not cost more than our British Museum & yet what do we have to compare?" (Drayton 2000, 137–38). The linking of public learning with imperial agenda was essential to the nineteenth-century view of national and economic achievement. Public interest and the encouragement of research went hand in hand, leading the naturalist Sir William Hooker in 1847 to remind the navy of the necessity of sending plants to the Museum of Economic Botany (Drayton 2000, 193). The strategy of public museums, gardens, and laboratories was essential to the expanding empire.

THE USES OF THE PUBLIC

The public concern with science has long been with us. Popular understanding and economic achievement were intimately tied even before the nineteenth century. Of course there was resistance. For example, at the end of the eighteenth century, when designs for the Royal Institution were being created, the architect was informed that his idea of an outside staircase, intended to allow artisans to witness lectures without interfering with their social superiors, should be dropped because "it was thought to have a political tendency" (Morus 1998, 18). Even so, the Royal Institution soon became the site of the remarkable experimental displays of Sir Humphry Davy and Michael Faraday and proved extremely popular (Gregory and Miller 1998, 20–21, 133–37; Morus 1998, 14). In that great century of scientific societies, there were seemingly endless efforts to bring the world of natural philosophy into a public comprehension. Thus, England's Zoological Society endeavored to create what was then mockingly regarded as a "Noah's Ark Society" but that soon became the London Zoo, into which nonmembers were first admitted in 1828. But this was an age that triumphed in the profitable, where patent applications exploded and where exhibitions trumpeted the accomplishments of nations. By midcentury, there had already been the French Exposition, the Zollverein Exhibition in Germany in 1844, and a movement in Britain toward exhibitions of Works of Industry that led ultimately to the Great Exhibition of 1851, in which not only British wares were displayed but even America challenged European technology (Drayton 2000, 193–94). The nineteenth-century state increasingly took a role in the promotion of the uses of nature. As Simon Schaffer has shown, in Britain, seemingly endless numbers of controls were legislated to bring science to bear on measurement and economic expansion—thus the establishment of the Board of Trade (1832), the Factory Inspectorate (1833), an observatory at Kew by the British Association for the Advancement of Science (1842), and the Excise Laboratory (1842) (Schaffer 1997a, 438–74). This undoubtedly owed much to the development of a cultural authority attached to science in which a public audience came to play a crucial role. As empires were "more obviously commercial," encouragement, enlightenment, and consumption merged. Above all, the Crystal Palace in 1851 made transparent the necessity of the public understanding of scientific and technological research. Thus, the exhibition in Hyde Park promoted both science and skill. Special trains were put on so that workers from provincial towns could see the power that mechanics, mind, and nature might achieve (Jacob and Stewart, in press; Pickstone 2000, 75, 78). Crystal Palace stood as the pinnacle of the long evolution of access to cabinets, lectures, gardens, expositions, zoos, and museums in the imperial spectacle of conquest and collection.

The superiority of the imperial state followed the appropriation of nature's laws for national objectives. Conquest, collecting, and observation were measured in a rapidly expanding trade in goods and were reflected in the growing manufacture of industrial power by European entrepreneurs. Access to collections, museums, sites of manufacture and research, and a natural understanding had once been something to control. Even when Matthew Boulton, in industrial Birmingham, preferred to keep visitors at bay while boasting of the power he produced, popular entrée into the world of science and technology became a necessity for the nation-state. Princely patronage was replaced by the patronage of governments that, in a liberal vision, sought to expand scientific knowledge. The new Natural History Museum in South Kensington in 1881 was as much a part of that sense of purpose as the Conservatoire des Arts et Metiers in Paris. Imperial superiority was reflected in such collections as much as in the ability to impose rules and measures in international trade. It is notable, for example, that when the British chemist and geologist James Smithson left a vast sum to the U.S. government, he did so expressly for an institution for the increase and diffusion of knowledge among men. The economic consequences of science and capital seemingly had not yet dawned on the American government. By then, the European state had learned to accept that benefits might accrue from investment in science—they had come a long way from a time when neither the Royal Society nor Charles II had done much to assist in the foundation of a Royal Observatory at Greenwich in 1675. By the First World War, national survival induced the British and German governments into establishing councils on industrial research.[5] These, it would seem, depended on conscripting an enlightened public interest to an imperial war effort.

SCIENCE, INDUSTRY, AND THE STATE

Government, whether of princes, republics, or the imperial state, and the broad public interest have repeatedly sought convergence. This became even more apparent in the twentieth century, particularly as applied science and technology expanded the arsenal utilized in international hostility. Certainly in the aftermath of two world wars, it was apparent that science could provide a crucial part in a call to arms. Powerful spokesmen of preparedness charted the course of science and state in the interwar years. Thus, Senator Elihu Root, chairman of the Board of Trustees of the Carnegie Institute and winner of the Nobel Peace Prize in 1913, stated shortly before the end of the First World War that "competency for defence against military aggression requires highly developed organized scientific preparations. Without it the most civilized nation will be as helpless as the Aztecs were against Cortez" (Jenkins 2002, 16). History has taught all kinds of lessons.

In the West, the circulation of scientific knowledge was linked to a democratic vision and to national survival—thus the enthusiasm of Vannevar Bush, president of the Carnegie Institution, who, in 1949, pronounced that "the technological future is far less dreadful and frightening than many of us have been led to believe, and that the hopeful aspects of modern applied science outweigh by a heavy margin its threat to our civilization" (Bush 1949, 2–3). The public, the amateur, and the professional had a place in the scientific world. Bush believed that "to accomplish all this we need first to clear the way for the really talented youngster to go to the top of the profession, there to become the research man, the teacher of others, the leader in new industries" (Bush 1949, 2–3). Bush even now, or perhaps especially now, makes stunning reading. His analysis of the Cold War world now seems all too familiar:

> Since the war ended, this elusive and powerful force, this mass concept, this public opinion, has ruled that we should enter wholeheartedly, in spite of irritations and annoyances, into the attempt to build some sort of United Nations. It has ruled that we should build a strong military machine and have it ready. It has stiffened our backs and frowned upon exposure of weakness or overreadiness to compromise. It has most certainly rejected any idea that we should become a conquering nation, or strike early ourselves in the attempt to avert a later and a more desperate war. It insists that we control the traitors in our midst, and somewhat bewilderingly that we do not sacrifice our essential freedoms in the process. It has even begun to insist that special and selfish interests be regulated within a compass that will not wreck the national strength we need. It has placed us on the path we now pursue, yet does not know exactly where it leads. (Bush 1949, 3–4, 246; see also Greenberg 1967, 74–80, 99)

We should not simply attribute efforts to expand public understanding, through museums, science centers, or the Discovery (or even the History) Channel to a considered or statist strategy. There was something much more subtle and long-standing at work in the transformation of Western culture. The new race was not in arms alone but in expanding the public support for science and industry. This has involved many imponderables and a scientifically illiterate perspective on the part of nonscientists and politicians contemplating intangible results. Consequently, the value of museums, collections, science centers, and hands-on demonstrations has been magnified by the political pressure that industry and state have brought to bear. It would be a mistake to see this, in the American circumstance, as simply a response to the gauntlet of Soviets in space. Even in the midst of the twentieth century, the call of science relied on historical comparisons. Thus, Glen Seaborg, winner of the Nobel Prize in Chemistry and chairman of the Atomic Energy Commission, would mobilize the past: "The educated man of today and tomorrow can no more ignore science than his predecessors of the Middle Ages could ignore the Christian church or the feudal system" (Greenberg 1967, 37). Seaborg was right: *Sputnik* had a long trajectory.

In the past three centuries, the unification of science and state has politicized the public understanding of research. Funding of science museums increasingly relies on governments, industry, and private foundations for which scientific literacy is but a means to an end. As Schaffer has suggested, "The problem for curators, is that authority and the facts are contemporaries of each other: one gets defined as the other does" (Schaffer 1997b, 31–39). This was the problem of portraits of nature that had confronted Cesi and the Accademia dei Lincei. The debate was not solely about objects but also about the authority to determine the facts of the natural world in a situation no less "conflicted and debatable" than issues like cold fusion, BSE, or SARS, where so much might be at stake (Schaffer 1997b, 31–39). It is not coincidental that at the height of the Cold War in 1950, the National Science Foundation in the United States was explicitly established by an act of Congress to "promote the progress of science." Science and the state were joined at the purse. But where access to science was concerned, accountability seemed to follow. This compounded the problem for politicians given to slavishly accept the expertise of scientists who testified before them. John F. Kennedy remarked in 1962 that society had to look after its own needs while scientists demanded its support (Greenberg 1967, 288).

So the politics of scientific research was invariably Janus-faced, looking for useful advantage and simultaneously at consequences, often unforeseen. The experiences of the two world wars made it clear that scientists must seek to manage public understanding. In so doing, magazines, newspapers, museums, and science centers all played an important part. Indeed, there has proved to be such a market for discussions of highly controversial scientific questions that it is not hard to find magazines featuring stories on genetic engineering, the relationship between crime and biology, or genetically modified foods that have many potential consequences for national economies as well as health. In a twist to this tale, philosophers as well as historians have engaged with the public once again and have filled the bookshops with popular tomes on genetics, technology, and even the so-called posthuman future that may follow our biotechnology revolution (for example, Fukyama 2002; Schwartz 2003; Tudge 2000; Wright 1999).

It is surely clear that facing hot topics such as Kyoto, mad cow disease, or informed consent in drug testing has made the business of science museums increasingly difficult and inevitably politicized. Indeed, one might surely wonder whether museums have a capacity to engender serious public debate on the social consequence of scientific research that has not already been compromised or reduced to the level of pandering. If so, this would be unfortunate. But perhaps the purpose of museums should be more a matter of raising awareness than inducing sophisticated analysis. As long as funding came from industry and government, it was inevitable that museums and collections would feel pressure when exhibits engaged controversial issues and engendered public or political heat, especially where scientific issues were unresolved, as with genetic engineering or global warming. Political liberals might feel inclined to address pollution, while conservatives prefer sometimes to save the money, both in the name of responsive politics (Kevles 1978, 171, 410 ff.). In such circumstances, those who witness the exhibits of science can matter. It is the exhibitionists who have become more responsive, attempting to engage audiences in more dramatic and directly physical ways. The utilization of IMAX theaters has delivered dramatic, edge-of-the-seat, scientific experiences and, in the Exploratorium of Frank Oppenheimer in San Francisco in 1969 or in numerous science centers since, revealed the broad range of connections between scientific principles through a wide variety of natural phenomena. Such adventures in nature's laws have allowed patrons to establish their own framework for comprehension (Oppenheimer 1987, 5–20; Schaffer 1997b, 31). As had long been the case, the public understanding was essential. The political imperative of the Cold War and its aftermath engaged the politics of access and has left us with a long-expanding audience and a deepening sense of accountability.

NOTES

1. Frederico Cesi to Cassiano dal Pozzo, October 4, 1622.

2. On the place of the Copernican universe, see Jardin (1996).

3. On the influence of Bacon, see Henry (2002) and Martin (1992).

4. On some excellent attempts to engage a modern public with these issues, see Pumfrey (2002) and Sobel (1996).

5. Compare Greenberg (1967).

REFERENCES

Altick, Richard D. 1978. *The shows of London.* Cambridge, Mass., and London: Belknap Press and Harvard University Press.

Bedini, Silvio A. 1994. Citadels of learning: The Museo Kircheriano and other seventeenth-century Italian science collections. In *Science and instruments in seventeenth-century Italy.* Aldershot: Variorum.

Bougainville, Louis-Antoine de. [1772] 1967. *A voyage round the world. Performed by order of His Most Christian Majesty, in the years 1766, 1767, 1768, and 1769.* Translated by John Reinhold Forster, F.A.S. Reprint, Amsterdam: N. Israel.

Bush, Vannevar. 1949. *Modern arms and free men: A discussion of the role of science in preserving democracy.* New York: Simon & Schuster.

Dettelbach, Michael. 1996. Global physics and aesthetic empire: Humboldt's physical portrait of the tropics. In *Visions of empire: Voyages, botany, and representation of nature,* ed. David Philip Miller and Peter Hans Reill. Cambridge: Cambridge University Press.

Drayton, Richard. 2000. *Nature's government: Science, imperial Britain, and the "improvement" of the world.* New Haven, Conn.: Yale University Press.

Fara, Patricia. 2002. *An entertainment for angels: Electricity in the Enlightenment* Cambridge: Icon Books.

Findlen, Paula. 1994. *Possessing nature: Museums, collecting, and scientific culture in early modern Italy.* Berkeley and Los Angeles: University of California Press.

Finocchiaro, Maurice A., ed. 1989. *The Galileo affair: A documentary history.* Berkeley and Los Angeles: University of California Press.

Freedberg, David. 2002. *The eye of the lynx: Galileo, his friends, and the beginnings of modern natural history.* Chicago: University of Chicago Press.

Fukyama, Francis. 2002. *Our posthuman future: Consequences of the biotechnology revolutions* 24. New York: Farrar, Straus & Giroux.

Goldgar, Anne. 2000. The British Museum and the virtual representation of culture in the eighteenth century. *Albion* 32 (summer 2000).

Greenberg, Daniel S. 1967. *The politics of pure science: An inquiry into the relationship between science and government in the United States.* New York: Plume Books.

Gregory, Jane, and Steve Miller. 1998. *Science in public: Communication, culture, and credibility.* Cambridge, Mass.: Perseus.

Henry, John. 2002. *Knowledge is power: How magic, the government, and an apocalyptic vision inspired Francis Bacon to create modern science.* Cambridge: Icon Books.

Isherwood, Robert M. 1986. *Popular entertainment in eighteenth-century Paris.* Oxford: Oxford University Press.

Jacob, Margaret C., and Larry Stewart. In press. *The impact of Western science: From Newton to the Crystal Palace Exhibition of 1851.* Cambridge, Mass.: Harvard University Press.

Jardin, Lisa. 1996. *Worldly goods: A new history of the Renaissance.* New York: Talese.

Jenkins, Dominick. 2002. *The final frontier: America, science, and terror.* London: Verso.

Jordanova, Ludmilla. 1989. Objects of knowledge: A historical perspective on museums. In *The new museology*, ed. Peter Vergo. London: Reaktion Books.

Kevles, Daniel K. 1978. *The physicists: The history of a scientific community in modern America.* New York: Knopf.

Martin, Julian. 1992. *Francis Bacon, the state, and the reform of natural philosophy.* Cambridge: Cambridge University Press.

Miller, David Philip. 1996. Joseph Banks, empire, and "centers of calculation" in late Hanoverian London. In *Visions of empire: Voyages, botany, and representation of nature*, ed. David Philip Miller and Peter Hans Reill. Cambridge: Cambridge University Press.

Morton, Alan Q., and Jane Wess. 1993. *Public and private science: The King George III Collection.* Oxford: Oxford University Press, in association with the Science Museum.

Morus, Iwan Rhys. 1998. *Frankenstein's children: Electricity, exhibition, and experiment in early-nineteenth-century London.* Princeton, N.J.: Princeton University Press.

Oppenheimer Frank. 1987. Exploratorium. In *Interactive science and technology centres*, compiled by Stephen Pizzey. London: Science Projects Publishing.

Pickstone, John V. 2000. *Ways of knowing: A new history of science, technology and medicine*. Chicago: University of Chicago Press.

Pumfrey, Stephen. 2002. *Latitude and the magnetic earth: The true story of Queen Elizabeth's most distinguished man of science*. Cambridge: Icon Books.

Schaffer, Simon. 1996. Visions of empire. In *Visions of empire: Voyages, botany, and representation of nature*, ed. David Philip Miller and Peter Hans Reill. Cambridge: Cambridge University Press.

———. 1997a. Metrology, metrication, and Victorian values. In *Victorian science in context*, ed. Bernard Lightman. Chicago: University of Chicago Press.

———. 1997b. Temporary contemporary: Some puzzles of science in action. In *Here and now: Contemporary science and technology in museums and science centres*, ed. Graham Farmelo and Janet Carding. London: Science Museum.

Schwartz, Maxime. 2003. *How the cows turned mad*. Translated by Edward Schneider. Berkeley and Los Angeles: University of California Press.

Sobel, Dava. 1996. *Longitude: The true story of a lone genius who solved the greatest scientific problem of his time*. New York: Penguin.

Stewart, Larry. 1992. *The rise of public science: Rhetoric, technology, and natural philosophy in Newtonian Britain, 1660–1750*. Cambridge: Cambridge University Press.

Tudge, Colin. 2000. *In Mendel's footnotes: An introduction to the science and technologies of genes and genetics from the 19th century to the 22nd*. London: Jonathan Cape.

Wright, William. 1999. *Born that way: Genes/behavior/personality*. New York: Routledge.

2

The Challenge and the Opportunity of Presenting "Unfinished Science"

John Durant

The very close interdependence of science and society first came to be generally recognized only in the second half of the twentieth century. Prior to 1950, science was generally regarded as a thing apart. To be sure, the Great War, in which science played a pivotal role, provided some pretty strong clues. But when the eminent physicist J. D. Bernal announced in 1937 that Marxism "removes science from its imagined position of complete detachment and shows it as part, a critically important part, of economic and social development," he did not yet speak for the generality of scientists, scholars, and politicians (Bernal 1937). Following the Second World War, of course, Bernal's basic point came to be very widely accepted—and this not on the authority of his beloved Marxism, but rather on the plain evidence of the senses. In an age of nuclear power, nanotechnology, and the NASDAQ, it does not require sophisticated political philosophy to discern that science is a critically important part of economic and social development.

Today it is commonplace that science and science-based technologies occupy a central place in our society. This basic fact has multiple implications for science as well as for wider culture. It means, for example, that decisions about what science is done and how that science is done are influenced by factors far beyond the narrow confines of the professional scientific community—by questions about the availability of research funding, about the potential distribution of benefits and risks, and about economic, environmental, ethical, social, and legal implications. By the same token, it also means that the wider community has a considerable stake in the outcomes of scientific inquiry. Across the industrialized world, citizens are increasingly reluctant to leave science to scientists, confident in the knowledge that "they know best." Reinforced by a general decline in deference toward authority and expertise of all kinds, the emergence of a critical cultural climate for science has placed new burdens and responsibilities on scientists themselves. No longer is it sufficient for scientists simply to obtain funding, to undertake research, and to publish results; increasingly, they find themselves obliged—by funders, other stakeholders and interest groups, and the mass media—to account publicly for what they are doing.

The shift of science to cultural center stage has profound implications for the work of science museums and science centers. For just as science and society are closely interdependent, so too are the science–society relationship and the work of science museums and science centers. In the nineteenth and early twentieth centuries, when science was still widely regarded as a thing

At-Bristol in Bristol, England, is a unique destination bringing science, nature, and art to life. Photo courtesy of At-Bristol

apart, cultural attitudes toward science and technology were generally cele-
bratory. Mirroring these attitudes, the great scientific and technical museums
of nineteenth-century Europe created exhibitions that were frankly tri-
umphalist: row upon row of marvelous machines testified to the progressive
harnessing of natural elements and forces to human purposes. In the mid-
twentieth century, as cultural attitudes started to shift, there was increasing
concern about the supply of scientifically and technically qualified labor to
meet the needs of rapidly expanding industrial economies, and huge efforts
were made to improve science and technology education. Once again, science
museums responded to the challenge. Hands-on interactivity—pioneered at
the Exploratorium and the Ontario Science Center in the late 1960s and then
spreading rapidly across North America, western Europe, and other parts of
the world—changed the focus of science museum exhibits from passive admiration of technical accomplishment to active learning of scientific and
technological principles.

*A young visitor at At-Bristol
learns by doing.* Photo courtesy
of At-Bristol

To the cultural preoccupation with the supply of scientifically trained manpower has been added in recent years a growing concern to respond appropriately to the increasingly critical climate of public opinion about science and technology. Though the extent of public disenchantment with science has surely been exaggerated (particularly in western Europe), there is no doubt that the 1980s and 1990s witnessed a series of high-profile public debates across the industrialized world in which science and technology featured as villains—or at least prime suspects—rather than as heroes. In discussions about issues as varied as energy and the environment, agricultural biotechnology and genetically modified food, and the use of animals in biomedical research, concerned citizens challenged the judgments of scientists and science policymakers and claimed the right to a greater say in decisions about the direction and oversight of scientific research. Here, I suggest, is one immediate and important source of current interest within the museum world in closer engagement with scientific research. This interest represents our community's latest response to the changing social circumstances in which we operate.

Having said this, I want to emphasize that the shift in focus represented by the phrase "public understanding of research" has the potential to be every bit as significant for the work of science museums and science centers as the shift more than a generation ago from passive spectacle to active, discovery-based learning. This is because the focus on scientific research requires an almost entirely different approach to that adopted in conventional hands-on exhibitions, and this different approach has radical implications for museums' relationships—with the scientific and technological communities, with their visitors, and with one another. In this chapter, therefore, I want to reflect on the deeper implications of the move into public understanding of research. I suggest that this move represents an invitation to museums to become fundamentally different sorts of places in the community—not secular cathedrals, as they were in the nineteenth and early twentieth centuries, nor yet educational playgrounds, as so many of them became in the late twentieth century, but rather public forums for active engagement between scientists and citizens in some of the most interesting, intriguing, and important issues of the day.

HISTORICAL REPRISE

A little over ten years ago I wrote something that still captures what I believe is the essential challenge facing museums in the area of public understanding of research:

I am struck by a curious shared weakness in the otherwise rather different contents of science centres and science museums. For both types of institution have a tendency to represent science in a way that divorces it from social reality. The image of science that I find in most science centres is one of clear, elementary principles waiting to be discovered by anyone with sufficient child-like curiosity and adult patience to search them out. By contrast, the image of science that I find in most science museums (including, it should be said, large parts of my own) is one of sure and solid progress in the mastery of nature. In both cases, science itself emerges as a fixed body of knowledge and practice, more or less totally beyond either doubt or dispute, and in both cases, two relevant social groups are strangely absent: first, the authors of all these achievements, scientists themselves; and second, the wider culture within which these people pursue their work.

In my view, museums should strive to find new and more effective ways of portraying science in the making. For only in this way can we be true both to the nature of science itself and to the needs of a general public which is continuously exposed to new (and often conflicting) scientific knowledge claims in the mass media. (Durant 1992, viii)

This passage comes from the introduction to a collection of essays that I put together for the London Science Museum in 1992. North American readers should note that the contrast it makes between science museums and science centers rests on the conventional British English distinction—not widely adhered to in American English—between institutions that own and display collections of intrinsic value (science museums) and institutions that do not (science centers). The difference in interpretive style between these two types of institution was already in process of being undermined in the early 1990s, as more and more science museums chose to adopt the distinctively interactive style of hands-on science centers. Since then, this convergence has continued apace to the point where today it is hard to tell the difference between many science museums and science centers. Only in universities blessed with traditional museums of the history of science does one still commonly find displays based largely or wholly around sequences of objects designed to display the progressive intellectual and practical mastery of nature; and even here, such an approach is now widely regarded as rather quaint and old-fashioned.

My main point more than a decade ago was, of course, that neither science museums nor science centers were engaged very closely with current or ongoing scientific research. While the former were preoccupied with celebrating the great scientific and technological achievements of the past, the latter were preoccupied with explaining well-established scientific and technological principles. In their different ways, therefore, both were involved mainly with the interpretation of what I term "finished science"—that is, science that has ceased to be the subject of serious debate among scientists themselves; neither group of institutions was substantially engaged in the radically different business of interpreting "unfinished science," or what Shapin terms "science-in-the-making" (Shapin 1992). This historical fact is somewhat paradoxical since most other forms of popular science communication (such as newspaper and magazine articles, books, and radio and television programs) have long concentrated on unfinished rather than finished science—and this precisely because the wider public has always been more interested in new or emerging scientific discoveries than in the discoveries of the past.

Since the early 1990s, a number of science museums and science centers on both sides of the Atlantic have become more interested in dealing with unfinished science. In the London Science Museum, for example, the attempt to engage with the world of contemporary science and technology represented the main thrust of exhibition development throughout the 1990s. Similarly, in the late 1990s, the Museum of Science in Boston undertook a major initiative designed to place the realities of ongoing scientific research in front of its visitors. The Wellcome Wing at the Science Museum in London (opened in 2000) and the Current Science and Technology program at the Museum of Science in Boston (launched in 2001) represent two significant—and significantly different—attempts on the part of relatively large and well-established museums to introduce the public understanding of research onto the museum floor in a vivid and sustainable way. The interest generated by the "Museums, Media, and the Public Understanding of Research" conference at the Science Museum of Minnesota in September 2002 testifies to the fact that these two museums were not alone in regarding this issue as of prime importance.

WHY FOCUS ON UNFINISHED SCIENCE?

Before going any further, I want to say a word or two about some key terms. I take the phrase "public understanding of research" to denote the analytical distinction between the intellectual products of science (such as data, evidence, models, hypotheses, and theories) and the intellectual processes of science (such as data collection, model making, hypothesizing, and theorizing).

All the intellectual products of science—past as well as present—are the results of research processes that are in principle open to being described and understood. Thus, a focus on public understanding of research need not necessarily imply an exclusive concern with the science of today as opposed to the science of yesterday. Rather, it implies a concern with the means by which scientific claims and conclusions are being or have been arrived at rather than with the contents of those claims and conclusions.

By contrast, the phrase "unfinished science" denotes what is essentially a sociological distinction between scientific claims and conclusions that are settled to the satisfaction of the scientific community (finished science) and scientific claims and conclusions that, for whatever reasons—the novelty of the subject matter, the availability of new research techniques, the absence or inconsistency of evidence, the paucity of theory—are unsettled within the scientific community (unfinished science). At any given moment in time, finished science represents the body of scientific knowledge that scientists take for granted as they go about their work, and unfinished science represents their work itself. Notoriously, finished science dominates the lives of most science teachers and students, whereas by contrast unfinished science dominates the thoughts and activities of working scientists.

Clearly, the boundaries between finished and unfinished science are not fixed. It is commonplace among exponents of science and scientific method that all scientific findings—however apparently "finished"—are open in principle to challenge and revision. This piece of conventional wisdom is reflected in the historical and sociological fact—familiar to anyone who has studied, say, the revolution in the biological sciences in the mid-nineteenth century or the revolution in the physical sciences in the early years of the twentieth—that what is taken for granted by the scientific community at one time (say, the fundamental truth of the axioms of Newtonian physics) can come to be regarded by that same community as in need of radical revision (say, following the Michelson–Morley experiment or the publication of Einstein's first paper on special relativity). A new observation, a new experiment, a new idea: these and many other things besides can change overnight the status of a particular body of scientific knowledge from finished to unfinished, and the results of such change are often profoundly disturbing as well as important.

If we are interested in public understanding of research, then clearly we can pursue this interest in any area of science—finished or unfinished, past or present. In this chapter, however, I am particularly concerned with the potential of unfinished science as a resource for the public understanding of research for two principal reasons. First, while finished science is the result of discoverable research processes, the fact that we know (or think we know) the outcome of these processes in advance makes it particularly difficult to obtain a clear and disinterested view of them. This is because we are always at risk of proverbial "wisdom of hindsight"—what the historian E. P. Thompson once termed "the enormous condescension of history." To be sure, historians are professionally expert at avoiding the more obvious pitfalls of such condescension, and even some science popularizers manage to steer clear of them. But there is nothing quite like the radical uncertainty of manifestly unfinished science for forcing people's attention to the processes by which scientific knowledge is established. Here, no wisdom of hindsight is easily available, and condescension is not an available option. With unfinished science, scientists and citizens alike frequently have little choice but to explore the various points of view on offer and then try to make up their own minds about the issues as best they can.

A second reason for focusing on unfinished science has to do with its intrinsic interest and potential importance to the wider public. Newtonian physics, Daltonian chemistry, and Bernardian biology are all scientifically interesting and important, but on the whole they do not now figure prominently in the public domain since their everyday applications and implications are mostly so familiar and so well established as to be largely taken for granted. By contrast, at any given point in time a significant amount of unfinished science is extremely prominent in the public domain. This is partly because novelty itself is a news value in science, just as much as anywhere else, and partly because the unfinished business of science often has important applications and implications that are unclear, uncertain, and/or contested. Does cold fusion offer the prospects of cheap and easily available nuclear energy? Does the memory of water offer scientific substance to the claims of homeopathic medicine? Does GM food offer a cheaper and more environmentally friendly solution to the world's food supply problems? Over the past few years, these and dozens of similar questions have been raised by any number of different areas of unfinished science. The point for science communicators, of course, is that every one of these questions is a potential resource for the public understanding of research.

THE CHALLENGE AND THE OPPORTUNITY OF UNFINISHED SCIENCE

Having made the case for focusing on unfinished science, in the remainder of this chapter, I turn next to a closer consideration of some of the more obvious differences between finished and unfinished science as far as science communicators working in science museums and science centers are concerned. Some key contrasts are set out in table 2.1.

Table 2.1. Finished and Unfinished Science and the Challenge for Museums

Finished Science	Unfinished Science	Challenge for Museums
Story complete	Story incomplete	How to identify the story?
Unchanging	Changing	How to track the story?
Significance clear	Significance unclear	How to tell the story?
Characterized by knowledge	Characterized by ignorance	How to deal with partiality?
Characterized by certainty	Characterized by uncertainty	How to handle doubt?
Scientists mostly agree	Scientists often disagree	How to handle controversy?
Attention focused on pay-off—"so what?"	Attention focused on process—"what's up?"	How to handle human & cultural dimension?

Exhibitions tell three-dimensional stories. When exhibitors deal with finished science, they generally know where they are: in scientific terms, at least, the story is likely to be complete, experts are likely to agree on what is and is not the case, and the significance of what has been established (in scientific terms) is likely to be clear. Of course, where the focus is on public understanding of research rather than on public understanding of the results of research, there is still room for alternative approaches and views. History is inevitably interpretive, and even in the case of finished science there is plenty of scope for historians to disagree about how particular bodies of knowledge have come to be established. Such disagreement, however, is essentially historical or sociological rather than scientific in character; by definition, finished science raises few if any serious scientific disagreements. For all these reasons, exhibitors who deal with finished science have the great advantage of being able to set about the interpretation of what is likely to be a relatively stable and unambiguous knowledge base.

Contrast this situation with the position that exhibitors find themselves in when they turn their attention to unfinished science. Now it is much harder to identify, track, and tell the story; and as exhibitors struggle to do these difficult things, they frequently find themselves having to deal with partiality, provisionality, and controversy. Experts will often disagree about what is and is not the case and why it is or is not important, and as often as not, attention will naturally come to focus—for scientific as well as historical reasons—on the processes, the personalities, and the politics of research. Lest all this should seem to be a recipe for disaster, however, it should also be observed that partiality, provisionality, and controversy are frequently the stuff of high drama. Unfinished science presents multiple opportunities to science communicators of all kinds—including exhibitors—precisely because the need to engage with the research process puts "the thrill of the chase" itself under the spotlight.

An example from my own experience will serve to illustrate the point. In the early 1990s, we developed in the London Science Museum a series of small, fast-turnaround, temporary exhibitions on contemporary science and technology. The exhibitions were called Science Box. A flexible, reusable exhibition display system allowed us to develop small (50–100 m^2) temporary exhibitions on single topics in periods of two or three months. One Science Box exhibition dealt with the health effects of passive smoking. At the time we worked on this subject, it was very definitely in the category of unfinished science. Expert evidence on the subject was still being actively collected and collated, and scientists differed on key questions such as the nature and the severity of the health effects of passive smoking. Argument was actively under way in the public domain, and partisan interest groups were actively lobbying on behalf of their various points of view.

All this presented the Science Box exhibition team with a considerable challenge. How should experts who were sharply critical of one another be consulted? How should lobbyists—some of whom applied direct pressure on us to deal with the issues in particular ways—be dealt with? And what about the commercial interests of the tobacco industry? Above all, how were we to ensure that we presented a clear and fair account of the issues to visitors? This last challenge was felt rather acutely, not least because as the exhibition team researched the issues, they found themselves increasingly persuaded of one particular point of view in the scientific debate. In the end, it was decided to minimize the risk of conscious or unconscious bias in the exhibition by being extremely open about both the exhibition and the scientific research processes. Visitors were informed that the health effects of passive smoking were currently under active scientific investigation, that experts disagreed among themselves, and that interest groups and lobbyists were campaigning on both sides of the argument. Relevant scientific evidence was presented in unusual detail—up to and including specific references to the relevant research literature, all of which was made available in the Science Museum Library for visitors who wanted to pursue matters further for themselves. Finally, visitors were informed that in the course of preparing the exhibition, the exhibitors themselves had come to the view that the balance of the available evidence lay on one side of the argument.

Passive Smoking is an example of an exhibition that came to focus extremely closely on aspects of the research process precisely because it dealt with science that was both unfinished and extremely controversial. Nothing serves to illustrate the distinctive character and qualities of scientific inquiry quite as well as the need to make sense of active argument and disagreement between experts working at the cutting edge of a particular research field. Here methods and techniques are refined (and rendered obsolete), observations are made (and disputed), hunches are confirmed (and dismissed), theories are validated (and invalidated), fashions are established (and exposed), and reputations are won (and lost). The struggle to secure new knowledge about the natural world exposes the workings of science—warts and all—to public view, and this presents the museum exhibitor prepared to work in this challenging area with several important opportunities.

First, the presentation of unfinished science obliges museums to engage with science and scientists in new ways. Except in those cases (such as some of the larger natural history museums around the world) where museums host significant scientific research activity based around their collections, the decision to present ongoing research to visitors requires museums to build new and closer links with the scientific community. At the very least, some sort of journalistic effort must be made to track and report particular kinds of scientific research. But in addition, researchers may be brought in to advise museum staff and/or to report their work directly to visitors, and aspects of the research process itself may even be relocated in the museum—as, for example, in the Wellcome Wing at the London Science Museum's Live Science facility, which allows museum visitors to volunteer to become subjects in ongoing biomedical research projects. When unfinished science first becomes the subject of serious attention in a science museum, that institution becomes (or ought to become) imbued with the research ethos of the scientific enterprise itself.

Second, the presentation of unfinished science obliges museums to engage with their visitors in new ways. No longer can the museum pretend to "have all the answers," and no longer, either, can it presume that the role of the visitor is simply to look, to listen, and to learn. When the science is unfinished, the story must be open-ended, and the true import of what is being dealt with must remain open to question. This situation creates new and potentially creative possibilities in the relationship between the museum and the visitor. Indeed, given sufficient courage on the part of the museum, it can be allowed to introduce a measure of equality between the exhibitor/presenter and the visitor that is truly liberating. The museum exhibitor or presenter who has the intellectual confidence to freely confess and even revel in his or her ignorance about what is "really going on" has the potential ability to empower the visitor to participate more fully in science. If ignorance and uncertainty come to be understood as preconditions for rather than barriers to research, then ignorant and uncertain visitors may be better encouraged to set out on the adventure of research for themselves.

Third, the presentation of unfinished science leads inevitably to the reexamination of the professional relationships among science museums and science centers. The costs of tracking the ongoing research process are very high—too high, certainly, for any but the largest and best-endowed museums in the world to undertake in any but the most carefully restricted areas of scientific inquiry. Just as newspapers long ago abandoned the notion of individually and independently gathering, sifting, and presenting the world's news for their readers, so museums committed to presenting current science and technology are now beginning to feel the need to abandon their (generally deeply entrenched) methods of working in splendid isolation from one another. What we need, surely, is the museum equivalent of the news media's wire services, that is, recognized sources of high-quality, up-to-date information about the ongoing research process that can be rapidly and cheaply accessed by individual science museums and science centers for purposes of presenting exhibitions and programs about particular areas of ongoing scientific research.

It is too early, probably, to specify the exact form such museum wire services should take. Almost certainly, they will comprise specially commissioned digital multimedia that are capable of being easily repurposed by particular museums or science centers. The reason for this is that existing generic science news services, while certainly useful, do not lend themselves readily to the needs of many science museums and science centers; instead, they require too much work (and cost) for purposes of creating lively, up-to-date displays and public programs on current science and technology. This being so, what we need are museum-originated materials that have already been compiled with a view to the distinctive needs of the exhibition floor. There would seem to be no reason, for example, why particular areas of research should not be allocated to particular, well-placed museums for regular tracking, information gathering, and digital dissemination. In this way, a multiple "hub and spoke" process of information exchange across the science museum community could bring high-quality, fast-changing contemporary science displays and programs within the reach of a significant number of museums and science centers around the world.

A NEW ROLE FOR SCIENCE MUSEUMS AND SCIENCE CENTERS?

We stand on the threshold of a new era in science communication. Across the industrialized world, there are calls for new forms of engagement between scientists and citizens as an essential precondition for the maintenance of public confidence in the ongoing research and development processes. Everywhere, monologue is out, and dialogue is in; authoritative expert pronouncement is out, and informed public debate is in (U.K. House of Lords 2000). In this situation, our culture urgently needs to find new kinds of social spaces where scientists and citizens can meet as equals to consider the state of the research process and the options—scientific, technical, economic, environmental, ethical, social, political, and legal—that we face. There is a role here for science museums and science centers that are prepared to work together in new ways around programs designed to facilitate closer public engagement with research. Such work will transform science museums and science centers in the twenty-first century, and, given a lot of innovation and hard work, it may also help transform our culture in ways that will provide benefits both to science itself and to wider society.

REFERENCES

Bernal, J. D. 1937. Dialectical materialism and modern science. *Science and Society* 2, no. 1.

Durant, J. 1992. Introduction. In *Museums and the Public Understanding of Science.* London: Science Museum.

Shapin, S. 1992. Why the public ought to understand science-in-the-making. *Public Understanding of Science* 1, no. 20: 27–30.

U.K. House of Lords. 2000. Science and society. Report of the House of Lords Select Committee on Science. London: Her Majesty's Stationery Office.

Section 2

PUBLIC UNDERSTANDING OF RESEARCH: THE BIG OPPORTUNITIES AND ISSUES

What are the central issues involved in presenting public understanding of research (PUR) programs in museums? After clarifying how PUR contrasts with "public understanding of science" and with "science literacy," we must decide how to deliver our strategy to our audience. We can achieve this only through a combination of good evaluation and inspired programming ideas that will almost certainly involve imaginative collaborations with research organizations and with other media. This is even more challenging than it sounds—in practice, PUR initiatives usually have to compete with more overtly populist programming.

Different Ways of Looking at Public Understanding of Research

Bruce V. Lewenstein and Rick Bonney

This book is about public understanding of research (PUR). But the very term means different things to different people. Thus, a big issue to address is the definition of PUR or at least a sense of the different meanings that it might convey.

Larry Stewart's overview in chapter 1 demonstrates that the interaction of public and research has a long history. But as a formal term defining particular programs or approaches, "public understanding of research" emerged at the U.S. National Science Foundation (NSF) in the late 1990s when Hyman Field, who had directed NSF's Informal Science Education program, started a new Public Understanding of Research initiative. He defined PUR as public education that helps laypeople understand what *current research* is being conducted; helps them consider what the social, ethical, and policy implications of new findings might be; and helps them recognize the importance of continued support for both basic and applied research (Field and Powell 2001). In Field's view, PUR should focus on cutting-edge research—on findings where "the truth" might not be certain but where the greatest excitement in science takes place. Field explicitly contrasted PUR's focus on "research into the unknown" with what he characterized as informal science education's focus on "established science knowledge."

An alternative definition, which has been less formally stated but which many practitioners have followed for years, highlights outreach activities that help laypeople understand the *process* of research. Just as introductory science textbooks often include a section on "the scientific method," practitioners of informal science education often stress the importance of introducing non-scientists to the processes of inquiry, questioning, evidence gathering, logic, and exploration that lead researchers to reliable knowledge about nature (Hein 1990). Different groups highlight different aspects of that process: while scientists focus on the formal "hypothetico-deductive method" or point to Karl Popper's definition of science as falsifiable knowledge, historians and sociologists of science have looked at the combinations of logic and social processes that lead researchers to their conclusions—and their often vigorous, even acrimonious disputes about conclusions (Bauer 1992; Collins and Pinch 1993; Ziman 2000).

While not mutually exclusive, these two approaches to defining PUR can lead to differing decisions about appropriate content for a PUR program, be it an exhibit, a lecture, a debate, a publication, a video, or a community-based project. If a museum is looking for speakers or demonstrators about dinosaurs, for example, does it need the "big name" who made the latest discovery or a good explainer who can show how the discovery was achieved? What is the role of history in an exhibit about genetics—background about DNA that helps explain the most recent discovery or the central core of a story line about James Watson, Frances Crick, Rosalind Franklin, and the process through which reliable knowledge about heredity was produced? Given limited resources and time, should designers of an exhibit on a fast-moving field like nanotechnology focus on an ability to rapidly change information or instead concentrate on creating instruments that will demonstrate the process of research into unseen worlds?

Field is unequivocal about the need to concentrate on public understanding of *current* research. "The results of many studies and experiments in which scientists are currently engaged will undoubtedly have profound impacts on the lives of citizens in developed and developing nations," he and colleague Patricia Powell wrote (Field and Powell 2001). "Yet few people even know what research is being conducted, much less understand why it is being done and what the potential implications may be. . . . The field of informal, public education is uniquely poised to reach the public at all levels, so that those who need the information most, i.e., those who make or will make decisions for themselves and their families, have access to accurate, up-to-date, unbiased, and substantive information."

Efforts to inform the public about current research are not new. In fact, many science journalists would argue that their main goal has always been public understanding of current research (Blum and Knudson 1997). Magazines, newspapers, and television programs frequently produce stories describing current research, often with the active support of scientific institutions (Porter 2002). In museums, however, the focus on current research is much less common (Farmelo and Carding 1997), even though cutting-edge scientific research is in fact at the foundation of some museums, such as those that focus on natural history. Because research is dynamic—with new results constantly changing the course of investigation—museum displays often avoid current research. Any exhibit or program that describes an investigation must be updated frequently, a process that is not so hard in a newspaper or even a periodic community program but that can be challenging or impossible in venues such as permanent exhibits.

The second PUR approach, helping the public understand research as a process, is also difficult to accomplish in a museum setting. Museums are great at displaying and interpreting objects, whether traditional collected objects or the constructed exhibits often seen in science centers. Museums have more difficulty displaying process and human activity (though the many examples presented elsewhere in this volume suggest that the challenge can be surmounted). Nonetheless, most educators consider presentation of process to be essential. Recall the proverb "Give a man a fish and you feed him for a day; teach a man to fish and you feed him for a lifetime."[1] The analogy is that if a museum can help someone understand how research is conducted—that scientific investigation involves observations and trials, controls and correlations, repetitions and revisions—then that individual should be able to understand and evaluate scientific claims and conclusions encountered in the course of daily life.

These two meanings of PUR—focus on the cutting edge or focus on the process—are not mutually exclusive, nor is conflict necessary between them. But they do reflect differing assessments of the important issues in the broad field of public communication of science and technology. To explore these issues, it is useful to recall similar debates that have shaped the field. Indeed, the first debate has been what to call it. As the field emerged in the 1940s and 1950s, it was called "public understanding of science," and the current NSF program on Informal Science Education is a direct descendant of the public understanding of science program created at NSF in 1958 (Lewenstein 1992). In the late 1980s, "public understanding of science" became a mantra in the United Kingdom after a Royal Society report bearing that title, and some commentators now refer to a public understanding of science "movement" (Miller 2001; Royal Society 1985).

The phrase "public understanding of science," however, has often carried the meaning of "public appreciation of and support for science and scientists" (Lewenstein 1992). Critics of this meaning have suggested that one outcome might well be more criticism of science, as nonscientists better understand the limitations of scientific knowledge. Or more public understanding might lead to more anger toward science as public knowledge develops about the linkages between scientific research and negative effects such as environmental pollution and industrial accidents on the scale of the 1979 Three Mile Island nuclear reactor accident or the 1984 Bhopal chemical explosion. To address these critiques, some commentators have begun using "public engagement in science," sometimes referring to the first definition of PUR (paying attention to and sometimes shaping or reacting to recent discoveries in science), while other times meaning the second (becoming involved in the scientific process without regard to current findings) (Association of British Science Writers 2003; House of Lords 2000; Leshner 2003).

These debates about whether public understanding is fundamentally about generating support for science or about gaining perspective that can be used for support, for criticism, or for some kind of more neutral edification draw on earlier disputes about "science literacy" that attempted both to define its components and to specify how it might be measured (American Association for the Advancement of Science 1993; Bauer 1992; Hazen and Trefil 1991; Holton 1983; Laetsch 1987; Miller 1983; Shen 1975; Thomas and Durant 1987; Trefil 1992). People who focused on science literacy often developed lists of facts, statements about specific scientific findings, questions about scientific institutions and the context in which scientific research is conducted, and questions about the processes of scientific research; scientifically literate persons were expected to be able to give the "right" answers (as determined by those creating the lists). One strand of the science literacy discussion has led to science education curriculum reform in the United States, especially the creation of the National Science Education Standards, which define the areas of knowledge that students should master (including both facts about the natural world and understanding of the logical and social processes of science) (Bybee 1997; National Research Council 1996; Project 2061 2001). Another outcome of debates about science literacy has been a series of formal quantitative models of science literacy that can be assessed via surveys of representative samples of national publics; these surveys, based largely (though not entirely) on the lists of facts and issues that people "should know," have now been conducted worldwide (see, for example, Miller 1998; Miller, Pardo, and Niwa 1997; National Science Board 2002).

Within the community of researchers, practitioners, and commentators concerned about public understanding of science (rather than science education in the schools), a number of critics have questioned whether quantitative measurement of "science literacy" is possible—or even whether science literacy is the right goal (Shamos 1995; Wynne 1995; Ziman 1992). Because the surveys usually show how little "the public" knows about specific aspects of science, the results are often accompanied by calls for efforts to improve science literacy. Fill the "deficit" of public knowledge, the reformers imply, and all will be well. Critics have suggested, however, that particular publics may have reasons for not knowing (for example, deliberate ignorance as a tool for managing uncertainty) or may simply have no need to know particular aspects of science and thus may choose to put their resources into other areas of endeavor (Michael, Grinyer, and Turner 1997; Ziman 1992). In addition, the "deficit model" often assumes a trust in scientific institutions that contemporary social research suggests is not always present—sometimes for good reason (Irwin and Wynne 1996). Quantitative researchers have developed a series of more elaborate and refined models to address concerns that social context is stripped from the quantitative studies (Bauer 2000; Sturgis and Allum, 2004), while critics continue to push for less precise but more comprehensive visions of what science literacy might be. The debate is clearly still in progress (Bauer, Petkova, and Boyadjjewa 2000; Bauer and Schoon 1993; Godin and Gingras 2000; Kallerud and Ramburg 2002; Office of Science and Technology and Wellcome Trust 2000; Roth and Lee 2002; Wynne 1996).

Two concerns of the critics of quantitative measurements are relevant for thinking about different perspectives on PUR. First is the concern that the survey approach to science literacy is too focused on facts. What the public needs, the critics suggest, is not more information about current findings but greater understanding of the processes by which researchers come to their findings. The perspective on PUR that highlights scientific processes without concern for current findings is closer to the position held by the critics.

A second concern is the critics' attention to the social context of scientific research. They argue, based on case studies, that members of particular publics made decisions about scientific findings based largely on trust. At a moment of controversy or conflict, people with incomplete knowledge or information will choose to trust the institutions in their community that have created bonds through previous interaction and open dialogue. The shift to discussions about "public engagement" referred to previously has in part been driven by these concerns about social trust. The goal of any PUR activities, the public engagement argument suggests, should be to create opportunities for experts and lay audiences to learn from each other—partly so that lay audiences can learn the science but also very much so that researchers will understand the public's concerns about their work and may even take those concerns into account as they direct their research projects. Often, public engagement activities such as consensus conferences have been created to respond to political controversy, such as genetic testing, xenotransplantation, or genetically modified foods (Einsiedel 2002; Einsiedel and Eastlick 2001; Irwin 2001; Joss 1999). Not surprisingly, the concept of public engagement troubles many scientists, for it implies that science can be appropriately guided by the choices and values of nonscientists. This idea directly conflicts with the belief that cutting-edge scientific research can proceed only when it seeks pure knowledge of the natural world and is free from political or social values and constraints.

In this complex stew of definitions and perspectives on public understanding, science literacy, and public engagement, the differing definitions of public understanding of research offer both challenge and hope. The challenge is to avoid bogging down in definitional lockjaw, unable to progress because of concerns about some particular activity or approach matching this or that category in one or another definition. Debating the differences is valuable because the process can highlight particular assumptions or perspectives that might otherwise be hidden. But the value can come at the cost of action.

The hope that emerges is precisely that which comes from the intellectual clarity arising from definitional debate. Focusing on *current research* is different than focusing on *process of research.* Focusing on bodies of knowledge is different than focusing on social and ethical implications. Focusing on the people who conduct research is different than focusing on the products of that research. No particular approach to public understanding of research, or public understanding of science, or science literacy is "correct." But we are all better off by understanding the components that make up these amorphous and overlapping fields. By exploring the various approaches, we can better see where our own activities fit into a matrix of possibilities and thus better understand the implications of choices we make about our projects. Such exploration leads to better and stronger PUR efforts.

NOTE

1. Attributed to Lao Tzu, called the "Father of Taoism," at www.brainyquote.com/ quotes/quotes/l/q121559.html (accessed May 21, 2003).

REFERENCES

American Association for the Advancement of Science. 1993. *Benchmarks for science literacy.* New York: Oxford University Press.

Association of British Science Writers. 2003. *Public engagement with science and technology.* www.absw.org.uk/PEST.htm (accessed May 21, 2003).

Bauer, H. H. 1992. *Scientific literacy and the myth of the scientific method.* Urbana: University of Illinois Press.

Bauer, M. 2000. "Science in the media" as cultural indicator: Contextualising surveys with media analysis. In *Between understanding and trust: The public, science and technology,* ed. M. Dierkes and C. Von Grote. Reading, Mass.: Harwood Academic Publishers, 157–78.

Bauer, M. W., K. Petkova, and P. Boyadjjewa. 2000. Public knowledge of and attitudes to science—Alternative measures. *Science, Technology and Human Values* 25, no. 1: 30–51.

Bauer, M. W., and L. Schoon. 1993. Mapping variety in public understanding of science. *Public Understanding of Science* 2, no. 2: 141–55.

Blum, D., and M. Knudson, eds. 1997. *A field guide to science writing: The official guide of the National Association of Science Writers.* New York: Oxford University Press.

Bybee, R. W. 1997. *Achieving scientific literacy: From purposes to practices.* Portsmouth, N.H.: Heinemann.

Collins, H. M., and T. Pinch. 1993. *The Golem: What everyone should know about science.* Cambridge: Cambridge University Press.

Einsiedel, E. 2002. Assessing a controversial medical technology: Canadian public consultations on xenotransplantation. *Public Understanding of Science* 11, no. 4: 315–31.

Einsiedel, E., and D. L. Eastlick. 2001. Consensus conferences as deliberative democracy: A communications perspective. *Science Communication* 21, no. 4: 323–43.

Farmelo, G., and J. Carding. 1997. *Here and now: Contemporary science and technology in museums and science centres.* London: Science Museum.

Field, H., and P. Powell. 2001. Public understanding of science versus public understanding of research. *Public Understanding of Science* 10, no. 4: 421–26.

Godin, B., and Y. Gingras. 2000. What is scientific and technological culture and how is it measured? A multidimensional model. *Public Understanding of Science* 9, no. 1: 43–58.

Hazen, R., and J. Trefil. 1991. *Science matters: Achieving scientific literacy.* New York: Doubleday.

Hein, H. 1990. *The Exploratorium: The museum as laboratory.* Washington, D.C.: Smithsonian Institution Press.

Holton, G. J., ed. 1983. Science literacy. *Daedalus* 112 (special issue): 1–251.

House of Lords. 2000. *Science and society.* London: U.K. House of Lords.

Irwin, A. 2001. Constructing the scientific citizen: Science and democracy in the biosciences. *Public Understanding of Science* 10, no. 1: 1–18.

Irwin, A., and B. Wynne, eds. 1996. *Misunderstanding science? The public reconstruction of science and technology.* Cambridge: Cambridge University Press.

Joss, S., ed. 1999. Public participation in science and technology. *Science and Public Policy* 26, no. 5 (special issue): 290–373.

Kallerud, E., and I. Ramburg. 2002. The order of discourse in surveys of public understanding of science. *Public Understanding of Science* 11, no. 3: 213–24.

Laetsch, W. M. 1987. A basis for better public understanding of science. In *Communicating science to the public*, ed. D. Evered and M. O'Connor. Chichester and New York: Wiley, 1–10.

Leshner, A. I. 2003. Public engagement with science. *Science* 299: 977.

Lewenstein, B. V. 1992. The meaning of "public understanding of science" in the United States after World War II. *Public Understanding of Science* 1, no. 1: 45–68.

Michael, M., A. Grinyer, and J. Turner. 1997. Teaching biotechnology: Identity in the context of ignorance and knowledgeability. *Public Understanding of Science* 6, no. 1: 1–17.

Miller, J. D. 1983. Scientific literacy: A conceptual and empirical review. *Daedalus* 112, no. 2: 29–48.

———. 1998. The measurement of civic scientific literacy. *Public Understanding of Science* 7, no. 3: 203–23.

Miller, J. D., R. Pardo, and F. Niwa. 1997. *Public attitudes toward science and technology: A comparative study of the European Union, the United States, Japan, and Canada.* Madrid: BBV Foundation.

Miller, S. 2001. Public understanding of science at the crossroads. *Public Understanding of Science* 10, no. 1: 115–20.

National Research Council. 1996. *National Science Education Standards.* Washington, D.C.: National Academy Press.

National Science Board. 2002. Science and technology: Public attitudes and public understanding. In *Science and Engineering Indicators—2002.* Washington, D.C.: U.S. Government Printing Office, chapter 7.

Office of Science and Technology and Wellcome Trust. 2000. *Science and the public: A review of science communication and public attitudes to science in Britain.* Vol. 2001. London: Wellcome Trust.

Porter, G., ed. 2002. *Communicating the future: Best practices for communication of science and technology to the public.* Gaithersburg, Md.: National Institute of Standards and Technology.

Project 2061. 2001. *Atlas of science literacy.* Washington, D.C.: American Association for the Advancement of Science and National Science Teachers Association.

Roth, W.-M., and S. Lee. 2002. Scientific literacy as collective praxis. *Public Understanding of Science* 11, no. 1: 33–56.

Royal Society. 1985. *The Public Understanding of Science.* London: Royal Society.

Shamos, M. 1995. *The myth of scientific literacy.* New Brunswick, N.J.: Rutgers University Press.

Shen, B. S. P. 1975. Science literacy and the public understanding of science. In *Communication of scientific information,* ed. S. Day Basel: Karger, 44–52.

Sturgis, P., and N. Allum. 2004. Science in society: Re-evaluating the deficit model of public attitudes. *Public Understanding of Science* 13, no 1.

Thomas, G., and J. Durant. 1987. Why should we promote the public understanding of science? In *Science literacy papers,* ed. M. Shortland. Oxford: University of Oxford Science Literacy Group, 1–14.

Trefil, J. 1992. *1001 things everyone should know about science.* New York: Doubleday.

Wynne, B. 1995. Public understanding of science. In *Handbook of science and technology studies,* ed. S. Jasanoff, G. E. Markle, J. C. Petersen, and T. Pinch. Thousand Oaks, Calif.: Sage, 361–88.

Wynne, B. 1996. May the sheep safely graze? A reflexive view of the expert–lay knowledge divide. In *Risk, environment and modernity: Towards a new ecology,* ed. S. Lash, B. Szerszynski, and B. Wynne. London: Sage, 44–83.

Ziman, J. 1992. Not knowing, needing to know, and wanting to know. In *When science meets the public,* ed. B. V. Lewenstein. Washington, D.C.: American Association for the Advancement of Science, 13–20.

———. 2000. *Real science.* Cambridge: Cambridge University Press.

4

Museums as Agora: Diversifying Approaches to Engaging Publics in Research

Albert A. Einsiedel Jr. and Edna F. Einsiedel

The Agora was the heart of ancient Athens. Literally meaning "marketplace," it was the locus of the business of everyday life. It was also the religious and cultural center, the venue where philosophers had intimate debates over ethical, religious, cultural, and political issues. Today, we observe some traditional museums changing into a modern-day museum agora, a public meeting place where citizens seek to discuss and understand scientific research and technological innovations as well as to learn about contentious issues and public policies that are associated with some of them.

Museums everywhere are undergoing changes as social, political, technological, and economic forces exert impacts on their repertoire of activities. These changes include changing conceptions of their audiences and how to interact with them. Discussions are taking place about the interaction of science, research, and public. One question that is relevant to science museums (but extends to other types) is whether the goal should be to focus on "science," on "research," or on the "social context" within which people make sense of their experiences with science and technology (Bradburne 1998). One outcome of those discussions is new attention to interactive public consultation processes as one tool for addressing public understanding of research.

Our task here is to discuss interactive public consultation processes in the context of museums. Our purpose is to explore ways in which new forms of public engagement, such as deliberative models of public consultation, can be adopted by museums to diversify their approaches to engaging the public in research.

Such a task is set with the recognition that the museum's traditional role of collecting, preserving, and interpreting for publics is necessary but is no longer sufficient in today's world. Museums have been exploring varied roles for themselves, including taking more active roles in helping publics and communities place themselves in a wider world and providing forums for critical thinking and continuing dialogue on issues of interest and concern (Bradburne 1998; Weil 1990).

Visits to museums and science centers can influence the public's perceptions of the nature of science. An Australian study (Rennie and Williams 2002), for instance, found that adults, after visiting an interactive science center, "were more likely to think that scientists always agree with each other, that scientific explanations are definite, and that science has the answers to all problems," leading them to feel more positive and comfortable with their relationship with science. While such perceptions may have public relations benefits to the science center, the study reported that many among the center staff "also felt there was room for improvement, especially in terms of how the nature of science was portrayed, and the representation of controversial aspects of science." By discussing the diversification of museum activities designed to enhance public understanding of scientific research, can we see if there is "room for improvement"?

THE ENGAGEMENT CONTINUUM
First, let us introduce the engagement continuum along which a museum's activities can be located. The continuum represents the degree to which the approach is passive or interactive. In promoting diversification, we mean the expansion of approaches to include both the passive and the interactive sides of the engagement continuum, approaches that are not mutually exclusive.

On the interactive side of the continuum, the public's understanding of research occurs in a social, economic, political, and environmental context of society. Further, the learners are regarded as experts in their own right, adults whose experiences, perceptions, beliefs, and concerns are valued and recognized as another valid way of knowing.

Engagement Continuum

PASSIVE _____ INTERACTIVE

Science in a vacuum   Science in context

Public as recipient   Public as an
of knowledge   inquiring expert

FIGURE 4.1
The Engagement Continuum

The passive side of the continuum can be suggestive of the traditional role of museums where content—whether it was artifacts, historical, artistic, or scientific knowledge—was presented without representations of context. This is increasingly recognized as being a less effective mode of interpretation. Some writers urge science museums to explore new models for engaging the community by creating environments in which informal learning can occur. Bradburne (1998), for instance, writes, "A learning society needs new institutions of informal learning, and institutions like Science North in Sudbury, the Science Alberta Foundation, the Ars Electronica Centrum in Linz, the ZKM in Karlsruhe, and the new Metropolis in Amsterdam all represent a new approach to the challenge of creating public informal learning environments" (245). At the same time, the passive mode is still very much in evidence in many museums that recognize that not all members of the publics are equally attentive to *all* topics *all the time*. Recognizing such factors as time constraints and diversity of interests, many members of the public do come to museums to learn and be educated—and when these can happen through inquiry learning, so much the better.

The interactive side is aware of publics as active participants in the process of making meaning out of a learning experience. The subject matter—scientific or cultural research—is also presented and understood in context. In the case of scientific knowledge, for instance, it is more effectively framed and understood in light of its social, historical, or political connections.

Museum activities on the interactive side of the engagement continuum are learner centered, collaborative, and, more important, inquiry based. Inquiry learning involves understanding knowledge in the context of authentic and personally relevant problems and meaningful tasks. Some museums, such as the Exploratorium in San Francisco, engage students, youth, and teachers in action research. They work collaboratively through problems and use their classrooms and the museum as living laboratories where exciting and meaningful discoveries are possible. (Inquiry learning is a large and complex subject for the purposes of this chapter. The Exploratorium Institute for Inquiry Web site offers definitions of inquiry learning as understood by museum science educators, teachers, artists, and scholars, among others.[1]) Unlike the traditional deficit model of learning, in which a teacher transmits absolute truths and neutral facts to knowledge-deficient learners, inquiry learning is reflective, exploratory, multidisciplinary, open, critical, yet respectful. It has elements of the constructivist museum concept (Hein 1995; Jackson and Hann 1994; Russell 1994) in that the learners' explorations and actions are important. The range of learning activities along the engagement continuum is exemplified in the types of museum experiences discussed next.

Lectures and Televised Programs

Lectures are at the passive end of the engagement continuum, although some scientists do encourage the public to ask them questions about their research during question-and-answer periods, thus making lectures somewhat more interactive for live audiences. This is not the case for audiences that view these lectures as delayed broadcasts. For instance, the American Museum of Natural History, in collaboration with Court TV, a national cable television network, showcased *Digging for Clues: The Story of Forensic Science*, a one-hour documentary that examines how modern forensic techniques have evolved from the exploration of the natural sciences. Three museum scientists discussed their research in biology, entomology, and physical anthropology, and forensic scientists from a range of other institutions described how their disciplines provided the base for today's scientific crime solving.[2]

Observing Scientists at Work

Another way for the public to understand research in science is to observe scientists as they conduct research in the museum itself. This experience, however, remains on the passive side of the engagement continuum. For instance, the public can view paleontologists at the Royal Tyrell Museum of Paleontology through special windows that offer a view of one laboratory where they examine fossils. The Natural History Museum scientists are also brought into the public eye in the Darwin Centre, which enables visitors to watch some of the 300 experts who work at the museum and discuss their research with them.[3]

There are limitations that restrict the nature of the engagement activities, such as when larger numbers of visitors and only a handful of scientists interact in an environment designed for scientific research rather than for informal inquiry and hands-on learning. For those learning experiences, the next type of activity offers more possibilities.

Expeditions and Travel Programs

Museums have brought groups of people to the field on expeditions and field studies. These are considered interactive to the extent that learners learn on-site and participate in the research activity. Here, the public's role can range from passive tourist to active researcher. To illustrate, the American Museum of Natural History has sponsored more than 1,000 expeditions in its 133-year history.[4] The Museum of Science in Boston offers expeditions to the Northwest Territories to view the aurora borealis and the Arctic's night sky and to trek Kilimanjaro and the Serengeti.[5] The Royal Tyrrell Museum of Paleontology sponsors weeklong field-integrated field research programs, offering the public an opportunity to work alongside the museum's scientists and technicians.[6]

OTHER MODELS FOR PUBLIC ENGAGEMENT

Workshops and Conferences

The public's understanding of research can be enhanced through workshops and conferences, as these forums tend to be more interactive. Participants often have opportunities to engage in dialogue with one another as well as with the researchers and workshop facilitators.

For instance, a decade ago, the Science Museum in London ran a series of three Women's Science Nights, especially for women aged 18 and older. Participants slept overnight in the museum after taking part in a program of hands-on workshops, demonstrations, talks by women scientists, drama presentations, and gallery tours.

Conferences can also be on the interactive half of the engagement continuum to the extent that the conferees are able to engage one another as colleagues in a manner similar to how participants at a professional and academic conference interact with each other. The American Museum of Natural History, for example, organized conferences on contemporary scientific topics that help illustrate the most current research on a given topic or how current research can be applied to significant social issues. It recently hosted a conference, "Sequencing the Human Genome: New Frontiers in Science and Technology," and another, "Conservation Genetics in the Age of Genomics." The sequencing of the human genome was recognized as the start of an extraordinary new era in science and technology but one that raised important social, ethical, and economic questions about the impacts of these technologies. The meeting on conservation genetics brought home the increasing importance of genetics research to the conservation of biodiversity.

Consensus Conferences and Other Deliberative Models

We now turn to the interactive end of the engagement continuum, where the consensus conferences and other deliberative models are found. These conferences are designed to bring about the public's deeper understanding of research as well as to provide them a forum to inform the social, ethical, economic, and political discourse surrounding the often controversial processes and outcomes of scientific innovation.

The Science Museum of London, for example, ran Naked Science, a series of events for adults only, in preparation for the opening of their Dana Center in 2003. This center aims to bring contemporary themes in science and technology to young adults (in the age range 18 to 40) through a range of events. By addressing only adults, the Naked Science series was able to tackle themes that would be unsuitable for family audiences—euthanasia, controversial vaccines, and so forth—in adult ways (G. Farmelo, personal communication, 2003).

In the past several decades, there have been increasing efforts to engage citizens on a number of political issues. This engagement has occurred most frequently on environmental issues and, more recently, on new—and typically controversial—technologies. These engagement mechanisms on technologies such as biotechnology can be characterized as having two key elements: they tend to provide citizens with a lead role in assessing technological questions, and they provide opportunities for dialogue and deliberation among citizens and between citizens and "experts." The consensus conference is an example of this deliberative model, which we briefly describe next.

The Danish Board of Technology pioneered the consensus conference process in the mid-1980s.[7] The Board was established at a time when public debate about biotechnology was rising around the plans to build production plants for genetically modified organisms in Denmark. The Board saw its role as redefining the process of assessing technology by broadening the evaluation process to include the general public. The consensus conference became one of several tools for this process of examining technological issues, one that puts citizens at the forefront of examining technological issues.

The consensus conference is usually convened around a controversial issue, say, genetically modified foods. Other topics taken up by consensus conferences include transportation issues, energy, the human genome, radioactive waste materials, gene therapy, municipal waste, and ozone in the upper atmosphere (see Loka Institute Web site for links to international examples).[8]

The organizers then go through several steps. First, participants are recruited by advertisement or by letters of invitation to a random pool. The final panel of about 15 to 20 participants is then selected on the basis of criteria designed to balance the group demographically and according to other criteria the organizing committee might consider relevant to the issue. A briefing paper prepared beforehand is then sent to the panelists as an initial resource base for learning about the given issue. These panelists get together in two briefing weekends where they 1) continue their learning process (for example, by initial discussions with two or three experts), 2) identify the key questions that need to be addressed on the given topic and start their first discussions among themselves, and 3) identify the types of experts they feel the need to hear from on the key questions they posed.

At the third and final meeting, which is open to the media and the general public, each of the experts gives brief presentations and is then questioned by the lay panelists. Members of the public also have an opportunity to ask questions of these experts. With the aid of a facilitator, the citizen panelists then hold a final deliberation among themselves and come up with their answers and recommendations to the questions they originally posed.

In the Canadian consensus conferences, there were 15 to 25 lay panelists and up to 15 experts. The number of experts depends on the types of questions the citizen panelists want to discuss (Einsiedel 2001a).

The consensus conference has been the typical model of deliberative public engagement on the controversial issue of genetically modified foods around the world, having been used in such countries as Australia, Canada, Denmark, Japan, South Korea, Switzerland, the United Kingdom, and the United States (Einsiedel 2001a). The consensus conference works well in multiple national and cross-cultural contexts, as shown in a comparative analysis of comparable conferences on food biotechnology held in Denmark, Canada, and Australia in 1999 (Einsiedel 2001b).

Other approaches that are similar in terms of in-depth public participation and dialogue and engagement with experts include scenario workshops, citizen juries, and a range of similar tools (see Renn, Webler, and Wiedemann 1995; for an overview of different theoretical and practical perspectives on public participation, see Joss 1999). The scenario workshop, for instance, uses as a starting point two to four narratives or scenarios on a given issue around which brainstorming sessions are then held and action plans developed. The citizen jury process works on a key question, examines "evidence" presented by a range of expert witnesses, and then deliberates on the evidence to come up with its "verdict" or recommendations.

The multinational EUROPTA Research Project, conducted between 1998 and 2002, illustrates how bottom-up processes referred to as "participatory technology assessment" have been employed to enhance the social embeddedness of novel science/technology innovations (Joss and Belluci 2002). One of the case studies is the U.K. National Consensus Conference on Plant Biotechnology, a joint initiative of the Science Museum, London, and the Biotechnology and Biological Science Research Council (for an overview, see Joss and Durant 1999). The Science Museum provided the logistical support for the public conference in which members of the citizens' panel met for two weekends.

Two other museum examples are La Cité des Sciences et de l'Industrie and the Australian Science Museum. The latter played a key role in cohosting a consensus conference on genetically modified food. To what extent these consensus conferences were successful in influencing political agendas and policy is a matter of speculation, but there is less doubt about their success in promoting communication between science and the public.

Why are museums well placed to host activities such as these? One reason is museums' long tradition of credible public service in the area of informal education in the arts, humanities, and/or sciences. Museums have credibility with the general public as well as with scientists. Compared with a research-intensive university, some of which operate university museums, museums designed for the public are relatively more populist and welcoming than the elitist university.

Another reason is that museums are physically accessible because they are usually centrally located and easy for most people to find. They are easy to access by private and public transportation, parking is readily available, and people in the surrounding communities are likely to visit them at least occasionally. They operate indoor and outdoor public-oriented facilities featuring meeting rooms and auditoriums furnished with the appropriate furniture, lighting, acoustical system, and audiovisual equipment that are specially installed for formal and informal public education. They have cafeterias, washrooms, coat racks, gift shops, and bookstores designed for public use. Museums also employ professional security personnel to protect these facilities and safeguard their users. These features make it easy and convenient to conduct public events such as public forums.

Although both the museum and the university try their best to make science more accessible and understandable to nonscientists, one can probably safely wager that most museums are more responsive to the general public's concerns than most universities. Today, as science is becoming increasingly specialized, esoteric, and pervasive in its impact on people's daily lives, who better than an institution engaged in facilitating representations to act as mediator between publics and the range of expert views? If museums can use exhibits effectively to show what science is about, they can be equally adept in portraying, as our earlier examples have shown, the complex interrelationships between science and society. If museums need new publics to engage, one set of publics could be the engaged citizens.

CHALLENGES

While there are many museums that engage the public in inquiry-based learning, there are a number of challenges that can hinder efforts to diversify their programming approach. First, there may be resistance to change within the organization. Public forums might be viewed as ancillary to, if not altogether outside the scope of, the traditional mission of museums built on their reputation acquiring exemplary collections and exhibiting artifacts. Robert Janes (1995) urges museums to experiment—through collective learning—on ways to engage the public. The American Association of Museums issued a report in the early 1990s that made a similar argument: that museums must adopt different modes of interaction with audiences in order to serve more diverse audiences.

Second, there may be a tendency to avoid politically controversial issues. Kreeger (1995) describes science museums that have faced criticisms from the public as well as from scientists. It is not unusual for organizations whose funding depends a great deal on maintaining a favorable and wholesome public image to avoid controversial topics that might attract negative publicity and alienate supporters. Even if a museum does not take sides in a controversial debate, there is a risk that the public may identify the museum with the controversy simply because it hosted the gathering. A recent example is the much-publicized *Sensation* exhibit at the Brooklyn Museum of Art that attracted greater attention when then–New York Mayor Rudolph Giuliani threatened to cut the museum' s financial support. The exhibit, according to one newspaper account, "featured, among other works [Giuliani] deemed offensive, a representation of the Virgin Mary by the British painter Chris Ofili that includes a clump of elephant dung and cutouts from pornographic magazines" (Smith 1999). Alan Friedman, director of the New York Hall of Science, who was serving as head of the New York city museum consortium (the Cultural Institutions Group), rallied his peers to sign a letter to Giuliani to express their concern over the proposed cuts (Able 1999).

There are arguably many controversies inherent in "typical" museum programs such that risk-averse museum boards and administrators may be reticent about hosting controversial forums. But museums could view controversial issues as opportunities to address salient community concerns that have serious policy implications for the community it serves. Moreover, atypical events may attract atypical museum visitors, as was the case when the Glenbow Museum in Calgary sponsored the Youth Curator Project, which attracted capacity crowds of teenage participants to *Youth and Media: AIDS, Fashion, Technology, Gang Violence* (Janes 1999).

Third, innovative and bold public engagement efforts may go unrecognized. Recognition of such efforts is another means of stimulating interest in alternative models of public engagement. This was the case in the United Kingdom when the St. Mary Redcliffe Journey into Science in Bristol and the Café Scientifique, founded in Leeds, both received Royal Society Millennium Awards, "not for instruction, but for debate on neutral ground" (U.K. Parliament 1999–2000).

Fourth, scarce funding may be a limiting factor. Although many science museums have a charter objective of promoting the public understanding of science, many are unable to obtain core funding for science communication in general and public affairs programming in particular. Pubic forums, which are a special case of science communication, cost money to organize. These public consultation activities can cost as little as $15,000 to as much as $90,000 in the United States and can be scaled up or down, depending on a variety of factors (Einsiedel 2002). To stage them, especially those in which admission is free, would require collaborative partnerships and targeted sponsorships. While this may be a difficult challenge in a very competitive environment, there are approaches that can be employed, such as targeting sponsors with direct interest in a given issue (for example, on a topic such as AIDS, seeking sponsorship from a pharmaceutical company producing an AIDS drug) and utilizing expertise in the community, such as those in local universities.

CONCLUSION

In seeking alternative ways to be more responsive to the public's need to understand research, some museums have expanded their public programs to include workshops, consensus conferences, and other inquiry-based learning activities. There are a number of positive reasons to include such deliberative and issues-oriented forums when museums decide to diversify their public programs.

Science museums have experienced staff members who practice science and inquiry learning. Typical public forums are often boring. Museum-sponsored interactive public forums could be made into more enjoyable learning experiences by integrating the relevant issues that affect the public, who appreciate finding solutions to important and urgent "wicked" problems.

Museums are looking for ways to respond more rapidly to the public's learning needs. Setting up some public meetings about salient issues relevant to practical, day-to-day life may take less time than organizing many formal exhibitions.

Not all museums have scientists on their staff, but many have access to a diverse network of scientists and other experts, including nonscientists, such as ethicists, policymakers, entrepreneurs, regulators, artists, and other scholars. Consensus conferences, for instance, typically involve diverse viewpoints and disciplinary traditions. Museums could extend their collaborative strategies to other museums and local and other organizations when hosting such conferences.

Modern museums have communication technology that can bring together the public and the experts online or on-site, synchronously and/or asynchronously (for a collection of essays about trends and issues as viewed by European museum experts, see Miles and Zavala 1994). Museums can connect with distant organizations (such as other museums and laboratories) where scientists are at work or where people unable to come to the museum might be located.

In searching for creative and bold ways to engage the public in critically thinking about various aspects of life, museums could offer the public a diversity of learning experiences. In addition to access to the museum's exhibits, to backrooms, and to the curators and researchers who work in them, museums could also encourage the public to access the knowledge in the backrooms of the scientists' minds and, together, explore critically the social context of scientific research and the relevant issues at hand.

NOTES

1. www.exploratorium.edu/IFI/resources/inquirydesc.html (accessed February 23, 2004).

2. www.amnh.org/programs/special/index.html (accessed February 23, 2004).

3. www.nhm.ac.uk/darwincentre (accessed February 23, 2004). See also chapter 17 by Sir Neil Chalmers in this Volume.

4. www.amnh.org/programs/special/index.html (accessed February 23, 2004).

5. www.mos.org (accessed February 23, 2004).

6. www.tyrrellmuseum.com/home (accessed February 23, 2004).

7. www.tekno.dk/index.php3?language=uk (accessed February 23, 2004).

8. www.loka.org/pages/panel.htm (accessed February 23, 2004).

REFERENCES

Able, E. H. 1999. Controversy and community (responding to "Sensation," an exhibition at the Brooklyn Museum of Art). *Museum News* 78 (November–December).

American Association of Museums. 1992. *Excellence and equity: Education and the public dimension of museums.* Washington, D.C.: American Association of Museums.

Association of Science-Technology Centers Inc. (by Inverness Research Associates, Washington, D.C.). 1996. *An invisible infrastructure: Institutions of informal science education.* Executive Summary, Vol. 1: Findings from a National Survey of Institutions of Informal Science. www.exploratorium.edu/IFI/resources/museumeducation/invisiblefindings.html.

Bradburne, J. M. 1998. Dinosaurs and white elephants: The science center in the twenty-first century. *Public Understanding of Science* 7, no. 3: 237–53.

Einsiedel, E. F. 2001a. Citizen voices: Public participation on biotechnology. *Politeia* 17: 63.

———. 2001b. Publics at the technology table: The consensus conference in Denmark, Canada, and Australia. *Public Understanding of Science* 10: 1–16. www.iop.org/Journals/pu.

———. 2002. Assessing a controversial medical technology: Canadian public consultations on xenotransplantation. *Public Understanding of Science* 11: 315–31. www.iop.org/Journals/PUS.

Hein, G. 1995. The constructivist museum. *Journal of Education in Museums* 16: 21–23. www.gem.org.uk/hein.html.

Jackson, R., and K. Hann. 1994. Learning through the science museum. *Journal of Education in Museums* 15: 11–13.

Janes, R. R. 1995. *Museums and the paradox of change: A case study in urgent adaptation.* Calgary: Glenbow Museum and University of Calgary Press.

Joss, S. 1999. Special issue on public participation in science and technology. *Science and Public Policy* 26, no. 5.

Joss, S., and S. Belluci, eds. 2002. *Participatory technology assessment: European perspectives.* London: Centre for the Study of Democracy.

Joss, S., and J. Durant, eds. 1999. *Public participation in science: The role of consensus conference in Europe.* London: Science Museum.

Kreeger, K. Y. 1995. Science museums attracting customers and controversy. *The Scientist* 9, no. 13: 1. www.the-scientist.com/yr1995/june/museum_950626.html (requires free registration for access).

Miles, R., and L. Zavala. 1994. *Towards the museum of the future: New European perspectives.* London: Routledge.

Renn, O., T. Webler, and P. Wiedemann. 1995. *Fairness and competence in citizen participation: Evaluation models for environmental discourse.* Dordrecht: Kluwer.

Rennie, L., and G. Williams. 2002. Science centers and scientific literacy: Promoting a relationship with science. *Science Education* 86, no. 5: 706–26.

Russell, T. 1994. The enquiring visitor: Usable learning theory for museum contexts. *Journal of Education in Museums* 15: 19–21.

Smith, D. 1999. A scientist rallies allies for besieged art museum. *New York Times,* October 4.

U.K. Parliament. 1999–2000. *Science and technology: Third report.* www.parliament.the-stationery-office.co.uk/pa/ld199900/ldselect/ldsctech/38/3805.htm#a30.

Weil, S. 1990a. The proper business of museums: Ideas or things? In *Rethinking the museum and other meditations,* ed. S. Weil. Washington, D.C.: Smithsonian Institution Press: 43–56.

———. 1990b. Rethinking the museum. *Museum News* 69 (March–August): 56.

5

Evaluating Public Understanding of Research Projects and Initiatives

Martin Storksdieck and John H. Falk

Evaluation has become an essential part of museum education and exhibition planning, execution, and administration.[1] Evaluation serves many purposes. Through front-end, formative and remedial evaluations, feedback from visitors helps guide the design of museum exhibits and programs. And through summative evaluations, the museum documents the impact of the visitor experience and ensures that the museum remains accountable to both its sources of funding and its public. As public understanding of research (PUR) efforts begin in museums and other institutions, the question arises whether there are special evaluation opportunities, challenges, or issues that need to be addressed or that the museum community should be aware of. More specifically, what type(s) of evaluation and assessment can realistically be accomplished around local PUR activities or even national PUR efforts?

In this limited space, we will not be able to address the "how to" of evaluation. This is done in excellent fashion elsewhere (Diamond 1999; Dierking and Pollock 1998; Taylor 1992). Rather, we would like to address a set of pertinent questions that museum professionals would have to answer before any evaluation should be conducted, including those on PUR activities: What are the goals for your exhibit/program, and what are the outcomes of your activities on those who experience them? These questions are at the core of any discussion about evaluation. Accordingly, we will focus our attention in this evaluation chapter on the issue of outcomes. Specifically, we will attempt to address the question, What are appropriate and realistic outcomes for PUR efforts in museums, and what are the implications of these decisions on assessment?

In order to begin a discussion about what could or should possibly be achieved by a PUR effort in museums, we would propose a hierarchy of issues that museum professionals need to consider. These are the following:

1. What is the nature of learning from museums?
2. What is the relative exposure to PUR that my program/exhibition provides visitors with? How does this experience fit into people's general framework for addressing PUR issues?
3. What are visitors' background knowledge of and interest in PUR efforts?
4. What is the nature of my PUR activity, and what is the most appropriate target audience for this activity?

In order to develop a realistic and audience-centered set of potential goals and objectives for a PUR effort, it is essential to begin from a clear understanding of how visitors make meaning in museums. It is important to appreciate in this context that museum experiences are only brief ephemeral events, embedded in the lives of people. Having reasonable expectations for the impacts of PUR efforts results from an appreciation that the changes in visitor understanding of PUR are directly related to the duration and nature of the exposure visitors are provided with, which in turn is always relative to the visitors' overall lifelong exposure to PUR. Within that framework of relative lifetime exposure, museum professionals have to take into consideration potential audiences' personal context, including prior knowledge and understanding, as well as their interest and motivation to learn about PUR topics. Finally, it is also important to understand and accommodate the social and developmental needs of the audience to be served. What level of information are the visitors capable of processing, and why have they chosen to participate in a PUR effort to begin with (that is, why are they visiting the museum that day)? Once museum professionals have developed some fundamental understanding of these four issues (relative exposure, personal context, and social context, and visitor agenda), they can begin to develop reasonable outcomes for any PUR effort and begin to develop a meaningful evaluation strategy, whether the evaluation is conducted in-house or by an outside evaluator. Let us explore each of these four areas in somewhat greater detail.

THE NATURE OF LEARNING FROM MUSEUMS

How Visitors Learn from Museums

All learning is a personally constructed, highly idiosyncratic, lifelong process of meaning making (Bruner 1990; Driver 1983; Pope and Gilbert 1983; Strike and Posner 1995). Unless we are forced to learn, say, as students in a classroom, most of what we learn in our lives we learn not because we have to but because we want to, because events in our life intrinsically motivate us to find out more (Csikzentmihalyi 1990; McCombs 1991; McCombs and Whisler 1989). We learn what we want, where we want, when we want, and with whom we want; in short, most human learning is free-choice learning—lifelong learning that is intrinsically motivated, nonassessed, and largely under the choice and control of the learner (Falk 2001; Falk and Dierking 2002). And while learning is a continuous process with knowledge derived from many different sources and in many different ways (Anderson 1999; Bransford, Brown, and Cocking 1999; Medrich 1991), there are a few important generalizations that apply to all learning situations—what people learn depends on what they already know and understand, whom they are with when they learn, where they are when they learn, and, perhaps most important, why they are motivated to learn in the first place (Falk and Dierking 1992, 2000). This perspective changes how we frame the question of how to evaluate museum experiences. It necessitates that we take the visitors' personalized standpoint seriously and assess their experience from their perspective. The implication of this constructivist, free-choice perspective on learning is that much, if not most, of what a visitor ends up learning from a museum experience is attributable to what the visitor brings to the experience—his or her unique, personal set of needs, knowledge, interests, and motivations—rather than attributable primarily to the quality of the museum exhibition or program itself. Hence, evaluation research needs to invest as much time in understanding what the visitors themselves bring to the museum in the way of their personal connections to research and science as in judging the "quality" of the PUR activities in the museum (for instance, the "attracting" and "holding" power of an exhibit).

Meaning Making and the Determination of Outcomes

Rather than assuming that every visitor will walk away with the meanings that museum professionals believed they would or should be achieving during their visit, learning should ideally be defined broadly and should principally emerge from the meaning visitors actually make of the experience (Ansbacher 2002; Dierking et al. 2002; Russell 2002). Visitors, after all, construct their own meaning and understanding of their museum experience, and this meaning and understanding varies greatly, depending on the visitors' background, age, experience, and knowledge; their social group; and the sociocultural and the physical context of the institution itself (Falk and Dierking 1992, 2000; Gregory and Miller 1998; Rennie 2001). Science learning, for instance, no matter how broadly defined, is not the only possible outcome of a museum visit. In fact, museums are visited for a multitude of reasons—for enjoyment, to spend quality time with family/children/friends, to experience something unusual, to take part in a culturally enriching activity, to learn new things or to reaffirm or solidify prior knowledge, or to reaffirm one's own identity, one's sense of self (Dierking et al. 2002)—and all these outcomes are valid from the visitors' perspective, though not necessarily appreciated by museum staff or funding agencies. In determining possible outcomes of PUR activities, museum professionals should acknowledge and embrace this breadth of possible outcomes. Simply put, visitors will decide for themselves what kind of outcome is right for them, and these outcomes are strongly influenced by the visitors' entering museum agenda. Don't get us wrong—we are not advocating that *anything goes*; it is important to determine and design for specific outcomes. However, whether or not these outcomes are achieved is only partially a consequence of what you, the museum professional, do.

This has important implications for evaluation. Clearly, we can measure whether any carefully calibrated and predefined outcome has been met with a precisely defined target audience. But that's only part of the story. In other words, one can fix the outcomes and see to what degree or for what percentage of visitors these outcomes have been met. But this does not necessarily provide a valid indication of what the true impact of an experience was on the public. The other approach, the one we would advocate, is to record emerging outcomes as well—whatever they are—in effect, letting the public itself tell you what they believe the impact of the activity has been. This approach allows the data gathering on both expected and unexpected outcomes and thus is far more robust and valid.

REALISTIC OUTCOMES BASED ON RELATIVE EXPOSURE TO PUR

Museum Experiences Are Not Isolated Events

"A better understanding of scientific research" or "a better/higher ability to judge current health science news and research that has been reported in the media" are typical goals for PUR activities. These may be laudable, ultimate (rather than proximate) goals, but they are also rather lofty goals. Evaluators, museum designers, educators, and scientists/curators are faced with the need to identify more proximate, pragmatic, and measurable goals—goals that are closely related to the potential impact that a program or exhibit could possibly have on participants or visitors. Whether goals are realistic is a function of three conditions: 1) the goals need to be connected to the actual museum experience of visitors; 2) visitors need to be inclined to embrace such a goal, and the goals need to be of vital importance to the visitors; and 3) the ambition of the goals needs to be calibrated to the relative exposure that the PUR effort provides visitors with. Museum experiences are not isolated events but rather events that become embedded within people's lives. Setting reasonable expectations for the impact of a PUR effort needs to be strongly tied to length and intensity of the experience itself, in other words, to the relative exposure of a visitor to the PUR activity. Is the PUR exposure a 15-minute visit to an exhibition, a 1.5-hour-long PUR-related family workshop at a museum, a 15-hour involvement in a citizen-science project, or a 15-day intensive exposure to current research from participation in a consensus conference on contentious science topic? Everything else being equal, each of these PUR efforts will significantly differ in its ability to impact its participants.

Immediate versus Long-Term Goals

Particularly complex potential PUR outcomes, such as a better understanding of the current research enterprise, may be hard to achieve in the short term. However, a PUR effort at a museum may trigger a thought process or may spark that additional degree of interest and attention that lets the visitor follow the topic of PUR later, after the visit. Since museum visits are not isolated incidences in peoples' lives and since research has shown that it is not possible to accurately judge the impact of a museum experience merely by talking to visitors as they exit the museum (Falk and Dierking 2000), longitudinal studies are necessary in order to record these long-term and sustained impacts of PUR activities.

VISITORS' PRIOR UNDERSTANDING AND INTEREST

Once a reasonable, ballpark sense of what a PUR effort should look like has been developed, based on the aspirations of the science community, informed by an understanding of learning from museums, and guided by a basic strategy of how to convey the messages (for instance, exhibition, program, forum, or Web site), two other key issues need to be considered: 1) prior knowledge and understanding of the public to be served and 2) their prior interest and motivation (visitor agendas). How much does the visitor already know about this topic? Are there major misconceptions that need to be addressed? What other exposure have visitors had, and in what form? How easy will it be for visitors to absorb the new information being presented into their preexisting mental schemas? How important are issues related to science and research for the visitor? Will the visitor actually have an interest in these themes? Answers to these questions help further define realistic and achievable outcomes for a PUR initiative.

Public Understanding of the Fundamental Nature of Science Inquiry

When people were asked about the nature of science and scientific inquiry in national surveys in the United States and across Europe (European Commission 2001; Miller and Kimmel 1997, 1999; National Science Board 2002), it turned out that the process of science is generally not well understood by the majority of the public. In fact, in 2001, only 30 percent of the U.S. public understood the basic nature of a scientific study (up from 27 percent in 1997), a rate that led the National Science Board (1998) to conclude that most Americans do not "understand the nature of scientific inquiry well enough to be able to make informed judgments about the scientific basis of results reported in the media."

These national and international findings are supported by a wide range of front-end, remedial, and summative studies conducted in the past few years. Several studies have revealed that science and natural history museum visitors possess a limited understanding of even the term "science" (Adelman, Dierking, and Adams 2000; Storksdieck et al. 2002). For instance, when visitors were asked their understanding of science during family programming at various science museum–type settings in the Philadelphia area, they mostly stated that science is "interesting," "important," and "necessary" or that "science is everything" (Storksdieck et al. 2002). Participants generally did not describe science as an organized process of inquiry. Instead, it seems that the most common perspective among these audiences of primarily low socioeconomic status was that "science equals everyday life"—a view, it should be noted, that was at least partly supported by the museums themselves as they strove to make science more interesting and accessible to these traditionally underserved audiences. Similar results have been found elsewhere. As part of an evaluation of the California Science Center's Creative World Exhibition, it was discovered that only about one-third of the Science Center's visitors possessed an understanding of how science and technology were related, and many of these individuals had only the most rudimentary grasp of that relationship (Luke et al. 2000). Most visitors thought that the two terms were synonymous or so close as to be indistinguishable. If the majority of visitors to science museums have only a limited understanding of the term "science," it is reasonable to assume that they will be significantly challenged when presented with the complexities of "current science" or "research." These findings need to be considered when designing evaluation studies for PUR efforts. Thus, it seems prudent not only to assess visitors' prior knowledge and understanding but to do so in a layered fashion. First, it must be determined what the public's understanding is of the most basic aspects of the scientific process, and then it must be determined what their understanding is of more detailed and/or advanced topics, such as biotechnology, nanotechnology, or science policy debates.

Interest in PUR

Ansbacher (2002) recently pointed out that any evaluation study of museum outcomes needs to begin by assessing the degree with which visitors actually engage and take part in the experience. Whether visitors will choose to attend to exhibits or programs depends largely on their interest in the topic. With limited prior knowledge about research and the scientific enterprise, will visitors actually show interest in PUR efforts in museums?[2]

Previous research indicates that visitors to museums seem more interested in the outcomes of science than in the process that ultimately created these outcomes (Mintz 1995). The results from several front-end studies and summative evaluations seem to indicate that, by and large, exhibits that portray the process of science are generally less interesting to visitors than are exhibits that provide results and findings (Luke, Coles, and Falk 1998; People, Places and Design Research 2000; Turner et al. 2001). When faced with a choice between science facts and science issues, science issues fare relatively poorly (Anderson and Holland 1997; Turner et al. 2001). The task, hence, lies in making PUR stories personally relevant to people and then to assess whether PUR efforts were successful in creating a personal link between science/research and visitors to science museums.

The National Academy of Sciences (NAS) plans to open a museum in its new National Research Council Building. The planners of the museum aspire to create a museum that will bridge for the public current scientific research with policy in ways practiced by the NAS. They intend to accomplish this primarily by addressing contentious science-based issues like global climate change and genomics research. During a front-end study conducted for this museum project, potential visitors to the museum were questioned about their hopes for the museum. The majority of respondents mentioned that they were most interested in the products of science, accurate scientific facts, and the role of science in their lives. They said they were least interested in learning how science is used to make policy decisions or to receive tools to help them make better personal, science-related decisions (Turner et al. 2001). In addition, typical PUR topics or themes (such as how to think like a scientist, meet the real experts, how scientists work, how chance is involved in scientific discovery, the scientific process and me, and the FDA and current food rules) were generally not favored by potential future museum visitors. When people were asked to rate their interest in a wide range of science-related topics, content-related topics like genetically modified food, cancer, bioengineering, and global climate change all were rated higher than the process-oriented "nature of science."

A front-end study conducted for the Carnegie Science Center interactive traveling exhibit *BioSci* found that potential visitors were both interested and enthusiastic about the exhibit and its potential content areas (biotechnology and medical technology). However, visitors were not particularly interested in the development cost of technology, availability and access issues, or the history of the technology development—all typical PUR topics (Anderson and Holland 1997). A summative evaluation of the New England Aquarium's *Nyanja! Africa's Inland Sea* exhibition explored whether visitors understood, among other messages, the role of scientific research in efforts to preserve and restore the threatened ecosystem of Lake Victoria. The exhibit designers decided to tell the story by embedding the biology into the customs and cultures of Lake Victoria residents and by using local scientists and their cooperation with U.S. scientists as a hook to interest U.S. museum visitors. A summative evaluation revealed that about only half the visitors recalled scientists or the research process in the exhibition, and interest in seeing more about research and scientists in future exhibits was only modest (People, Places and Design Research 2000).

In summary, recent studies seem to indicate that only a portion of those interested in science may also be interested in the nature, process, and mechanics of science. In fact, while most respondents in front-end and summative studies at science museums and similar institutions express a high interest in science per se, they are often lukewarm at best when it comes to understanding the research endeavor in more detail. It is therefore important that evaluators record visitors' prior interest and attentiveness to PUR issues during all phases of the evaluation process.

National Baseline Data

At this stage of the PUR movement, it would be useful to collect some solid baseline data on the public's understanding of science and research, including people's current understanding of research practice and the scientific enterprise, people's interest and current attention to PUR topics, and the extent of the public's perceived personal connections to research and the scientific enterprise. These studies should be done across the United States, preferably on location (science centers, science museums, zoos, aquariums, planetariums, and other science-related museum-type settings). These data could provide the background for comparisons for every subsequent front-end and summative evaluation on PUR efforts in museums.

Such baseline data would help remedy a significant shortcoming in current assessments of the impact of museum experiences on visitors. In traditional cost-benefit analyses of programs and projects, the yardstick of success is not whether the project achieved positive results but whether it performed better than the next-best alternative. In PUR terms, the question would not be whether a project, program, or exhibition succeeded in providing the public with some measurable change in understanding or appreciation but whether that program or exhibition achieved these goals more effectively and efficiently than some other PUR initiative—for the envisioned target group. In other words, we advocate that background studies be conducted to allow the field to set realistic and comparable goals and objectives that can be measured against preexisting data. We also advocate that summative evaluations be made accessible so that specific PUR initiatives can be assessed in comparison to other PUR initiatives, not necessarily as an exercise in "who does it best" but in order to learn, as an emerging field, what works best for what kind of purpose. The notion of comparisons with baseline data and similar other efforts and the idea that museums would have to think beyond achieving a marginal benefit would have profound implications for both the practice and the evaluation of PUR (and arguably all informal science education) efforts in museums.

WHO ARE WE DESIGNING PUR ACTIVITIES FOR?

PUR efforts can take on many forms, depending on which conceptual level of research and/or science they address. We would propose the following hierarchy of five conceptually different levels of increasing complexity and abstractness. The five levels range from the actual process of day-to-day research to an understanding of current research to aspects of science and society and how they affect our understanding of the history and philosophy of science:

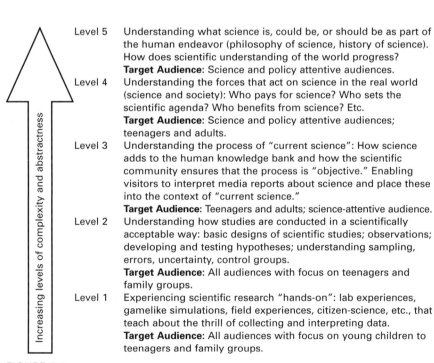

FIGURE 5.1
Five Levels of Museum Experiences

These five levels are distinguished primarily by their degree of abstractness, their appeal to differently aged visitors to science museums, and the likelihood that visitors to science museums possess appropriate levels of prior knowledge and understanding to allow them to engage with these topics. We assume that as we progress through this hierarchy, it will be increasingly more difficult to achieve positive results with an ever more narrow pool of potential visitors for whom the experience would be highly appropriate. Also important to note is that most museum experiences are social in nature and that most visitors come as part of a social group. Typically, museum groups are heterogeneous with respect to age, gender, interest, and prior knowledge (Luke et al. 1998). This heterogeneity has an important impact on what can reasonably be presented in a PUR exhibition or program and should also be kept in mind when designing evaluation studies to assess these experiences.

The following are some selected examples of evaluations and lessons learned from them for each of these five levels of PUR effort:

Level 1: Experiencing scientific research "hands on" through lab experiences, gamelike simulations, field experiences, citizen science, and so on that teach about the thrill of collecting and interpreting data. An example for a PUR activity in this category is the Science Museum of Minnesota's Experiment Gallery, where young visitors explore such phenomena as gravity, resonance, and energy transformation through a host of hands-on activities, or the New York Hall of Science's Biochemistry and Astronomy Discovery Labs, which are set up for families or small groups who can conduct their own experiments about science in everyday life and which encourage primarily young visitors to experience the process of actually gathering data or even generating data and then deriving some conclusions from them. These activities teach experimentation. Evaluation should therefore focus on participants' experiences and should attempt to measure or observe exactly what participants were engaged in.

A summative evaluation of the New York Hall of Science's Biochemistry Discovery Lab revealed that in visitors' minds, the popular images of chemistry explosions and boiling liquids were supplemented with an image of quieter chemical reactions of biochemical systems (Sulston and Weiss 2001). In effect, visitors' perspective on a certain branch of research (biochemistry) had been expanded. The evaluation also showed that half the groups were taking a lab notebook home. Taking materials home from a museum visit is not only a valuable vehicle for continued interest in the science content but, even more so, a sign of interest in experimentation since lab notes are the core of recording any experimentation. The summative evaluation did not specifically address PUR aspects. However, since it already used the type of questions (open ended) that would be useful for a PUR evaluation, it could have easily been expanded to directly address PUR issues.

Level 2: Understanding how studies are conducted in a scientifically acceptable way, including basic designs of scientific studies: observations, developing hypotheses, testing hypotheses, understanding sampling, errors, uncertainty, and control groups. Like level 1 projects, level 2 efforts, for instance, the citizen-science project PigeonWatch, can be assessed by focusing on participants' actual experience and any learning that may directly follow from it (provide observation skills, teach about bird behavior and pigeons in particular, and the process of data collection in general), and it would be inappropriate to assess the program on its ability to explain the scientific process itself. *Girls at the Center (G.A.C.)*, for instance, is a collaborative effort between the Franklin Institute Science Museum in Philadelphia and the Girl Scouts of the U.S.A. The program provides science experiences for 6- to 17-year-old girls and an adult partner (a parent, guardian, or other significant adult) in economically disadvantaged communities across the country. A five-year longitudinal study of 324 participants suggested that the program succeeded in immersing girls and adults in the activities of doing science observing, classifying, experimenting, and hypothesizing (Adelman et al. 2000). Findings suggested that participation in *G.A.C.* improved girls' self-reported interest in and attitudes toward science and began to influence their perceptions of themselves as "scientists" as well as their ability to recognize connections between science and everyday life. The program also positively influenced adults who had participated along with girls. Adults were much more aware of the importance of science learning for girls and how to support and facilitate their science learning inside and outside of school. These outcomes persisted over time as well. This study suggested that outcomes needed to be defined broadly and that they needed to extend beyond the narrow cognitive perspective. In fact, the girls did not improve their understanding of science itself much during the program, yet a comprehensive approach toward evaluation allowed researchers to address a wide range of additional outcomes that documented the success of the program.

Level 3: Understanding the process of "current science": how science adds to the human knowledge bank and how the scientific community ensures that the process is "objective," enabling visitors to interpret media reports about science and place these into the context of "current science." Level 3 PUR initiatives may aim mostly at empowering people to evaluate media reports about current science, from the newest claims on what will reduce one's risk of heart attack to being able to form informed opinions about science-intensive topics like global warming or genetically modified foods. The Current Science & Technology Center (CS&T) at the Museum of Science in Boston addresses these aspects through its live multimedia presentations and its Science Theater programs. Sometimes openly addressed but always implicit in these presentations are aspects of how the scientific enterprise comes to advance over time. As part of a formative evaluation, visitors to presentations on the multimedia stage of CS&T were asked in open-ended questions to describe the nature of the presentation and the likely target group. Results suggested that audiences often focused on the science content of the presentations rather than the science processes (Storksdieck 2003). Summative evaluation will have to take into consideration that 20-minute presentations, no matter how impressive, provide visitors with only a brief exposure to a topic. Instead of assessing how these presentations may impact visitors' understanding of current science processes, evaluation will have to focus on the role these brief exposures have on visitors' overall efforts to assess the outcomes of current science.

Level 4: Understanding the forces that act on science in the real world (science and society): Who pays for science? Who sets the scientific agenda? Who benefits from science? and so on. Level 4 PUR activities include citizen science and consensus conferences like those conducted at the Science Museum in London or the German Hygiene Museum in Dresden and public debates on contentious science topics like the ones hosted by the Cité des Sciences et de l'Industrie near Paris. Evaluators may be faced with a range of very divergent outcomes that extend far beyond the individual participants. Joss (1995) concluded in a general discussion on evaluating consensus conferences that the "desired outcomes of consensus conferences (public debate, public involvement in policy making) are complex, difficult to observe, and made up of different parameters reacting in different ways." How do such general goals get translated into measures that are generally accepted? Joss made the following conclusions for the evaluation of citizen consensus conferences:

- The aims of the evaluation should be clear to all involved since support for the evaluation process is important for the success of the evaluation.
- Planning needs to be done well in advance since research strategies and methodologies need to be embedded into the overall process of the conference.
- Participation should be voluntary and should focus on the "actors" rather than the individual.
- Methods should be unobtrusive and subtle so as to not burden participants and so as to fit smoothly into the conference proceedings themselves.
- Qualitative methods should be used since they fit the nature of the activity and lead to richer data and more useful results.

An evaluation of a series of consensus conferences on human genetics research in the Netherlands in 1994–1995 utilized a variety of mostly quantitative methods (observations, questionnaires, quasi experiments, surveys, content analysis, and media analysis) to address a broad range of aspects of the conferences, including the process itself; effects on participants' values, attitudes, and knowledge (opinion); dissemination of information to the public; and effects of the conference on policymaking (Mayer, de Vries, and Geurts 1995). While evaluations that assess a broad range of independent outcomes have the potential to yield comprehensive results, they are also very complex and necessitate a great deal of resources.

However, complex evaluations can be conducted even with limited financial support. Based on previous experiences in Denmark, the German Hygiene Museum in Dresden experimented in 2001 with a citizen conference on genetic diagnostics (Zimmer 2002). The experiment was evaluated comprehensively with a pre-/postdesign and a control group, employing a mix of quantitative and qualitative methods (all based on self-report) and defining the scope of the evaluation extremely broadly, from direct impacts on participants (knowledge acquisition and opinion building) to impacts on group behavior and group dynamics to the societal impact of the citizen conference (for instance, on the media and on policymakers). The results were generally positive, though policymakers and scientists were dissatisfied with the outcome of the conference: participants grew more critical toward some of the diagnostic techniques rather than more accepting. It turned out to be crucial for assessing the overall value of the conference that evaluation was embedded into the process and that outcomes were defined broadly and on a variety of different conceptual levels. Despite its complex design, the evaluation itself was budgeted at 12.7 percent of the total cost of the project.

Level 5: Understanding what science is, could be, or should be as part of the human endeavor (philosophy of science, history of science). How does scientific understanding of the world progress? At this point, we are not aware of any pure PUR effort that directly and solely addresses this level of abstractness, though college-level courses in science, science teacher continuing education workshops and courses, or guest speaker series at science museums for science museum staff could potentially touch on these issues. In general, PUR efforts that aim at level 5 will likely be associated with professional development of some sort. Evaluation should be embedded in the activity, for instance, by allowing participants to reflect in writing or as part of a group discussion. Here again, longitudinal measures would be essential.

An exhibition that addresses various levels of abstractness and that also contains elements of level 5 may be the *Mysteries of Çatalhöyük* exhibition at the Science Museum of Minnesota. The exhibition was unusual in that it focused on the process rather than the results of an archeological dig in Turkey. Exhibit designers told the story of this particular excavation site by exposing visitors to the reality of archeological research, including the many open questions that still remained unanswered, and by featuring the scientist involved in the research. The summative evaluation (People, Places and Design Research 2002) listed particular challenges with this PUR approach to interpreting archeology:

- Most exhibitions about digs feature artifacts, whereas this exhibition was about the scientific process much more than about the "finds."

- The perception of scientists as technical experts was challenged by showing researchers as normal people at work.
- Visitors' cultural connection with Çatalhöyük was weak.
- The dig project was still in its early stages, with many unanswered questions that may have left some visitors dissatisfied since visitors normally expect facts and answers.

The summative evaluation focused on the research process and found that three of visitors' top-of-mind comments about the subject matter and interpretation of this exhibition included how we study the past (archaeology, the nature of the work, how a dig works), learning about an ancient culture, and comparisons between past and present. Visitors, hence, identified the research theme of the exhibition. When prompted with structured questions, visitors again chose statements that indicated that they recognized the context of the exhibition: "It's a good typical story of an archaeological dig" and "A place where scientists are asking lots of questions but don't have many answers yet." "Unanswered questions" were identified in a front-end study as a potential conceptual problem for many visitors. However, 80 percent of visitors in exit interviews described an archaeologist's work as "advancing knowledge by raising new questions." The summative evaluation asked a multitude of more detailed questions about the "daily work" of scientists, and responses revealed that the exhibition was successful in conveying not only the structure and process of science but also the daily routine and social context of scientific research. In that sense, the exhibition is a good example for conveying scientific research on multiple conceptual levels, and the hierarchical design of the summative evaluation (first the emerging answers to open-ended questions and then specific structured questions) proved valuable in capturing the exhibition's impact on visitors' understanding of research.

CONCLUSION

All evaluation must start with a discussion of outcomes. Defining the right kind of outcomes and framing the debate about goals and objectives for any activity is not an easy matter, particularly within a museum context where there are typically many different factions and points of view to be reconciled (for instance, funders, scientists, designers, educators, and marketers). This is all the more difficult when it comes to PUR since PUR efforts attempt to convey not just factual but also process knowledge. Setting realistic outcome goals for PUR efforts in museums requires museum professionals to address four important issues:

1. What is the nature of learning from museums?
2. What is the relative exposure to PUR that my effort provides visitors with?
3. What is my audience interested in, and what is my audience's prior understanding of research and the scientific enterprise?
4. What is the type of PUR activity I am providing, and for what type of audience should I provide it to?

In addition, a range of other aspects have been discussed that museum professionals should consider as they embark on evaluations of PUR efforts:

- Evaluation starts with the visitor experience. Evaluation outcomes should, hence, be derived from the actual experience of visitors.
- Predefined outcomes are useful in guiding programming since each outcome needs to be linked to at least one program element; however, predefined outcomes may not or need not be the only positive outcomes achieved.
- Allow visitors to self-define outcomes. Let visitors express in their own words how they gained from the experience (emerging outcomes).
- It is important to clarify outcomes and associated audiences, either by defining the nature of a PUR effort first and then focusing on an appropriate target group or by choosing a target group and then deciding on the most appropriate PUR effort to best serve that target group. In addition, researchers should acknowledge the important role played by social interactions and the very real likelihood that visitor populations will be comprised of individuals with widely divergent levels of experience, knowledge, interest, and ability (for instance, family groups).
- General goals discussed for PUR efforts are often abstract. It is important to break those down into smaller, more proximate outcomes.
- PUR efforts may have to assume very basic prior knowledge and limited interest in "science and research as a process." Summative evaluations, therefore, need to establish solid baseline data on visitors' prior knowledge and

understanding and interest in PUR in order to ascertain what may be only incremental changes.

- Various studies on PUR suggest that people need to be introduced to the first principles of scientific research before they can realistically be expected to gain a deeper understanding of the scientific research process. It may be necessary to define layers of outcomes that are appropriate for different types of visitors.

Finally, we would strongly advocate for a national study to establish a baseline for the public's understanding of research in the United States. Such a systematic and coordinated background study would provide a foundation for designing effective PUR efforts since it would permit such efforts to be grounded in a current understanding of the knowledge and interests of potential audiences for PUR efforts at museums across the country. It would also provide a quantitative baseline against which to measure the effectiveness of all new PUR efforts, a process that could significantly enhance the accountability of informal science education efforts nationwide.

NOTES

1. We will use the generic term " museum" to refer to a wide range of institutions, including science centers, natural history museums, science and technology museums, zoos, aquariums, and other similar settings.

2. Program or exhibit designers are faced with serious problems when a front-end study reveals that potential visitors have little prior knowledge, that there is a high potential for misconceptions, and that potential visitors exhibit little to moderate interest in a topic.

REFERENCES

Adelman, L., L. D. Dierking, and M. Adams. 2000. Phase II: Summative evaluation final report, years 3 and 4, Girls at the Center, The Franklin Science Museum and Girl Scouts of the U.S.A. Unpublished technical report. Annapolis, Md.: Institute for Learning Innovation.

Anderson, D. 1999. Understanding the impact of post-visit activities on students' knowledge construction of electricity and magnetism as a result of a visit to an interactive science centre. Doctoral Ph.D. diss., Queensland University of Technology, Brisbane, Australia.

Anderson, D., and D. Holland. 1997. Front-end evaluation report—*BioSci*. Unpublished technical report. Annapolis, Md.: Science Learning Inc.

Ansbacher, T. 2002. What are we learning? Outcomes of the museum experience. *Informal Learning Review* 53 (March–April).

Bransford, J. D., A. L. Brown, and R. R. Cocking, eds. 1999. *How people learn*. Washington, D.C.: National Research Council.

Bruner, J. 1990. *Acts of meaning*. Cambridge, Mass.: Harvard University Press.

Csikzentmihalyi, M. (1990). Literacy and intrinsic motivation. *Daedalus* 119, no. 2: 115–40.

Diamond, J. 1999. *Practical evaluation guide*. Walnut Creek, Calif.: AltaMira Press.

Dierking, L. D., M. Cohen Jones, M. Wadman, J. H. Falk, M. Storksdieck, and K. Ellenbogen. 2002. Broadening our notions of the impact of free-choice learning experiences. *Informal Learning Review* 55 (July–August 2002).

Dierking, L. D., and J. H. Falk. 2003. Optimizing out-of-school time: The role of free-choice learning. *New Directions for Youth Development* 97 (spring): 75–88.

Dierking, L. D., and W. Pollock. 1998. *Questioning assumptions: An introduction to front-end studies in museums*. Washington, D.C.: Association of Science-Technology Centers.

Driver, R. A. 1983. *The pupil as scientist?* Milton Keynes, U.K., Open University Press.

European Commission. 2001. Europeans, science and technology. *Eurobarometer* 55, no. 2 (December 2001).

Falk, J. H. 2001. Free-choice science learning: Framing the discussion. In *Free-choice science education: How we learn science outside of school*. New York: Teachers College Press, 1–20.

Falk, J. H., and L. D. Dierking. 1992. *The museum experience*. Washington, D.C.: Whalesback Books.

———. 2000. *Learning from museums*. Walnut Creek, Calif.: AltaMira Press.

———. 2002. *Lessons without limit: How free-choice learning is transforming education*. Walnut Creek, Calif.: AltaMira Press.

Gregory, J., and S. Miller. 1998. *Science in public: Communication, culture, and credibility*. New York: Plenum Trade.

Joss, S. 1995. Evaluating consensus conferences: Necessity or luxury? In *Public participation in science: The role of consensus conferences in Europe*, ed. S. Joss and J. Durant. London: Science Museum with the support of the European Commission Directorate General XII, 89–108.

Knapp, M. S. 1997. Between systemic reforms and the mathematics and science classroom: The dynamics of innovation, implementation and professional learning. *Review of Educational Research* 67, no. 2: 227–66.

Korpan, C. A., G. L. Bisanz, C. Boehme, and M. A. Lynch. 1997. What did you learn outside of school today? Using structured interviews to document home and community activities related to science and technology. *Science Education* 81: 651–62.

Luke, J. J., K. S. Büchner, L. D. Dierking, and B. O'Ryan. 2000. Creative World Summative Evaluation, California Science Center. Unpublished technical report. Annapolis, Md.: Institute for Learning Innovation.

Luke, J. J., U. Coles, and J. H. Falk. 1998. Summative evaluation of DNA Zone, St. Louis Science Center. Unpublished technical report. Annapolis, Md.: Institute for Learning Innovation.

Mayer, I., J. de Vries, and J. Geurts. 1995. An evaluation of the effect of participation in a consensus conference. In *Public participation in science: The role of consensus conferences in Europe*, ed. S. Joss and J. Durant. London: Science Museum with the support of the European Commission Directorate General XII, 109–24.

McCombs, B. L. 1991. Motivation and lifelong learning. *Educational Psychologist* 26: 117–27.

McCombs, B. L., and J. S. Whisler. 1989. The role of affective variables in autonomous learning. *Educational Psychologist* 24: 277–306.

Medrich, E. A. 1991. Young adolescents and discretionary time use: The nature of life outside of school. Paper commissioned by the Carnegie Council on Adolescent Development for its Task Force on Youth Development and Community Programs.

Miller, J. D., and L. Kimmel. 1997. *Public attitudes toward science and technology, 1979–1997, integrated codebook.* Chicago: Chicago Academy of Sciences, International Center for the Advancement of Scientific Literacy.

———. 1999. *Public attitudes toward science and technology, 1979–1999, integrated codebook.* Chicago: Chicago Academy of Sciences, International Center for the Advancement of Scientific Literacy.

Mintz, A. 1995. *Communicating controversy: Science museums and issues education.* Washington, D.C.: Association of Science-Technology Centers.

National Science Board. 1998. *Science and Engineering Indicators—1998.* NSB-98-1. Arlington, Va.: National Science Foundation.

———. 2000. *Science and Engineering Indicators—2000.* NSB-00-1. Arlington, Va.: National Science Foundation.

———. 2002. *Science and Engineering Indicators—2002.* NSB-02-1. Arlington, Va.: National Science Foundation.

Ogbu, J. U. 1995. The influence of culture on learning and behavior. In *Public institutions for personal learning,* ed. J. H. Falk and L. D. Dierking. Washington, D.C.: American Association of Museums, 79–95.

People, Places and Design Research. 2000. Summative evaluation of *Nyanja! Africa's Inland Sea* at the New England Aquarium. Unpublished technical report. Northampton, Mass.: People, Places and Design Research.

———. 2002. Summative evaluation: Visitors' experience of *Mysteries of Çatalhöyuk* at the Science Museum of Minnesota. Unpublished technical report. Northampton, Mass.: People, Places and Design Research.

Pope, M., and J. Gilbert. 1983. Personal experience and the construction of knowledge in science. *Science Education* 67: 193–203.

Rennie, L. J. 2001. Communicating science through interactive science centers: A research perspective. In *Science communication in theory and practice,* ed. S. M. Stocklmayer, M. M. Gore, and C. Bryant. Dordrecht: Kluwer, 107–21.

Rogoff, B., and J. Lave, eds. 1984. *Everyday cognition: Its development in social contexts.* Cambridge, Mass.: Harvard University Press.

Russell, B. 2002. The cloisters: Outcomes of the museum visit. *Informal Learning Review* 54 (May–June 2002).

Sless, D., and R. Shrensky. 2001. Conversations in a landscape of science and magic: Thinking about science communication. In *Science communication in theory and practice,* ed. S. M. Stocklmayer, M. M. Gore, and C. Bryant. Dordrecht: Kluwer, 97–105.

Storksdieck, M. 2003. Staff presentations remedial evaluation, Current Science and Technology Center, Museum of Science, Boston. Unpublished technical report. Annapolis, Md.: Institute for Learning Innovation.

Storksdieck, M., K. Haley Goldman, M. Hendrix, and L. D. Dierking. 2002. Families exploring science together: Year two evaluation report. New Jersey State Aquarium; the Academy of Natural Sciences; The Franklin Institute Science Museum; Philadelphia Zoo. Unpublished technical report. Annapolis, Md.: Institute for Learning Innovation.

Sulston, I., and M. Weiss. 2001. Summative evaluation, Pfizer Foundation Biochemistry Discovery Lab at The New York Hall of Science. Draft of an unpublished technical report. New York: New York Hall of Science.

Taylor, S., ed. 1992. *Try it! Improving exhibits through formative evaluation.* New York: New York Hall of Science.

Turner Custard, P., L. D. Dierking, and M. Storksdieck. 2001. Koshland Science Museum front-end evaluation final report. Unpublished technical report. Annapolis, Md.: Institute for Learning Innovation.

Zimmer, René. 2002. *Begleitende Evaluation der Bürgerkonferenz "Streitfall Gendiagnostik."* Karlsruhe: Fraunhofer Institut fur Systemtechnik und Innovationsforschung.

6

What about the Audiences? Tailoring PUR Programs for Museum Visitors

Heather Mayfield

Scientific research is and always has been very much a minority pursuit. These days, it directly involves scarcely one person in a thousand in most Western countries (Pyerson and Sheets-Pyerson 1999). Furthermore, the work of research scientists—unlike that of those who follow a narrow specialty in the arts—is neither readily comprehensible, nor relevant, nor enjoyable for most of us, even those who have a strong background in science. So why should the 999 or so out of every 1,000 members of the public who do *not* participate in scientific research care about it, let alone make any effort to understand it?

That question is, I believe, fundamental to any worthwhile discussion of how scientific research can be effectively promoted in society. Too often scientists tacitly assume that the benighted lay population (sometimes dubbed "the great unwashed," if only in private) would better appreciate the value of research and therefore be more willing to support it via tax dollars if only there were more publicity to promote the researchers' causes. This is the classic top-down approach to science communication: scientists decide what the public should know and think about science and then press for more resources—in museums, television, radio, the Internet, and other media—to spread their messages (Bodmer and Wilkins 1992). The failure of this approach is the underlying impetus for the current campaign to promote the public understanding of scientific research (PUR).

I want to argue here that if we really wish to engage the public effectively with current research, a goal I strongly support, then we need to think much more carefully about our audiences—their needs, wants, knowledge, attitudes, and behavior. It is vital to decide the goals we are seeking to achieve before we commit substantial resources to them. For example, is our top priority to persuade the public of the need to fund research, to teach them about the latest findings, to encourage children to take up science careers, or what? And for those of us who work in museums, it is important that we adopt an empirical approach to the comparatively new field of PUR, seeking continually to learn from each other's successes and failures.

So I shall look at the PUR challenge pragmatically, from a bottom-up perspective, that is, from the point of view of the audience. I begin by asking why it is worth promoting public understanding, awareness, and appreciation of science. Then, having considered what audiences might usefully derive from such programs, I ask how scientific research might most effectively be promoted and how such PUR ventures might be funded and supported. Finally, I turn to what seems to me the crucial practical point at this stage in the history of PUR: the need for more high-quality information about our audiences' attitudes toward contemporary research. Only when we have such information, I shall argue, can we effectively plan PUR projects that collectively stand a chance of being successful from the audiences' points of view.

WHY DO IT AT ALL?

The sociopolitical case for promoting PUR in a democracy is well rehearsed (Bodmer 1985). We are all familiar with the high-minded notion that citizens must be empowered by not only a basic education but also by information that enables them to exercise their democratic rights as voters. A government is unlikely to spend substantial amounts of money on basic research if it believes that electoral reaction will be hostile. In some cases, public indifference or opposition to a research project can be such that legislators will feel able to let it wind down (the *Apollo* moon-landing project in the 1970s) or to close it down completely (the Super Collider project in the mid-1990s). It is therefore plainly in the interests of researchers to persuade others of their work's practical utility, intellectual value, and moral legitimacy and to communicate something of the passion that drives their enterprise. Economic arguments can be powerful, too: it is often argued that a strong research base has always been vital to the sustenance of a strong economy.

Although self-interest is a powerful motivator for those in the research community who work to promote PUR, it is hard to deny the worthiness of the case for society as a whole, even if it is unlikely to command a high place on national political agendas (scientific research is rarely a critical issue in elections). It is only when science issues make the headlines that we see just how poor the public's understanding of the nature of scientific research really is. Witness, for example, the poor quality of the continuing public debates in the United States about stem-cell technology (Radford 2003) and in the United Kingdom about genetically modified organisms (GMOs). Despite the thoughtful and well-informed features in newspapers and other quality information in the media, the level of public engagement in these issues is less than adequate, and, perhaps in consequence, the trust among those involved in frontline research and other participants in this exchange seems to be gradually diminishing in most Western democracies. This demonstrates how ineffective previous attempts to promote PUR have been. British Prime Minister Tony Blair surely had a point when, in the heat of the 1998 GMO crisis, he questioned the worth of a decade of PUR initiatives in the United Kingdom (Farmelo 1997). Despite the apparent success of all those well-intended ventures, the response of the research community to the national crisis was flat-footed, the reporting in most of the influential tabloid newspapers verged on the hysterical, and the public remained patently unable to handle a crisis involving new scientific research.

It was the GMO crisis, together with the mad cow disease debacle two years earlier, that brought to a head the increasing dissatisfaction with the top-down approach to science communication in the United Kingdom (Jasanoff 1997). There emerged a strong consensus in favor of dialogue between the public and scientists (U.K. House of Lords 2000), although whatever the buzzword "dialogue" means, it certainly betokened a wish to move toward a more even-handed approach to discussion among the parties involved than the old-style lecture delivered *from* the scientist *to* the public. In addition, the spirit of the new approach was to focus less on the need to pass information and facts to the public and more on the importance of giving laypeople the opportunity to discuss topics in science that are of special interest to them rather than topics that the scientists deem important. The upshot of all this was that the rather patronizing phrase "public understanding of science" was replaced by "public-science dialogue." Scientists were no longer in the driving seat—in the United Kingdom, the public were now codrivers.

This change seems to me to be a great opportunity for science museums. Instead of focusing on passing information and facts to visitors (something we do rather poorly), the new agenda encourages us to create forums that bring our visitors together with scientists in nonthreatening environments—something we have been in the past and still are ideally suited to do. In this way, it may be that one of the future key roles of the science museum is to serve as a place where practicing scientists meet informally with the public with neither having the upper hand in setting the agenda. Science museums could become the live interfaces between contemporary research and the public, something no other medium can provide.

This vision brings with it the challenge of attracting a truly representative public, not just the predominantly white, prosperous, middle-class "usual suspects." Most science museums have two principal audiences: schools and families. It is an uphill (though vitally important) struggle to attract visitors from parts of the community that do not feel so comfortable in our environments. And it is by no means clear that an emphasis on contemporary research in its broadest sense is going to bring in the new audiences we would all like to attract. As our colleagues in marketing departments understandably remind us, what sells museum tickets in large numbers are exhibits not on recondite scientific research but on tried and trusted popular themes, such as dinosaurs, sports, and space travel. It is this aversion to taking risks with our audiences' tastes, born of the precarious finances of most science museums, that makes it so difficult for contemporary research to get a foothold in science museum exhibits.

There is, however, no reason to despair. Audiences continually voice their wish for content that is changing, up to date, and relevant to their lives. No one wants to revisit a stagnant museum, whether it is real or virtual. Here, then, is the core of a rationale for including much more content about current research in science museum exhibits: if we choose our topics well and treat them in ways that have strong appeal to our audiences, modern research could form the basis of continually refreshed content.

Wellcome Wing, Science Museum, London, in the Who Am I? *gallery.* Photo courtesy of Science Museum, London

WHAT WOULD WE WANT AUDIENCES TO GET OUT OF RESEARCH EXHIBITS AND PROGRAMS?

In most developed countries, particularly the United States, the public are quite well disposed to science. However, for most of the time, in the words of Gregory and Miller (1998), the public pay "civil inattention" to science. The goal of a PUR program should be to overcome this indifference and to give its audience a sense of genuine engagement with research. By this I mean not so much to engineer an actual involvement in research (although that would be desirable whenever possible) as to create a feeling that the audience's input somehow makes a difference. Visitors to the London Science Museum have consistently expressed their wish that their input, gathered at exhibits where feedback is invited, be used constructively, perhaps to form part of an updated display or a wider multimedia public consultation or even a report to a body that monitors public opinions and feelings about science-related issues. What audiences certainly do not wish is to spend time entering their views, only to find out that their opinions are filed in the waste bin.

For me, one of the most important challenges of involving the public in discussions of contemporary scientific research is to make this involvement genuinely constructive. To achieve this, a museum must be clear about its principal purpose in presenting this type of programming. Is it, for example,

- to help the participants learn about the underlying science?
- to provide an entertaining event for visitors?
- to underpin some part of the school curriculum?
- to give scientists opportunities to meet the public?
- to supply feedback to interested organizations?
- to be part of a campaign to change public attitudes?
- to illustrate to the director or the board that the museum is keeping up to date?
- to make a funder or sponsor feel good about reaching out to the community?
- to influence public policy? or
- to attract new audiences?

Each of these could be a legitimate aim of a PUR program, and there are many others, too. The trap to avoid is to be unclear about priorities, with the result that presentations become unfocused and banal.

Most museums have much to learn from other media about dealing with new science in ways that are accessible and compelling to large audiences. Every day there is an abundance of examples from newspaper reports and features and from television and radio sequences of the classic journalistic practice of clearly identifying the audience, making it clear why the story is so relevant, and then delivering the story's "who, what, when, where, why, and how" together with catchy hooks to the audiences personal lives and a strong preference for the concrete over the abstract (White et al. 1993).

Although museums will never have the resources to react to events as quickly as, for example, newspapers and television, exhibit developers will have to become adept at best practices in science journalism if they are to be successful in competing with other media. These communication skills could valuably be brought to bear in displays and programs that focus on stories that evolve relatively slowly, giving exhibit developers time to prepare material that audiences will not readily find elsewhere. Examples of suitable themes include Mars landings and other space missions, searches for extraterrestrial intelligence, and high-profile international meetings on topics of potentially great public interest (AIDS, climate change, and so on).

There is potential, too, in taking advantage of local science and technology stories. Most science museums could do much more to seize opportunities to focus on local engineering projects and science research being done in their area by local universities and companies. In this way, a museum could aspire to be the "science hub" of their community: the place where scientists can meet informally with local people while museums provide the communication skills necessary for mutual reward.

What has been missing in the tried-and-tested formulas of science communication is a component that gives the audience an awareness of the underlying processes of research. This omission, along with the unimaginative and fact-based curricula taught in many schools and colleges, is in large part responsible for public ignorance of the nature of science. How many of those outside the scientific world realize that when research results appear, they are only provisional and therefore open to question? How many appreciate that successful scientific enquiry involves not only logical reasoning but also imaginative thinking? And how many understand that science is, above all, a human activity and so reflects the weaknesses as well as the strengths of its participants?

Easy though it is to rattle off aspects of the nature of scientific research, it is hard to come to a consensus about what constitutes the core of this nature. The unfortunate science wars of the late 1990s demonstrated the extent of the disagreements about this between, on the one hand, those practicing science and, on the other, many commentators on the subject, notably in the field of the sociology of science (Labinger and Collins 2001). Occasionally, exhibit developers can get into deep trouble when they tread into this dangerous area. Look, for example, at the furor over the *Science in American Life* exhibit at the Museum of American History at the Smithsonian Institution in Washington, D.C. (Molella 1997). This innovative exhibition, undeniably popular with audiences, introduced many social elements into its theme but fell foul of many scientists by including material that they deemed unnecessarily negative and therefore not the sort of science they wanted to see in the show. Somehow, museum developers need to find ways of tackling these issues.

Without an appreciation of the nature of scientific research, it is impossible to appreciate the true meaning and value of a new research result. The problem is that it is extremely hard to convey this nature without being dull—something no journalist would dare to do. But perhaps there is an opportunity for museums here. With the more leisurely pace of a museum visit and the wide variety of experiences in a typical exhibit, we stand a better chance of bringing in by stealth important points about the nature of research. Impressive progress has been made in this field at Boston's Museum of Science, whose staff have been developing entertaining exhibitions about the processes of scientific investigation since 1991 under the banner "science is an activity."[1] Other exhibitions, for example, at the Rose Center for Earth and Space at the American Museum of Natural History in New York, have subtly, yet powerfully, introduced themes about the nature of research into the narratives of their displays and films.[2]

Whatever one's priorities, many of the most popular themes in topical research will be ones that audiences find controversial. What museums have to do is to find ways of enabling their users to engage in controversy that give them more than they could derive from other media. One of the key challenges here is to provide programs that have a life beyond their duration rather than to organize events that are simply "talking shops." One attractive possibility is to make museums local channels through which the public can have a voice in controversial issues. This agenda of empowerment (to use the management jargon of the 1990s) is much more easily described than delivered. To achieve it, museums would need to radically rethink their relationships with each other, with other media, and with their audiences.

WHAT WOULD WE DO?

When museum professionals last met with research scientists to discuss how research could best be presented in museums (Farmelo and Carding 1997), they concluded that the way forward involved ever closer collaboration among museums, media, and research organizations. Although that conclusion remains true today, it would be churlish to deny that progress has been made since 1996. The touring exhibition on AIDS, organized by the Association of Science–Technology Centers,[3] and the Bionet virtual exhibition project in Europe, coordinated by the European Collaborative for Science, Industry and Technology Exhibitions,[4] are prime examples of a burgeoning spirit of collaboration among science museums in North America and Europe. There remains, however, huge scope to increase the degree of collaboration among museums in the production of material on contemporary research. At the moment, the field is dominated largely by the comparatively well-resourced institutions—notably, La Cité des Sciences et de l'Industrie à Paris (La Cité), the Museum of Science in Boston, the Deutsches Museum in Munich, and London's Science Museum—with the smaller museums understandably unable to participate. For audiences, the potential rewards of collaborations to share content in contemporary science among the fraternity of museums are enormous.

With or without such collaborations, it is essential that museums become much more savvy and imaginative in setting up relations with other media. The audience data underline the key issue: museums reach a relatively small number of people compared with their counterpart providers in television, radio, and newspapers. What is more, many of these other media reach parts of the community that most museums can now only dream of attracting, such as teenagers and senior citizens. To be sure, demographic trends toward an ever increasing proportion of over-65s in the population indicate the pressing need for museums to do much more for the elderly members of the community; we should move away from our tendency to think of seniors as volunteers and toward thinking of them as one of the most-valued visitor sectors. It is easy to imagine how one might begin to implement a strategy to attract these visitors in greater numbers—perhaps by presenting exhibits on themes of special interest to seniors, such as Viagra and research into its potential female spin-off and into advances in research into conditions that affect the elderly. It is not fanciful to imagine drug companies being willing to fund programs like this.

It is also easy is envision the potential benefits for the public of cross-media collaborations. For example, if museums did more to provide high-quality information, advice, and facilities for television and radio (possibly by supplying well-informed and eloquent presenters and ready-made recording locations), one could imagine that museums would gain much more publicity, ultimately resulting in increased visitor numbers. Such collaborations already happen locally and with the Discovery Digital Networks (notably by the Royal Ontario Museum in Toronto), but there is undoubtedly plenty of opportunity for museums to raise their game, maybe in some cases to become recognized as major content providers for local television and radio stations.

Perhaps we might one day move toward a new vision in which the public gets its science news from providers that are set up to respond quickly (television, newspapers, radio, and the Web) and then use museums to follow up on the stories. In this way, museums would not attempt to participate in the labor-intensive business of news production, but would play to their strengths as places where people can reflect on stories at leisure after the other media have lost interest.

As science museums work more and more closely with other media, it's a safe bet that museums will quicken the pace at which they work and become even more audience focused. It would be unfortunate if museums were ever wholly to espouse the profit-driven values of commercial television, but there is certainly much that museums can learn from the audience centeredness of most other media. Despite a lot of progress, there are still too many museum exhibits that seem to be intended to please museum professionals rather than the visitors.

One of the key trends in the commercial media over the past decade has been to promote audience involvement. We are now moving rapidly away from the old programming style in which experts broadcast one-way to audiences. Increasingly, audience feedback is part of the program via phone calls, e-mail, and text messages. It is in this climate (driven in part by the growth of the Internet and "reality television") that the "dialogue" style of science communication has flourished.

It is vital that museums respond to these changes in the media climate and become more generous-spirited places—less didactic and more welcoming in their responses to visitors' opinions and feelings. We are moving into an era when visitors are coauthors of content, not merely the passive recipients of expert knowledge. Several museums have begun to move in this direction, producing exhibitions that plainly value the visitors' input and make their opinions part of the show. Examples are displays on contemporary science at the Tech Museum of Innovation in San Jose,[5] the (temporary) genetics exhibit at the American Museum of Natural History in New York (which featured fascinatingly illuminating comparisons between visitors' views and national data), and the exhibits in the Wellcome Wing at London's Science Museum.[6] In programming, too, there are signs of a move toward a style that is more respectful of audiences' views and that gives the public as loud a voice as the experts. The science and society program Forum des Sciences, now well under way at La Cité in Paris,[7] is showing the way here, with well-resourced events and complementary exhibits (real and virtual) on topical and controversial themes that involve the public and other media in new and imaginative ways.

In order to connect with a wider public, museums will have to build on the new learning strategies that they have been developing over the past decade, recognizing the many ways in which people best absorb information and relate to it (Gardner 1993). One consequence of this is the recognition that many people are tempted to engage with science-related content through works of art (Ede 2000). This notion has led to some imaginative arts-based exhibits on contemporary sciences, such as at the Deutsches Hygiene-Museum in Dresden,[8] in the Wellcome Trust's Sci-Art project in the United Kingdom,[9] and at the MIT Museum (with arresting contributions from the leading quantum chaologist Eric Heller). Artists who work at the frontier of contemporary digital technology are increasingly on display in leading art galleries, such as Bill Viola (Guggenheim Museum in New York), Perry Hoberman (Kiasma Museum in Helsinki), and Ranjit Makkuni (the 2002 award winner at the Austrian-based Ars Electronica in 2002).[10] By working more closely with such artists, museums could reach audiences that would otherwise remain foreign to them.

If museums are serious about reaching new audiences and not just preaching to the converted, it is vital that programs are presented outside the walls of museums. Although most museums regard their homes as their core asset, it is possible to envisage museums that do not have a single spatial location and that reach their audiences through new technology and flexible deployment of resources. Apart from the burgeoning of virtual museums,[11] several other projects are developing ideas that make little or no use of a central location in "real" space (as opposed to cyberspace). For example, Andrea Bandelli and his collaborators in Turin, Italy, are developing some extremely imaginative ideas based to some extent on "the science center without walls" conceived by Canada's Science Alberta Foundation. The Turin project[12] is run by an agency that organizes activities and projects and produces them in collaboration with other institutions without a permanent "bricks-and-mortar" location. The project has had some remarkable successes, notably a series of events presented in April 2003, at a former Fiat car factory in Lingotto that is now a sort of "urban center," with shops, several offices, a concert hall, and some faculties of the university.

It will be fascinating to explore the consequences of dropping the centrality of the building in our conception of a museum, for the uncomfortable fact is that many people have no wish to visit the museum environments we have created; in some sectors of society, museum visits are extremely rare apart from mandatory school trips. If we wish to reach these nonvisitors, it would be more productive not to try to attract them through our doors but to visit them in places they frequent in large numbers—shopping malls, airports, sports stadiums, and so forth. Properly targeted exhibitions presented in busy places such as these could introduce research to parts of the community that would otherwise scarcely dream of visiting a science exhibit. To be successful, such exhibits would have to be populist to an extent that would make many conservative museum professionals uncomfortable—that is, the balance would have to tilt from information toward entertainment, and the tone would have to be much less high-minded than the one used in most displays. I, for one, believe we should welcome such a shift toward a more visitor-centered approach.

This brings us to the question of the stance museums should take when they present contemporary science. Should they strive to be a promoter, a skeptic, or an honest broker? Many supporters of museums, including many funders, governors, and governments, take it for granted that museums are supporters of the scientific enterprise. Yet, I wonder if unquestioning support is always a good thing, especially now that museums aspire to be places that debate controversial scientific issues. If we are to play this role in facilitating dialogue, then surely we have to be openly neutral so that we cannot be validly accused of being in the pockets of any particular lobby. If such accusations were made to stick, the museum would forfeit the trust of its visitors and soon cease to be a viable forum for tackling controversy.

Nor should science museums be narrow-minded about what constitutes a scientific topic. Discussions of many issues arising from contemporary science benefit hugely from contributions from experts in other disciplines. Big bang cosmology, xenotransplantation, the search for extraterrestrial intelligence, vivisection, biological weapons—all these topics might naively be interpreted as suitable for comment only by specialist scientists. But the discussion can be immeasurably enriched if experts in other fields are invited to the table. This is the thinking behind the programs at the London Science Museum's new Dana Centre in its new Wellcome Wolfson Building. Its programs, targeted at young adults (in the age range of 18 to 40) bring together not only scientists but many other specialists, including ethicists, politicians, and sociologists. Using a grant from the Wellcome Trust, we have developed and delivered *Naked Science*, a program that sought to push the boundaries of science communication by experimenting with topics that would not normally be regarded as suitable for the traditional family audience. In addition, we are trying new formats that go beyond conventional lecture and panel formats.

Examples of our *Naked Science* events include the following:

- *Do Scientists Need to Destroy Embryos for Research?*—attended by 100 adults (55 percent female), with an accompanying online discussion.
- *The Science of Beauty*—a series of overlapping events, presented in an art gallery, including an artists' gallery tour, an object-handling session, talks with holistic therapists, and poetry readings.
- *Animals or Human Embryos: Which Should We Value More?*—an experimental event in which the audience was divided into four focus groups to discuss controversial issues in depth before reporting back to the entire gathering.
- *Motherland—Is DNA the Key to Finding Your African or European Roots?*—presented in the form of television show (à la Ricky Lake), organized in collaboration with the BBC and an independent production company. Of the audience of 112, about 90 percent came from the Afro-Caribbean community.

In the new Dana Centre, we intend to build on what we have learned from the *Naked Science* events—its disasters as well as its triumphs—by inviting stand-up comedians, dancers, actors, and poets to perform in the Centre. Our long-term hope is to recast the grammar of public-science discourse.

Wellcome Wing, Science Museum, London, in the Who Am I? *gallery.* Photo courtesy of Science Museum, London

HOW WOULD WE MAKE IT HAPPEN?

It is usually easiest to secure commercial funding for museum projects when their themes are aligned with those of wealthy branches of industry, eager (in the time-honored phrase) to "put something back into the community." How could museums persuade such funders to support PUR programs? Above all, museums would need to demonstrate that the promotion of PUR is central to their missions, not an activity they pursue when the mood takes them.

The Liberty Science Center in New York has been particularly successful in developing and delivering funded programs that involve young audiences in solving contemporary engineering problems, thereby introducing them to the method of research. The Center's annual Panasonic Challenge for high-school students, which began in 1991, involves setting an engineering problem that must be solved with the aid of some given kit.[13] The generous prizes include scholarships for the overall winning team and Panasonic equipment for special category winners.[14]

Even more remarkable is the Center's *Live from . . . Cardiac Classroom,* funded by Johnson & Johnson. This program uses two-way videoconferencing technology to connect 75 middle- or high-school students to a cardiac surgical suite at Morristown, New Jersey's, Memorial Hospital. For two hours while open-heart coronary bypass surgery is in progress, students are immersed in a one-of-a-kind learning experience that extends their knowledge and understanding of anatomy and physiology, lifestyle choices that determine health consequences, the diversity of careers in the medical field, and how research and new technology are changing the health and medical profession.[15]

More commercial funding for PUR programs in museums would be welcome, but for the moment the overwhelming majority of resources for these activities will come from organizations that aim to promote research. In the United States, this funding comes principally from the National Science Foundation, and in the United Kingdom it derives from the research councils and the Wellcome Trust. In the late 1960s, it was the Trust that funded the largest-ever building program of science centers in the United Kingdom when it co-funded the creation of several new centers, each of which now plays an important role in promoting PUR.

THE NEED FOR MORE RESEARCH

The idea that science museums should focus on contemporary research is extremely radical—so radical that it would be foolish to embark on such a program without a lot of evidence that there is demonstrably an appetite for our proposals. We need much more research to inform our knowledge of the audiences we are targeting. Potential funders would need this information, and they will rightly insist on seeing hard evidence for the need we have identified.

If there is to be a concerted campaign for museum programs that focus on contemporary research, then it seems to me that it would be worthwhile to initially fund a formative evaluation project that probes the prior knowledge and attitudes of the audiences we are seeking to target. What aspects of research most interest and concern the public? What does the public know and feel about science research? Where do they currently obtain their information, and do they trust it? If not, why not? At the moment, our information on these and related questions is mainly anecdotal or conjectural, and there is a pressing need for hard data to inform our planning. Perhaps the PUR community should work with the Visitor Studies Association on a national (or even international) project to tease out the answers to these questions.[16] This lively association, based in Colorado, meets annually, furnishing excellent opportunities to meet with world-leading experts in the field of evaluating museum programs.

There does exist a substantial body of research data on previous PUR projects, although the various evaluations are by no means of uniformly high standards in terms of their methodologies or their data quality. Still, too much of these data remain on the hard disks of the originating institutions, and too little of it is shared. Some of the evaluation results can be sensitive: no museum wants to make public the visitors' verdict that it has rewarded the munificence of a funder with a turkey of an exhibit. However, the great majority of research findings are uncontroversial and are potentially valuable to other organizations.

Setting up an international clearinghouse of evaluation data for PUR projects would be a hugely valuable innovation. Such a collection should include data not only from museums but from projects in all other media. There is much to be learned from evaluations of audience responses to research coverage on Web sites and in radio and television programs.

The problem here is the widespread aversion to publicly admitting that a project has failed. In my view, museums should take the lead and resolve to be much more balanced in our presentations to colleagues at conferences and seminars. Just as we should be proud of a resounding success, we should also take pride in an honorable failure that enables us to learn from mistakes. Such failures are often as valuable as successes. If we were to make this culture change, the community would be able to advance its PUR initiatives more swiftly, ultimately to the benefit of our audiences. They care nothing for the vanity of producers, only for the product.

ENVOI

It is hardly surprising that the current impetus to improve the public understanding of contemporary scientific research is coming from contemporary scientific researchers and those who wish to support them. The thrust of my arguments here is that, in order to achieve their aim, the scientists would be well advised to abandon their proselytizing style of presenting to the public in museums and instead be much more focused on the audiences that they are seeking to influence. Such an approach will entail thinking through precisely what we are trying to achieve in promoting PUR, trying out various ways of doing it, and evaluating carefully new programs to see which of them are most effective in achieving our goals. What is needed, then, is for scientists to approach the PUR challenge with the same imagination, logical rigor, and rational self-criticism that they bring to their work in science. In short, scientists need to be more scientific.

NOTES

1. Further details, including valuable evaluation reports, are available at www.mos.org/exhibitdevelopment (accessed February 24, 2004).

2. www.amnh.org/rose (accessed February 24, 2004).

3. www.astc.org (accessed February 24, 2004).

4. www.bionetonline.org (accessed February 24, 2004).

5. www.thetech.org (accessed February 24, 2004).

6. www.sciencemuseum.org.uk (accessed February 24, 2004).

7. www.cite-sciences.fr/francais/ala_cite/college/flash.htm (accessed February 24, 2004).

8. www.dhmd.de (accessed February 24, 2004).

9. www.wellcome.ac.uk/en/1/pinpubactexh.html (accessed February 24, 2004).

10. www.aec.at/en/index.asp (accessed February 24, 2004).

11. www.museumlink.com/virtual.htm (accessed February 24, 2004).

12. www.torinoscienza.it/lab-vr (accessed February 24, 2004).

13. www.panasonic.com/indUStrial/creativedesign (accessed February 24, 2004).

14. In the United Kingdom, there is a similar initiative: the annual Young Engineer's Design Awards, where the finalists traditionally exhibit their design solutions in the Science Museum (accessed February 24, 2004).

15. Students interact directly with all members of the surgical team to better understand the teamwork, experience, and differentiated skills required to mend a broken heart. Liberty Science Center educators, audiovisual staff, and volunteers facilitate the audio and video interactions while surgical instruments, materials, and devices circulate around the room and questions come in a steady stream from the engaged audience. The program began in 1998 as a result of the imagination and vision of Liberty Science Center Board member and cardiologist William A. Tansey III. (accessed February 24, 2004).

16. www.visitorstudies.org (accessed February 24, 2004).

REFERENCES

Bodmer, W., ed. 1985. The public understanding of science: Report of an ad hoc group, endorsed by the Council of the Royal Society, U.K.

Bodmer, Sir Walter, and Janice Wilkins. 1992. Research to improve public understanding programmes. *Public Understanding of Science* 1, no. 1.

Ede, Sian, ed. 2000. *Strange and charmed: Science and the contemporary visual arts.* Calouste Gulbenkian Foundation.

Farmelo, Graham. 1997. From big bang to damp squib? In *Science today: Problem or crisis?* London: Routledge, 175–91.

Farmelo, Graham, and Janet Carding, eds. 1997. Introduction. In *Here and now: Contemporary science and technology in museums and science centres.* London: Science Museum Publications, 26–27.

Gardner, Howard. 1993. *Frames of mind: The theory of multiple intelligence.* London: HarperCollins.

Gregory, Jane, and Steve Miller. 1998. *Science in public: Communication, culture and credibility.* London: Plenum Trade Press.

Jasanoff, S. 1997. Civilization and madness: The great BSE scare of 1996. *Public Understanding of Science* 6, no. 3.

Labinger, J. A., and H. M. Collins. 2001. *The one culture? A conversation about science.* Chicago: University of Chicago Press.

Molella, Arthur. 1997. Stormy weather: Science in American life and the changing climate for technology museums. In *Here and now: Contemporary science and technology in museums and science centres,* edited by Graham Farmelo and Janet Carding. London: Science Museum Publications, 131–38. (For a perceptive review of the exhibit, see Exhibits and Expectations, *Public Understanding of Science* 4, no. 3 [1995]: 305–13.)

Pyerson, L., and S. Sheets-Pyerson. 1999. *Servants of nature: A history of scientific institutions, enterprises and sensibilities.* New York: Norton.

Radford, Tim. 2003. Stem cell technology. In *Frontiers 02: Science and Technology, 2002–2003.* London: Atlantic Books.

U.K. House of Lords. 2000. Science and society—Third report. February. www.publications.parliament.uk/pa/ld199900/ldselect/ldsctech/38/3801.htm.

White, Stephen, Peter Evans, Chris Mihill, and Maryon Tysoe. 1993. *Hitting the headlines: A practical guide to the media.* Malden, Mass.: Blackwell.

7

Dangerous Ground?
Public Engagement with
Scientific Controversy

Xerxes Mazda

One Sunday afternoon in July 2001, the Science Museum in London held a séance. In a darkened Victorian library, 30 members of the public joined hands and witnessed a series of objects moving mysteriously across a table. Of course, it was a trick. Or was it? The Science Museum did not comment either way. Some participants truly believed they had witnessed a paranormal event. Others were angry. They were suspicious that the facilitator, a well-known psychologist who specializes in debunking paranormal beliefs, was collaborating with the Science Museum, of all institutions, to waste time and money with cheap stunts. The séance did more than attempt to contact the dead. It tackled head-on the controversy over the supernatural, probing the rift between skeptics, for whom the subject is unworthy of rigorous scientific consideration, and believers.

I consider this one of the more unusual attempts by the Museum to engage the public with controversy in scientific research. This chapter covers more typical areas of controversy: vivisection, genetically modified food, nuclear energy, vaccination, and Internet censorship, to name but a few. What follows is my personal account of seven years of work at the Science Museum on public engagement with controversy and the things we have learned in the process. I hope that some of our findings will prove useful to other institutions.

Although this chapter focuses on the work of the Science Museum in London, it should be considered against the international backdrop of increasing public engagement with scientific controversy. The idea of tackling scientific controversy is by no means new. Journalists have long focused on controversy as a way into the sometimes distant and opaque world of scientific research. However, the past few years have seen a steady rise in efforts to engage the public in these controversies. Some early indicators included consensus conferences, which are joined today by the extensive opportunities the Internet provides to vote or express an opinion on a wide range of hot scientific issues (Joss and Durant 1995). Museums have also been increasingly using feedback on scientific controversy as a way to engage the public in issues in science and technology. Early examples from the United States include those at the Tech Museum of Innovation in San José and the Monterey Bay Aquarium, where visitors could record their opinions on controversial issues from the television V-Chip, to ocean conservation. Today, opportunities to offer feedback in exhibitions have become the norm, with many museums, such as the Museum of Science in Boston running programs looking at scientific research and controversy.

Ever since its foundation in the nineteenth century, the Science Museum has struggled, with varying degrees of success, to interpret contemporary science and technology alongside its history (Mazda 1996). The difficulty of this endeavor has altered over time as science and technology have moved on, and the expectations of people visiting the Museum have changed. Certainly over the past few decades, the subjects covered by the Museum have become increasingly difficult for visitors to understand. At the same time, public concern over perceived problems with science and technology has grown.

In the early 1990s, this triggered the Museum to explore more effective ways to engage visitors with issues arising from contemporary scientific and technological research. This led to several new initiatives: for example, from 1991 to 1998, the museum produced the Science Box series of small (approximately 500 square feet) temporary exhibitions that covered topical issues in science and technology such as the hole in the ozone layer, genetically modified food, and chaos. Our experiences with these exhibitions partly informed the content of the Wellcome Wing, a new building containing six highly interactive exhibition areas over four floors, focusing on the relevance to visitors of issues in contemporary science and technology.

In parallel with this trend, we have been increasingly looking at ways of engaging visitors, not just with research, but specifically with the controversies that arise from this research. This has culminated in one of our current projects, *Naked Science*, an experimental series of highly participatory events that tackle controversies in contemporary science and technology.

The Museum's Visitor Research Unit is monitoring the effectiveness of these experimental approaches through an evaluation program that has benefited as much from our failures as from our successes. The following is my individual perspective on one aspect of the work of this unit: evaluations of the exhibits that engage the public with controversy in scientific and technological research.

This chapter is divided into three parts. The first section looks at reasons for introducing museum visitors to research controversy and suggests the role that exhibitions and events that encourage dialogue can play in the public's exploration of this controversy. The second section introduces two key areas that the Science Museum has evaluated in detail: the things that motivate visitors to take part in exhibits containing dialogue and the types of controversial subjects that engage visitors. The third section introduces three potential questions that the Museum is currently tackling through evaluation: whether a subject can be too controversial, whether a museum can produce an unbiased and neutral exhibition or event, and the balance between providing information and encouraging visitor debate.

Most important, there are some issues that are controversial to scientists but not to the general public. For the purposes of this chapter, I am interested only in the issues that the general public finds controversial. If an issue is not relevant enough to our visitors for them to engage with it, or if no one seems to be disagreeing over the issue, then it lies beyond the scope of this chapter.

WHY MUSEUMS SHOULD COVER CONTROVERSY

The Visitor Research Unit repeatedly finds evidence that visitors enjoy engaging with controversy and think it is something that museums should cover. This is expressed in several ways, as when the public tells us that they feel distanced from science. They view scientists as living in ivory towers, surrounding themselves with mystery. However, visitors do want to challenge and understand why scientists do what they do and what drives them to do it.

Scientists, historians, and sociologists recognize that controversy is an integral part of the way science and technology develop (Engelhardt and Caplan 1987). Indeed, the process of challenging the status quo is a key approach to many aspects of our lives today, from the arts, law, and politics to science and technology (Gater 1999). This makes covering controversy an essential part of the work of presenting scientific or technological change. To not do so would be to propagate a simplistic, linear approach to scientific change where discoveries progress smoothly toward the latest accepted theory or gadget.

The public, who rarely have any cause to be involved firsthand in research, are often made aware of scientific research only when it is expressed in terms of controversy. Latour has described how the main output of a research lab is the published peer-reviewed paper, which remains the main evidence of research in the public domain (Latour and Woolgar 1986). Journalists use their skill to turn the more promising of these papers into discussions of controversial issues for public consumption. Museums are increasingly following the same tactics.

Controversy is also a useful way for museums to introduce social issues and raise visitors' awareness of the political, economic, and environmental angles to current scientific debates. Ignoring controversy would inaccurately represent issues in contemporary science and technology, as it would imply that there is no room for future changes of direction. The skilled exhibit developer illustrates scientific controversy by choosing examples that are controversial and relevant to both scientists and the public.

If used properly, controversy can engage visitors and enhance their overall experience. Controversy has the potential to make ordinary subjects more interesting. By using it as a lens through which to look at scientific or technological innovation, exhibition developers can make such subjects attractive and compelling to the public.

USING DIALOGUE TO EXPLORE CONTROVERSY

In 2000, a new piece of jargon entered the U.K. science communicator's lexicon: dialogue. A government report on science and society described how "the crisis of [public] trust has produced a new mood for dialogue" (U.K. House of Lords 2000). The report recommended that institutions involved in the public understanding of science, including science museums and science centers, should catalyze debate and dialogue between scientists and the public as one way of breaking down suspicion and mistrust. This report reflected a more general mood within the science communication sector. For example, the National Museum of Science and Industry (NMSI), the family of museums that includes the Science Museum, created a new vision shortly after this report appeared: "We engage people in dialogue to create meanings from the past, present and future of human ingenuity."

Dialogue and debate are especially useful in dealing with controversy. Issues surrounding controversy are often abstract and complex and are difficult to cover using traditional exhibition media, such as interactives or object-based display. Exhibit developers face the constant danger that exhibitions tackling controversy will become text heavy, with little appeal or motivation for visitors to engage with them.

Yet if visitors take part in debates themselves, exploring scientific controversy through dialogue-based exhibits and events, the issues will often come to life. We have been testing this approach at the Science Museum since 1996 and are now confident that engaging visitors in debate is a key part of our exhibition methodology. The rest of this chapter looks at some of the ways we have attempted to encourage visitors to explore scientific controversies through dialogue and some of the lessons we have learned from our evaluation.

EVALUATING VISITOR MOTIVATIONS

For an exhibit designer, it is essential to consider what motivates visitors to engage with controversial issues through dialogue (Gammon and Mazda 2000). This was something we researched in the first part of our evaluation program, which involved studying early interactives we called "discussion exhibits." These were simple components of the Science Box exhibitions and allowed visitors to join debates by writing their opinions about issues covered by the exhibition. Today, areas for visitor comments are common in museums and art galleries, but at the time they were relatively rare in science museums. The two discussion exhibits that we evaluated as part of this program were attached to the following Science Box exhibitions:

- *Future Foods?* (1997) looked at the science and issues behind genetically modified food.
- *Join the Great Fat Debate* (1998) introduced visitors to the issues around Olestra, a manufactured substitute for fat.

Our evaluation methodology included questionnaires, focus groups, observation of visitors using the exhibits, and an examination of the comments that people left. From this evaluation, we were able to establish three basic rules for the things that motivated visitors to write their comments and the things that motivated visitors to read the comments that other visitors had left.

Three things that motivated visitors to write comments are the following:

1. *An outlet for anger.* Visitors appeared to use the discussion exhibit as an outlet for their anger and frustration with issues in the exhibition. Many comments showed genuine passion—words were written in capitals or heavily underlined. Specific points raised in the exhibition appeared to have catalyzed visitors to express opinions drawn from their own knowledge, experience, and prejudices. For example, one visitor wrote about genetically modified food,

   > Where is the democracy? It is the consumers who do not benefit. The companies who produce it are there to make a profit! All genetically engineered food should be banned or at the very least labelled in shops so we are not hoodwinked into buying it

   Another visitor commented that

   > Olestra adds no calories to the diet. It cannot be used by the body. How much has it cost to develop and how much profit do the manufacturers want to get back from it? Twenty-five years of testing is an awful lot of investment. Why do we need it? Answer: we don't, but someone thinks they can profit from it.

2. *A wish to cause change.* Visitors seem to be motivated by the belief that their comments would be read by manufacturers and policymakers. This belief is not particularly surprising, as public opinion is often gauged using market research. A *Future Foods?* focus group participant voiced the belief of many visitors when she said,

   > I think it is a very controversial topic and a lot of people are very upset about it. It stirs emotions. So I think they're trying to find out what people think, and then they can use that to focus their marketing strategy to counteract, because after all they're selling a product of some sort.

3. *A desire to scribble graffiti.* This appears to be a powerful motivation for visitors to use discussion exhibits. Many of the comments that were left would best be described as graffiti. For example, of the 2,259 comments left in *Future Foods?*, well over half the comments were unusable "graffiti." The

largest proportion of these were scribbles, and some were obscenities.

Three things that motivated visitors to read other visitors' comments are the following:

1. *Powerful language.* The comments that visitors leave make compelling reading, in large part because of the emotive language used. For example,

   > I am a molecular biologist, and GM [genetically modified] food scares me to death.

   and

   > GE [genetic engineering] is not an extension of existing selective breeding. GE is clumsy and dirty. In some processes tiny particles of tungsten are fired into the chromosomes of host cells [...] its like firing a cannon-ball at a butterfly with a maggot and an appleseed attached and hoping it sticks in the eyeball and not the wing. Stop it you silly people.

   The visitor who wrote this latter comment had a working knowledge of genetic engineering yet uses more emotive and expressive language than the often bland, balanced language employed by museums. Ultimately, this makes the comment more readable.
2. *Perceived imbalance.* Visitors felt that the *Future Foods?* exhibition was biased in favor of genetically modified food.[1] For example,

   > This exhibition boldly states that risk assessments examine all potential effects that GM could have on our health and environment then goes on to list impressive sounding committees. This is a ridiculous and scientifically inaccurate claim. It is impossible to assess how a gene pool will behave—just as nobody foresaw the impact of introducing new species in Australia or New Zealand.

   Visitors seemed to value the comments of other visitors, as they were seen to be redressing the perceived imbalance in the exhibition. A focus group participant expressed the observation that the written comments appeared to be saying the opposite of the exhibition, which possibly led to some balance. This was echoed by a the visitor who wrote, "This seems to be a very agribusiness dominated exhibition. The only doubts are ours, the punters, on these slips of paper."

3. *Personal relevance.* The discussion exhibits were valued by visitors because they allowed issues to be tackled from the point of view of the visitor rather than of a scientist, exhibit developer, or manufacturer.

We used our understanding of these six motivations when we were designing the content of the second generation of dialogue exhibits, the *Tell* interactives in the Wellcome Wing. These differ from discussion exhibits by being entirely computer based, in keeping with the high-tech flavor of the Wing. Twelve *Tell* points are scattered throughout the exhibitions in the Wing. Visitors begin by watching a series of short video clips that introduce a range of different views on the controversial subject; then they can either find out more about the subject, read the comments that other people have left, or type in their own comment. We designed *Tell* to be flexible, with a fully networked content management system and centralized database of visitor comments, which allows us to display visitors' comments at many places in the Wing.

We wanted the formative evaluation of the *Tell* points to answer two questions:

- Can we discover any rules for predicting which subjects and formats of questions visitors find controversial and engaging?
- What types of technology (such as video, audio, or typed feedback) encourage visitors to leave the longest and most engaged responses?

I discuss our findings regarding the former question in the next section.

EVALUATING WHICH SUBJECTS VISITORS FIND CONTROVERSIAL

How wonderful it would be if we could predict which subjects visitors would find controversial. A definitive list would be ideal. Frustratingly, we have so far found this impossible. We even found it very hard to produce simple rules for defining controversial areas. Subjects that we thought were topical and would tap directly into people's fears, such as the "big brother" threat of electronic surveillance, engaged visitors at only a very superficial level. Conversely, subjects that we feared had been overexposed, such as animal experimentation, proved to be highly active issues.

We believe that it is worth persisting in trying to find simple rules for subjects that can engage visitors, as the wrong question can lead to a low quality of interaction. We could rationalize this using the motives to read and write: as visitors find an issue less controversial and less emotive, they feel more detached from it, and their anger and desire to effect change weaken. The graffiti effect begins to dominate, and the comments they write are less compelling for others to read, thus downgrading the overall visitor experience.

We decided that there were two separate effects at work: the format that we used for the question and the subject of the question. We were able to test both of these as part of the evaluation for *Tell*. Overall, we tested around 25 different subjects and question formats by leaving a prototype system in the museum and analyzing visitors' responses and nonresponses. We backed this up with observation and questionnaires. The questions we tested were related to the four main areas of science and technology covered in the Wellcome Wing—biomedicine, digital technology, future technologies, and breaking news stories.

Using the results of this evaluation, we found that the most important rules for asking questions are the following:

1. *Ask open questions.* This may be obvious in hindsight, yet much to our surprise, we often accidentally asked closed questions during the evaluation period. We found that visitors would consistently respond just "yes" or "no" to closed questions. For example, the question "One in five people will suffer from depression during their lifetime. Are drugs the answer?" elicited overwhelmingly "yes" or "no" responses, although a few visitors explained their reasoning: "I do not think drugs are the answer. I think the answer is to right whatever you did to make yourself unhappy."

   As a way of trying to avoid closed questions in the future, we stipulated that all questions should begin with "Tell us what you think about [add subject]." Using this formula, the question above became "Tell us what you think about treating depression with drugs," which produced a range of more interesting responses.

   When we looked at the more successful subjects, we concluded that to produce engaging exhibitions, it was important to do the following:

2. *Ask questions to which you can give several answers.* We found that if the exhibit developer could think of five or more different angles on an issue, visitors would think of these and more. Issues with potentially many different points of view encouraged a much richer input from visitors, and this increased visitors' motivation to read the comments.

For example, one of our recent exhibitions looks at the controversial findings of a U.K. researcher on the effects of the triple measles, mumps, and rubella vaccine (the MMR vaccine). He suggests that this vaccine can damage children's bowels and cause autism. This finding hit the national headlines and caused confusion among concerned parents as to whether to vaccinate their children. As part of the exhibition, we asked visitors to "tell us what you think about the MMR vaccine." This unleashed a wide range of points of view, including the following:

- There are too many contradictory statements for parents to be able to make up their minds.
- Take the vaccine, as the risk of getting mumps, measles, or rubella is greater than the risk of side effects from the vaccine.
- We should believe what doctors say, as they are honest people and would not compromise our lives.
- We should stop all injections and combat disease through a wholesome, organic lifestyle.
- It is selfish for one parent not to vaccinate their children, as their health then relies on all other parents doing so.
- Take the vaccine unless there is 100 percent proof that it causes serious side effects.
- Don't take the vaccine unless there is 100 percent proof that it is safe.
- I'm a doctor, and any link is unproven.
- Side effects might be caused by the cocktail of jabs that young children are given, not just the MMR vaccination.

In contrast, when we asked the question "Tell us what you think about Internet censorship," visitors raised only three points:

- The Internet is good for finding out information: "I think the Internet is great because you can get information for your homework."[2]
- The Internet supports freedom of speech: "Freedom of speech is so rare in this world that we should be thankful for the rights we as citizens have. If you don't like what you see nobody can force you to look."

- The Internet is bad and needs censorship: "The Internet is a new medium of communication and open to abuse. Let's censor it before it has the ability to corrupt young minds."

The limited variety to visitors' responses reduces the motivation for other visitors to read the comments and engage with the exhibit.

We have been more successful in discovering issues that visitors find controversial through a current piece of research that supports our *Naked Science* events. We have been asking visitors to describe the underlying elements that make issues controversial for them. This has the advantage that it is much quicker to do than testing individual questions and analyzing the results, but has the disadvantage that visitors often behave very differently from how they say they will behave. From our work so far, we suggest that it is important to do the following:

3. *Ask questions that cover risk or moral issues and that are personally relevant.* We have so far conducted four focus groups looking at our *Naked Science* events. Participants in these groups have told us that they would consider issues controversial if they had one of four attributes. They could involve risk, and risks to people's health would be especially controversial. They could include moral or ethical dimensions. They could be issues where people felt helpless. And they could have personal or social relevance. Different types of audiences put different emphasis on which aspect was more important in making an issue controversial for them. Examples of issues that cover several of these attributes include the potential misuse of science and the commercial use of science. For example, focus group participants suggested that they would want to engage with the issue of companies patenting part of a genome whose function had not yet been discovered.

A key finding for making an issue engaging is to make concrete something that would otherwise be abstract. One way of doing this is to encourage visitors to explore how the issue will affect real people, such as the visitors themselves. For instance, people are far more engaged in thinking about what it feels like to be the world's first clone than by a general question on the rights and wrongs of cloning.

Having looked at two of the key areas that the Science Museum has evaluated in detail, I will briefly consider three potential questions that the Museum is currently tackling through evaluation. The first of these is whether a subject can be too controversial for a museum to cover.

ARE SOME SUBJECTS TOO CONTROVERSIAL TO TACKLE?

How would you do an exhibition on abortion? A fetus in a jar, a graph of teenage pregnancies, pictures of pro-life protesters? How about an exhibition on animal experimentation?

Are these subjects too hot for museums to handle? The recent past is littered with examples of exhibitions that were considered too controversial: the *Enola Gay* and *Science in American Life* at the Smithsonian spring to mind (Gieryn 1998; Molella 1997). As the Science Museum has increasingly tackled controversy in its exhibitions, this question has become ever more important. For example, the Wellcome Wing contains a whole floor devoted to biomedicine within which visitors expected us to tackle animal experimentation. However, we were concerned, rightly or wrongly, that if handled badly, this could spark acts of vandalism or more extreme forms of terrorism. We are now facing similar issues regularly with *Naked Science*, our experimental series of events.

I am going to argue that no subject is too controversial for a museum to cover but that the museum is able to make subjects more or less controversial by the way they are tackled. This has been backed up by focus groups who were quite explicit that they didn't believe that there were any controversial subjects and even went further to suggest that they would consider it demeaning of the museum to assume that they had not considered the issues or were not intelligent enough to do so.

What a refreshing contrast this presents to the view of museum professionals who often undertake painful and contorted self-censorship when tackling controversy, supposedly with visitors' best interests at heart. Indeed, it is not unusual for museums to cancel exhibitions and events over concerns that they are too controversial well before they have made it off the drawing board. Perhaps museums would be better off asking the public before jumping to conclusions.

The Science Museum has its fair share of cancellations. We have recently withdrawn two *Naked Science* events, as we considered they were inappropriate in the light of national or international events. In hindsight it is hard to know whether the decision was justified. For example, in the aftermath of the anthrax attacks in the United States, we canceled an event on bioterrorism because of internal concerns over attracting terrorists. In retrospect, perhaps we were justified in canceling it, but for a different reason. At the time, everyone was very tense. Visitors would have wanted hard facts: How likely is it to happen to me? How can I protect my children? How can I spot a bioterrorist? As the event would not have offered the answers, it would have been very frustrating for those who took part.

More recently, we withdrew an event on natural death, as it coincided with the discovery of two murder victims, and we believed that running the event would have courted accusations of sensationalism from the public and the press. Whenever tackling controversial issues, we need to be aware that the public draws a fine line between being controversial and being sensational. The cynical creation of sensational news by newspapers and television channels is a well-known way of boosting circulation and viewing figures, and the public are not beyond suspecting museums of adopting similar tactics. Needless to say, the difference between controversy and sensationalism is often difficult to judge.

At this point, I must give a word of warning. The opposite side to believing that no subject is too controversial if it is tackled properly is believing that every subject can be made controversial if it is done the right way. This is a very tempting belief: controversy could be a universal panacea. After all, subjects that visitors find controversial are more engaging.

There are many dangers to this approach in addition to inadvertently becoming sensationalist or insensitive. For example, in an effort to be controversial, exhibit developers could distort the content and messages of an exhibition, focusing on elements that are not central to the subject they are covering. They could also inadvertently sacrifice material that would be more interesting to visitors than the controversial elements.

I will now turn to the second issue we are currently addressing: whether an institution, such as a museum, or an exhibition can be considered neutral by its visitors.

CAN MUSEUMS AND EXHIBITIONS BE NEUTRAL?

The name "Science Museum" is synonymous with neutrality and trust, and these associations have a commercial value. We have recently been able to realize some of this value in a project that the Museum's commercial arm undertook for British Nuclear Fuels (BNFL). This company is involved with all aspects of the nuclear industry, including manufacturing fuel, designing and running nuclear power stations, processing waste, and decommissioning old facilities.

BNFL had suffered criticism in the past, particularly from antinuclear groups, over the exhibition at its visitor center at Sellafield in Cumbria, located on the site of Britain's largest nuclear plant. Recently, BNFL took the unprecedented step of engaging the Museum as a "trusted third party" to produce an editorially independent exhibition to look at the issues surrounding the way we generate our electricity, including the role of nuclear power. The exhibition does not seek to tell visitors the "answers" but rather enables visitors to explore the issues and express their opinions. Even so, there was a degree of risk involved in the project—if we had put a step wrong, we would have eroded hard-earned loyalty and trust from the public and scientists alike.

Yet, we felt that through using techniques such as engaging visitors in dialogue, we were well placed to face the challenge of developing an exhibition that would be perceived by the majority of visitors as unbiased. In this case, we defined the exhibition to be unbiased if as many people thought it was pronuclear as thought it was antinuclear. One area of this exhibition comprises large-scale floor and wall projections of comments left by visitors alongside those of environmentalists, scientists, the nuclear industry, government, and so on. Gratifyingly, when we evaluated this area, visitors overwhelmingly rated the comments as being balanced.

This evaluation underlines two key ideas. First, what counts is whether visitors perceive an exhibition to be neutral, not whether the museum has tried to make the exhibition neutral. I can illustrate the difference between these two points of view with an experiment we tried when developing *Join the Great Fat Debate*. We attempted to make one of the computer interactives as neutral as we possibly could. This interactive presented three points of view from three professionals working in the field. One of them was "pro," one "anti," and the third "balanced." The interactive began by each professional talking, with an image of them on screen. They spoke for exactly the same amount of time, made the same number of points, and responded to the points that each other made. The order in which they appeared was randomized for each visitor, and when visitors told us that they found one of the people's accents untrustworthy, we had all three scripts said by the same actor. We gave ourselves full marks for neutrality, yet many visitors told us that our exhibition was biased in favor of Olestra.

It is not really surprising that exhibit designers are unable to produce exhibitions that are perceived as neutral—there are simply too many variables. To start with, the way visitors use an exhibition precludes the possibility of building one that is neutral. Even in small exhibitions, visitors do not read every word, follow prescribed routes, or spend the same amount of time on each area, even if they reach them at all. In addition, different media have different impacts on the visitor: our evaluation has repeatedly shown that interactive exhibits are more popular, hold visitors' attention for longer, and are more memorable than text panels.

The second point illustrated by the BNFL evaluation is that it is constructive to define a neutral exhibition as one where the same number of people think it is biased one way as think it is biased the other way. This definition is one we have begun to adopt in the place of describing a neutral exhibition as one that the majority of visitors think is neutral. It is not surprising that visitors almost always view an exhibition on controversy to be biased. If the topic covered in the exhibition is truly controversial, visitors will color their perception of the exhibition by their personal views. In the same way as we believe that the newspapers that reflect our political views are truthful and unbiased, so we believe that exhibitions that reflect our views are balanced. We will perceive an exhibition that challenges our point of view, no matter what the justification, to be biased toward one side of the argument.

But ultimately, even when we seem to have succeeded in producing a balanced exhibition about a controversial topic, the results have been disappointing. It seems that when we play safe, we produce exhibitions that visitors find dull, mundane, and uninformative. For example, we worked hard to create a Science Box exhibition on genetic diseases that would be fair and balanced. In the process, we took a subject that people find controversial and failed to make it engaging. As one visitor said, "It still left a lot of questions, it didn't answer anything . . . you get things like that in doctors' waiting rooms."

Perhaps in some instances we can afford to be more courageous in the way that we tackle controversy. Rather than attempting to be neutral or attempting to be perceived by visitors as being neutral, we should clearly take one point of view, sometimes in a challenging and provocative way. We certainly have a lot to lose if we get it wrong. We will also need to reexamine the often-repeated mantra that museums are neutral public spaces, arenas for dialogue and debate, and blank slates that can be used by different groups of people to put across their points of view.

I will now turn to the difficult issue of striking the balance between presenting information and engaging visitors in a debate.

HOW MUCH INFORMATION DO VISITORS NEED?

We hear the same thing again and again. Visitors want facts from reliable sources—from experts. They don't want to get their facts from other visitors. This came out clearly in the focus groups for the BNFL visitor center. Visitors told us that other peoples' opinions would be misleading. Instead, they wanted to be presented with straightforward "facts" that would help them make their own minds up about the issues.

Similarly, focus groups for *Naked Science* events tell us that they need more information. They find debates ill informed when they perceive that the contributors, ordinary people such as themselves, don't really know enough in order to join in and are unable to back their arguments with scientific "facts."

However, once their desire for trustworthy information has been met, visitors are genuinely interested in what other people think. This is, after all, one of the things that motivates visitors to take part in dialogue. This points to a delicate balancing act. We need to provide information from a source perceived by visitors as being reliable so that they feel comfortable taking part in the debate but not so much that they become passive spectators. Ultimately, there will be some subjects on which visitors will feel happier contributing than on others. The more relevant subjects become to visitors' own lives, the more of an "expert" the visitor becomes in the subject and the more confident they will be to contribute.

Interestingly, despite demanding more information before they are able to engage in debates, the visitors we have watched using exhibits such as *Tell* and *Join the Great Fat Debate* will often leave their own comments before they have explored the background information. We suspect that many visitors get a lot of their background information from the comments and opinions of other visitors.

As a way of summarizing our findings, I would highlight the three things I bear in mind when engaging visitors in controversies on science and technology:

1. Visitors really do appreciate reading or listening to other visitors' points of view. This adds an extra dimension to many exhibitions, and it is worth putting a lot of effort into motivating visitors to make a contribution so that there is something worthwhile for others to engage with.

2. Visitors will always want hard facts from a reliable source. For any form of dialogue to be meaningful, they need to feel that there is an informed input. This may be in the form of information sheets, an exhibition, or even a live "expert," but without "facts," visitors will be reluctant to engage.
3. Visitors will never perceive your exhibition or event to be neutral, but this is not a reason for giving up. If the same number of visitors think that it is biased one way as think it is biased the other, you are likely to be close to producing a balanced exhibition.

Finally, for me, one of the greatest rewards that comes from engaging visitors in dialogue over research controversy is the pleasure I get in marveling at the quality of the contributions that visitors make or simply having my preconceptions challenged. I will finish with one of my favorite comments from the *Future Foods?* exhibition:

> Just look at the capabilities of man in lesser areas. Can we say that we have the technology to transport oil by sea for example, without side effects for the sea? Why certainly. We have the technology to do so, but how often does it actually prove true? The seas are littered with disasters and general oil pollution the world over. I could have chosen any of hundreds of human concerns. Now let's take a more critical example. The food supply of the world. Do we have the technology to modify it? Well maybe, we are not sure about the side effects. Do we think that the gains will materialise without any side effects? I don't honestly think so. Man is not yet so clever as to master relatively straightforward things without mishap, the possibility of a group of scientists modifying our food supply in such a fundamental way without incident is beyond our experience of human nature.

Food for thought indeed.

NOTES

This chapter summarizes the work of the Visitor Research Unit and other Science Museum staff who have interpreted contemporary science from 1993 to the present: Emma Birch, Georgina Bishop, Alex Burch, Tom Campbell, Karen Davies, Owain Davies, Jackie Donovan, Neil Fazakerley, Ben Gammon, Yvonne Harris, Sarah Hunt, Lisa Jones, Chris Parkin, Nicola Perrin, Jo Siems, and Deborah White.

1. This view was not unusual (see Levidow 1998).

2. All quotes in this section come from unpublished reports by the Science Museum (1999).

REFERENCES

Engelhardt Jr., H. Tristram, and Arthur L. Caplan, eds. 1987 *Scientific controversies: Case studies in the resolution and closure of disputes in science and technology.* Cambridge: Cambridge University Press.

Gammon, Ben, and Xerxes Mazda. 2000. The power of the pencil: Renegotiating the museum-visitor relationship through discussion exhibits. In *Museums of Modern Science*, Nobel Symposium 112, ed. Svante Lindqvist. London: Science History Publications.

Gater, Catherine. 1999. Exhibitions and expectation: A study of controversy in museum exhibitions and the consequences for the public understanding of science. M.Sc. thesis, Imperial College of Science, Technology and Medicine, London.

Gieryn, Thomas F. 1998. Balancing acts—Science, Enola Gay and history wars at the Smithsonian. In *The politics of display*, ed. Sharon MacDonald. London: Routledge.

Joss, Simon, and John Durant, eds. 1995. *Public participation in science: The role of consensus conferences in Europe.* London: Science Museum Publications.

Latour, Bruno, and Steve Woolgar. 1986. *Laboratory life: The construction of scientific facts.* Princeton, N.J.: Princeton University Press.

Levidow, Les. 1998. Domesticating biotechnology: How London's Science Museum has framed controversy. *European Association for the Study of Science and Technology Review* 17, no. 1: 3–6.

Mazda, Xerxes. 1996. The changing role of history in the policy and collections of the Science Museum, 1857–1973. Science Museum Papers in the History of Technology.

Molella, Arthur. 1997. Stormy weather: Science in American life and the changing climate for technology museums. In *Here and now: Contemporary science and technology in museums and science centres,* ed. Graham Farmelo and Janet Carding. London: Science Museum Publications.

U.K. House of Lords. 2000. Science and society—Third report. February. www.publications.parliament.uk/pa/ld199900/ldselect/ldsctech/38/3801.htm.

8

Improving Public Understanding of Scientific Research: A View from the Research Side

Chris Paola

At present, the great majority of scientific researchers interact with the public on only a limited basis, if at all. In the long run, this situation is not good for either the research community or the public that funds it. The purpose of this chapter is to discuss some of the obstacles to greater involvement in the public understanding of research (PUR) from the point of view of a member of the research community and to suggest some possible solutions. I can hardly presume to speak even for the whole research community in my field (earth sciences), let alone for all of science. However, I believe that I am typical in two respects: first, I have had little engagement in PUR activities in my professional career, and, second, in general I support the idea of PUR, but I am not sure exactly what I could do about it. I have tried to keep my comments as general as possible.

OBSTACLES TO PUR

Most scientific researchers are interested in improving public understanding of their own work and of research in general. Though researchers are as diverse in their interests and desires as members of any other group, in general the stereotype of the lonely genius working on arcane problems in a remote academic laboratory has little to do with the reality of research. On a pragmatic level, publicly funded researchers understand that they have a stake in convincing the public that their money is being well spent. More important, most scientific research is ultimately driven by a passion to understand. Few people so motivated do not enjoy telling others about their work. So my first point is that, for the most part, the present low level of involvement of the scientific research community in PUR is not due to some widespread lack of interest among researchers. It is due primarily to reasons of institutional and personal inertia and to the range of other pressures on researchers' time. Specifically, I see the main present obstacles to greater involvement of researchers in PUR as the following:

1. *A perception that the public would not be interested.* The technical complexity of most research makes it difficult to communicate to someone with little background in the field in question (this is increasingly a problem even within research communities, let alone with the general public), or, equivalently, the scientific content of the work could not be presented to the public without gutting it.

2. *Time pressures.* Doing research at a high level is time consuming and extremely competitive. For faculty researchers, PUR work would have to compete for time with existing activities, such as teaching, advising students, and administrative work, in addition to funding, carrying out, and communicating research itself. Nonacademic researchers also have a comparable if differently structured load of competing activities already.

3. *Lack of readily available means of involvement in PUR.* Most researchers are not aware of how they might communicate their research to the public. Very few young researchers or graduate students, outside of fields like paleontology that have been traditionally associated with museums, even think about museum work or PUR as a possible career path.

4. *Lack of incentives.* At present, there are few institutional incentives within the normal academic evaluation process to recognize and reward PUR activities by faculty and students, with the exception of very high-profile activities that call attention to the institution (such as being quoted in the *New York Times*). Without a well-understood system of support and recog-

nition, commitment of significant amounts of time to PUR is not in the career interests of most professional researchers. Unfortunately, this is especially true of younger scientists, who in many cases are the ones who would have the most to offer to the public.

WHAT COULD BE DONE

As for most complex problems, there is no simple way to deal with these issues. However, there is good reason to think that we could make significant progress from the research side with a few fairly modest steps. The most effective way of influencing the behavior of researchers is via the major federal funding agencies since these provide most of the funding for scientific research. This cannot and must not be done simply by adding new requirements to the existing research-funding structure. The research community, which by and large is already pushing itself to the maximum to do what it is doing now, would not respond well to being ordered to do more without either the financial resources or the institutional recognition to support it.

A good model for influencing the behavior of U.S. researchers is provided by a series of steps that the U.S. National Science Foundation (NSF) has taken to encourage the participation of undergraduate students in NSF-funded research projects. The "default" mode for most researchers at graduate institutions is to employ graduate students and postdoctoral associates in research programs. NSF has changed that culture substantially in recent years by providing small supplements to existing research grants to allow undergraduate participation and by encouraging panelists and reviewers to consider undergraduate participation in evaluating proposals. (I do not know to what extent other agencies use a similar model, but even if they do not, the influence of NSF on the research community is such that NSF-inspired habits are likely to diffuse into other programs.) I do not see any reason why a similar approach could not be taken to foster PUR activities in research grants. Furthermore, since most developed countries fund academic research by systems that are more or less comparable to that of NSF, I do not see any reason why the approach I suggest in this chapter would not work in other countries.

Based on this model and on general experience, I think the following ideas would provide a practical route to expanding PUR activities from the academic research side:

1. *Integrate PUR into mainstream research funding.* From the point of view of a researcher, I believe that it is essential that PUR be incorporated into existing research grant programs rather than via a set of special PUR initiatives. PUR programs separate from mainstream research funding would be much less effective in entraining mainstream researchers who are faced with a dauntingly complex array of funding programs and sources as it is.

2. *Include PUR in proposal evaluation.* The most effective way to encourage researchers to build PUR activities into their publicly funded research is also the most obvious: make it clear that adding PUR activities to a proposed project will increase its chances of being funded. This is best done by direct contact between PUR program directors and technical program directors within the funding agency. In the U.S. NSF system, the so-called Criterion II for proposal evaluation, which involves assessing the broader societal impacts of a given project, provides a natural avenue that PUR could take advantage of. Many researchers are still uncertain as to how best to fulfill this criterion, so specific practical suggestions for using PUR to enhance the broader impact of research would likely be well received.

3. *Provide real (financial) support for PUR activities.* It is neither fair nor practical to ask people to add activities to standard research grants without providing them the means to carry them out. Encouraging PUR activities will not work unless it is combined with supplemental funding to pay for the additional activity. One way of doing this would be through the following:

   a. *Graduate PUR assistantships.* As it is, many graduate students in the sciences are supported by working as research or teaching assistants. So a PUR assistantship would be a natural extension of the existing graduate support system. Graduate students would work for one or more semesters on PUR activities related to their research projects and would receive their regular (typically half time in the United

States) graduate stipend for doing so. PUR assistantships could include working in or with a museum, the media, or any other nonacademic PUR organization. From the researcher's point of view, having a student do a PUR assistantship would be at worst no different from having her or him do a teaching assistantship as many graduate students do for at least part of their course of study. Depending on the arrangement, a PUR assistantship could be more directly related to the research project than a teaching assistantship, however. From the student's point of view, a PUR assistantship would be an opportunity to learn about a whole new area where they might apply their training. A comparable program could probably be devised for undergraduate students as well.

b. *Recognize PUR activities as part of academic service.* This is a process that must be top-down, so one would have to start by convincing academic leaders (presidents, deans, and provosts) that it is in the long-term interest of academic institutions that their faculty be seen participating in PUR activities. This should not be hard to do. Many university administrators recognize the value of having their faculty be visible to the general public—as long as it does not take too much time away from their research. At a more pragmatic level, incorporating PUR into the existing grant system will also automatically align PUR with the academic incentive system, which places a high premium on receipt of federal research grants.

c. *Provide central resources in support of PUR.* Even if all the previously mentioned incentives were in place now, many researchers would not know where to begin adding PUR activities to their research projects. It is, at least at present, simply not part of our training. An immediate way to begin overcoming this problem would be for agencies like NSF to provide centralized information resources on potential PUR collaborators across the country. These could be categorized by, for example, research themes, PUR institution, and geographic location.

WHAT SHOULD PUR BE?

I would like to close with some thoughts about what we should be communicating about research. Clearly, the groups who will define what PUR should be are the organizations directly involved in funding it and carrying it out. We researchers are not necessarily the best judges of what it is about scientific research that can most effectively be communicated to the public. That notwithstanding, the research community has a stake in how this central part of our lives is communicated to the general public.

It seems to me that PUR really has two parts: understanding research results, which is an extension of the general public understanding of science, and understanding research as a human activity. With regard to the first, there is little doubt that the first concern of the research community is accuracy. We realize that the general public cannot be expected to appreciate the nuances and technical details of our work, but it does seem reasonable to insist that what is communicated be accurate at the level at which it is presented. In general, accuracy seems to be a greater issue when dealing with the media than when dealing with museums. A second aspect of research results that often is not communicated well to the public is the uncertainty of scientific results. In part, this is probably related to the public perception that science deals in "facts" and that "theories" are just facts that somehow have not quite solidified yet. The reality is that the only "facts" we have are raw observations, which are nearly useless until and unless they are placed in the context of some sort of theory. Theory is the real lifeblood of science, but it is always provisional—it is and must be open to improvement based on better information or better ideas. It is precisely the mutability of scientific theories in the face of new observations that separates science from dogma. In any case, it does not seem to me that we have done a good job of communicating the idea that uncertainty, debate, and changes to prevailing ideas are not "problems" but, rather, the normal heartbeat of the scientific enterprise. This may not be comforting when there are societal decisions to be made (such as how to deal with global warming), but it is and must be presented as a sign of strength, not weakness.

As important as it is to communicate the results of research, it seems to me that PUR could equally well be taken to imply "understanding of research as a human enterprise." I believe that many in the research community would feel equally passionate about communicating what it is like to do scientific research and why we love it as we do about specific research results. Some of the human aspects of scientific research that PUR programs could communicate are the following:

1. *The social nature of scientific research.* Very few members of the public are aware that scientific research is a highly social activity. It is rare for researchers today to work in isolation, and my own experience is that the practice of science is actually far more social than that of the humanities. The public misperception is inadvertently reinforced by media coverage, which tends to focus on charismatic individuals rather than on teams.

2. *The role of intuition in science.* Most people are taught somewhere along the line that there is a "scientific method" that is followed in doing scientific research. In reality, while there are algorithms and methods for solving specific kinds of problems and for collecting data, there is no method for doing research. Scientific findings must be objectively reproducible, but that does not mean that actually doing science is impersonal. Scientific research is highly creative, and the methods people use to do it are as varied as the ways people create art or music. The best and most valuable scientific insights come not from rote analysis of data but from intuitive leaps informed by a deep understanding. There is no "method" for doing this.

3. *Scientific research is not as removed from ordinary life as people think.* Any number of things that most people do in their daily lives are essential parts of scientific research: solving mysteries, following trails, discovering new ways of looking at something, solving puzzles, and interpreting clues.

Though most members of the general public do not yet know it, the scientific research enterprise in the United States and other developed countries will soon face a critical shortage of researchers. In some fields, like computer science, the problem is already acute. Combating this shortfall could well be the most important practical social contribution PUR could make. Both the continuing underrepresentation of women and other groups in science and the ongoing need to recruit scientists and engineers from abroad are symptoms that we are not attracting and developing all the scientific talent that we need and that is potentially available. Communicating the latest results of scientific research in the most exciting ways possible will help. Equally important is to overcome the stereotype of science as a remote, cold-blooded activity practiced by isolated social misfits in white lab coats.

The heart of science is simply an unending dialogue with nature. Like any good dialogue, you must engage both your mind and your passions—but the lab coats are strictly optional.

NOTE

I would like to thank David Chittenden of the Science Museum of Minnesota for encouraging me to write this and Deborah Schoenholz for editorial support. My participation in PUR has been supported by the U.S. National Science Foundation through the National Center for Earth-Surface Dynamics.

9

New Alliances to Promote the Public Understanding of Research

Peter J. Bruns and Mark D. Hertle

BACKGROUND: THE PROBLEM

For the public to support research, it needs to know its potential and the limits of this very human endeavor. Scientific research takes many forms and deals with nature from subatomic to cosmic, from fractions of seconds to the age of the universe, so details of specific varieties of research vary enormously. But common principles can be communicated to the public. One way to do this is by active partnerships between science practitioners and teachers. Scientists from the academic and applied sectors can join with educators from many segments (museums, school systems, and institutions of higher education) to bring together their special skills and perspectives in order to create innovative ways that capture the essence of the doing of science. While this may be what we want, the truth is that there are few examples we know of that achieve this synthesis. In this chapter, we explore elements of the problem, identify various groups that could contribute solutions, and finally provide two examples of novel and very effective partnerships.

Discovery is the heart of research. For practicing scientists, this means finding new answers to questions that are often themselves new. This can understandably be a very heady experience. It is exciting to work out a protocol and watch the data roll in with an answer to a cleverly conceived question.

On the other hand, the reality is that many steps and missteps occur before this rare eureka moment can occur. What part of this process does the public need to know? As scientists and educators, we certainly think there's excitement. But they must also understand elements of the reality that puts constraints on what we know and what we find: the need to verify and feel confident about the data, to test and compare, and to relate to an already existing body of knowledge. Any practitioner knows that drudgery and hard work are part of the fabric of research, that failures typically far outnumber successes. How much of this does the public need to know, and why? We suspect at least a bit. After all, this may be the part of research that is most human, to which people can connect and through which scientists are finally seen as people doing interesting things worth knowing. In addition, the public needs to understand that healthy skepticism is a natural part of research, so that cautious statements mean not lack of understanding but, rather, an understanding of possible pitfalls and unknown factors, an understanding that every so-called fact is always subject to continued scrutiny. Perhaps the true scientific method is not the formal work plan that is often taught to schoolchildren but, instead, a variable series of actions that successfully joins imagination and reality.

Finally, research is not done just for the fun of it. There is a real and accumulating body of knowledge behind all that work, and research is done to add to that body of knowledge. Any effort to connect people with science should include real information about what we already know. Public understanding of research (PUR) cannot be divorced from public understanding of science.

In short, programs aiming to promote PUR must convey the human side, with all its strengths and frailties, along with some of the product, the state of the art today. This requires a careful balance of technical terms and facts with some kind of real experience. Program planners must always be sensitive of the need to include both content and process. To do this for the general public is a tall order, one that generally requires input from a broad group of people. We think there may be great utility in the formation of new alliances to bring people with special but unique strengths as contributing members to the final project. In the following section, we review several different sources of expertise that could be brought to such partnerships.

THE PLAYERS

The Research and Higher-Education Community

Obviously, scientists are at the heart of the doing of research, and programs that show what research is all about must include this community. On the other hand, working researchers do not generally have experience in disseminating their practice or their products to the general public. Recent mandates for them to do this have not been overwhelmingly successful. The NASA and National Science Foundation (NSF) requirements for scientists and science and technology centers to do outreach have fostered a bit of this activity, but even here the successful programs have often been organized and run by staff members who are not necessarily engaged in the research activities themselves. Although these staff members may know how to build programs, they lack the personal perspective that researchers themselves bring. On the other hand, the researchers lack knowledge of how to best reach particular audiences. Thus, outreach strategies that rely solely on practicing scientists by themselves can be highly inefficient. Even worse, they can result in failure, even after considerable effort. Failure here can create lasting problems: the public becomes even more certain that science is an occult art that cannot be understood (or trusted?), and scientists feel confirmed that the public cannot understand what they are doing or why they do it. Thus, practicing scientists must be involved, but generally they should be only one part of an effective team.

K–12 Educators

Teachers know how to reach people across the educational spectrum, including those with minimal scientific knowledge. Like scientists, teachers rely on public support of their endeavor and have a vested interest in programs that increase PUR. To have the greatest impact, teachers should reach beyond their students; it is universally recognized that the home environment has an enormous influence on student interest and learning. Of course in some measure many teachers are themselves somewhat inexperienced in understanding the true nature of research. Many K–12 science educators have little science background; even those with science degrees may have very little personal experience with research. In addition, they often need help in keeping up with the fast pace of contemporary science. But the good ones know how to teach. Thus, teachers are a vital resource to bring students (and ideally students' families) and ideas to the arena, but again this group by itself does not have the expertise or resources to go it alone.

Museum Educators

This group uniquely takes applied and basic ideas, facts, and concepts from the world of research and presents them to diverse groups of people in a wide array of settings. As such, they are well suited to deliver some of the previously discussed concepts and products to the general public. They are in the interesting middle ground of so-called informal education. Their programs and products aim across the complete gamut of society, from children to adults, from people with no background and with only a marginal interest in science to practicing professionals who are intrigued by science beyond their own fields. Moreover, museum educators are often in the enviable yet challenging position of having families as their customers.

The good news about informal education is the boundless opportunity; the bad news includes the lack of a reliable structure and predictable audiences. Students come to higher education voluntarily (in fact, higher education often chooses its students in a highly competitive process). Public K–12 educators get their students delivered to them by society's laws and expectations, but museum educators must recruit their audience. Museums also can assume little. They are unable to require prerequisite courses or experiences of their students. Thus, this part of the potential compact understands the need for a broad range of educational practices that can reach eclectic groups with variable backgrounds and interests. It is sensitive to the need to draw in the subjects, and it is expert at educational marketing in ways the others rarely employ or even know.

In summary, advancing PUR involves a diverse collection of inputs and targets. In our view, it is an exciting opportunity for new levels of collaboration between professionals traditionally separated by culture, practice, and funding sources. In an effective synthesis, the science community can join in by contributing research-based practices and activities (the joys and pains of doing research) and current ideas in science. School systems and teachers can bring forward audiences and contribute effective teaching methods and supportive curricula, and museum educators can provide the delivery system, using methods that combine formal and informal education techniques.

In the following sections, we provide two examples of programs funded by the Howard Hughes Medical Institute (HHMI) that we think exemplify elements of this synthesis. We include them here mostly as examples of successful collaborations between professional educators from various sectors, although we must emphasize that this sort of alliance is a moving target in which different settings and communities yield major differences in program details. The first collaboration included a museum, a medical center, and a city school system and resulted in a whole suite of activities, including an addition to a systemwide curriculum. The second, an inquiry-based middle-school project, was developed in a museum and has been exported to an international market via an international research scholars program.

BIRMINGHAM, ALABAMA: A GROWING ALLIANCE

This example involves a partnership among the University of Alabama (UAB) Medical College, the McWane Science Center in Birmingham, and the Birmingham public school system. The story of the development of this relationship and the products and activities that resulted is illuminating. The activities started with a teacher enhancement course at the medical school, led by Professor Steven Hajduk of the UAB Department of Biochemistry. In this, his first venture into outreach, Hajduk developed an active program and a working relationship with

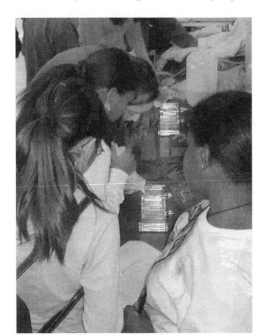

Students load their DNA samples for analysis by gel electrophoresis. Photo courtesy of University of Alabama at Birmingham. Photo by Mary Connolly

the local school system but needed a better venue, so he turned to the laboratory facilities and staff of the newly opening McWane Center. Once connected, they continued the teacher program and added a series of daylong lab activities at McWane for high-school students. Included in the student-centered activities were four separate modules (on DNA fingerprinting, sickle cell anemia, protein structure, and protein–protein interactions) that are inquiry based and engage the students in lab discovery. More than 200 teachers have now gone through the lab-based teacher enhancement program, and about 2,400 students per year, from every high school in Birmingham, work on the modules in the laboratory. The material was developed using university experts and is delivered by staff from the Center together with graduate students and undergraduates from the university.

Although these accomplishments were exemplary by themselves, the partnership moved ahead, creating and using an additional outreach laboratory at the McWane Center. Scientist–educators, hired by UAB but located at McWane, run the facility, and McWane contributes a full-time educator (as well as graphic design, exhibit development, and other expertise). In addition to the formal offerings for high-school students, one of the laboratories is used, in part, for a year-round student science club in which the members do semester-long authentic research in a variety of topics (such as sequencing the genome of parasitic microbes). The facility is also used for public drop-in programs that last approximately one hour and connect to a current traveling exhibit. For example, a *Jurassic Park* exhibit was complemented by a DNA extraction/gel electrophoresis activity in the laboratory. Similarly, a student exercise in isolating extremophiles from nature (in this case, bacteria from Antarctica), developed collaboratively with an expert from the university, was adapted to accompany a Mars exhibit and later an IMAX movie and exhibit on the Shackleton expedition in the museum. The laboratory exercises and exhibits reinforce each other.

Meanwhile, laboratory-based genetics and microbiology curricula have been created by UAB in partnership with Birmingham city schools, and both have been adopted by the district and implemented citywide. The curricula provide modules for laboratory activities to be done in the classroom, such as transformation of bacteria with DNA that confers antibiotic resistance and the ability to express a fluorescent protein. Use of the modules is evaluated using instruments developed by McWane staff, and the McWane laboratory is used in the summer to prepare teachers to teach the labs.

In summary, this three-part collaboration has brought together some of the best of each part of the community. Scientists have extended their research, the museum provides public access and facilities, the schools bring forth teachers and students, and the university engages undergraduates, graduate students, and postdoctorals to help staff the projects. This collective uses current scientific research to provide the basis for teacher enhancement, student curricula, and informal student research experiences and to enhance museum exhibits. Everyone wins.

EXPORTING A MUSEUM ACTIVITY FOR CHILDREN THROUGH THE SCIENCE COMMUNITY

How young a public is fair game for programs that advance the understanding of research? As discussed previously, understanding the nature and products of research can play a key role in broadening the understanding of science for high-school students and adults; as such, efforts should aim to promote both the process and the current state of scientific understanding for audiences of this age group. In contrast, research experiences for young children should focus largely on discovery and excitement. Effective projects can be designed that

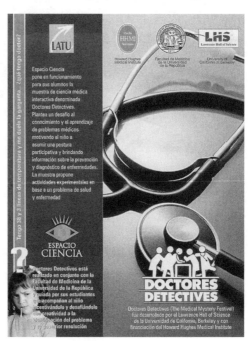

Flyers announcing the Doctores Detectives *exhibit were circulated throughout Uruguay; more than 150 people, including government and academic dignitaries, attended the formal opening. The exhibit is housed at Espacio Ciencia, the science museum operated by the Laboratorio Technologico del Uruguay (LATU).* Photo courtesy of Lawrence Hall of Science. Photo by Mary Connolly

help children find answers to interesting questions by an inquiry-based process, even though the information may already be well known.

The *Medical Mystery Festival*, developed by the Lawrence Hall of Science, of the University of California at Berkeley, uses this approach to engage kids and convey basic health and lifestyle intervention messages to middle-school students. Ten stations, which can be easily set up and can be done in any order, provide activities for students to observe and measure characteristics of their own physiology. Each station also simulates test results for one or two of eight fictitious patients. Students record these findings on the Patient Charts and their own (or their family's) test results on the Student Personal Record or Family Record. Examples of activities the students perform at the stations include performing a simulated urinalysis to determine if the patient has a urinary tract infection, comparing skin photographs of known rashes with photographs of a patient's skin, and using eye charts to test vision. Students arrive at a diagnosis and check their answers and learn about their own bodies and healthy lifestyles. This interactive museum exhibit was designed to travel; activities are often set up in a community setting, such as a library or church, to engage children's families.

Students perform a simulated urinalysis to determine if their "patient" has a urinary tract infection. Photo courtesy of Lawrence Hall of Science. Photo by Mary Connolly

A major target group for the project was Hispanic Americans, so materials were partially translated into Spanish. This and the easy portability of the project led us to propose collaboration between Mary Connolly of the Lawrence Hall and a Uruguayan scientist, Dr. Rafael Radi, whose research was already being supported through HHMI's International Research Scholars program. Dr. Radi had expressed a significant interest in science education outreach to his community and eagerly accepted the challenge to import the collection of materials. In collaboration with Espacio Ciencia, a science museum in Montevideo, Uruguay, the *Medical Mystery Festival* has been translated, literally and culturally, into *Doctores Detectives*, to be used as an exhibit at Espacio Ciencia. Medical students from the Universidad de la Republica will assist with the exhibit's interpretation for visitors. This venture has been so successful and represents such a cost-effective leverage of the original HHMI grant to the Lawrence Hall of Science that we are planning to duplicate the exhibit for installation in Buenos Aires, Argentina, under the sponsorship of another international scholar.

Thus, a museum project that was designed with the assistance of the medical science community in this country has been disseminated internationally through a collaboration with overseas scientists, clinicians, and their students. Even though the project relies on discovery rather than genuine research, it

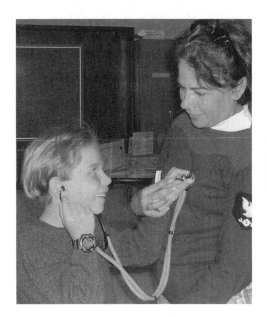

A student compares resting and active heart rates. Photo courtesy of Lawrence Hall of Science. Photo by Mary Connolly

presents the foundations of research and will have scientists available to broaden the learning experience. This will be a first step in extending an understanding of research well beyond our borders.

CONCLUSION

In this chapter, we have proposed that new and highly productive partnerships can be formed to develop, deliver, and disseminate active experiences that promote the understanding of research to a wide audience. For the greatest impact, scientists should partner with educators from all parts of the educational spectrum, including those who work at formal as well as informal educational institutions. Research is a process with a product, and alliances such as we present here can bring powerful additions to science education.

It is our hope that methods can be found to support, encourage, and reward these kinds of groupings and efforts. Although traditional funders of educational innovation should be involved, local sources of support from school systems, local governments, and even industry should also be included since effective partnerships as described here enhance community learning. However, in addition to securing financial support from various sources, the separate institutions need to foster efforts to bring these traditionally distinct but parallel efforts together and to credit their own faculty, staff, and students for these nontraditional group efforts. In the end, it is clear not only that effective partnerships allow individual members to share the burden, but also that the entire effort can deliver new kinds of goods and services in which the whole is greater than the sum of the parts.

10

Collaboration and the Public Understanding of Current Research

Larry Bell

Science centers around the world are grappling with the many issues involved in adapting traditional museum methods to the task of presenting current research to a public more familiar with dinosaurs than stem cells and dioramas than interactives. The challenges these offer to presenters are diverse:

- Adding new material quickly and keeping things up to date
- The ever-growing body of knowledge to keep up with
- Adopting new styles of presentation appropriate to the goal
- The often unfamiliar and nonintuitive nature of current research topics
- Getting access to experts who can help
- Finding internal and external sources of funding needed to do the work

The Museum of Science in Boston has been very active in developing new educational capabilities through its Current Science and Technology experiment. Over the past three years, we studied what other science centers and similar organizations are doing to bring what is going on in science today into their exhibits and programs. For nearly three years, we have operated the Current Science & Technology Center in the Museum. The Center is built around live presentations that are offered several times each day and a series of changing exhibits. We have also looked carefully at the work of the Antenna team at the Science Museum in London and related efforts at the Exploratorium, the Monterrey Bay Aquarium, the American Museum of Natural History, the Maryland Science Center, and the Liberty Science Center. The greater part of what these institutions do is based on unique artifacts and exhibits. But when they delve into really current science and technology, they tend to rely more on a variety of media that are replicable. This fact alone suggests the possibility that sharing our work and collaborating with like-minded institutions may be an effective strategy for contributing to the public understanding of today's scientific research.

Participants at the "Museums, Media, and the Public Understanding of Research" conference in St. Paul, Minnesota, in September 2002, discussed several needs that science centers and other informal venues for science education have in connection with addressing public understanding of research. Several of the discussions led to ideas about collaboration. Efficiencies beyond what we currently achieve in exhibit and program development are essential to undertake the challenge to be current, up to date, and constantly changing. One can argue that it is possible for the public to understand the nature of scientific research without understanding lots of current research, but for the purposes of this discussion, assume that the goal is to familiarize the public with a variety of current and ongoing research efforts.

The first half of this chapter focuses on discussions at the conference in St. Paul: challenges presented by the goal to advance public understanding of research (PUR), ideas about what kinds of things we might share through collaboration, barriers that we will need to overcome, and some of the benefits of collaborating in this work. The second half reflects on the author's experience with several collaborations among science centers in an attempt to identify key characteristics that lead to the success of a collaborative effort.

CHALLENGES FOR PRESENTERS

Traditionally, science and technology centers have been at the forefront of public science education, but early methods were static and did not involve interaction or discourse. The more recent and widespread development of interactive exhibits and media presentations has invited the public's participation but has been limited, by both format and technology, to exploring perceivable phenomena or acquiring more detailed information. PUR efforts require more creative approaches both for actually engaging the audience and for keeping up with the ever-changing subject matter. Participants at the PUR Conference in St. Paul identified a number of challenges for themselves in taking on the challenge to build public understanding of research:

- It is not unusual for the development cycle of a new exhibit to be three or four years long and the cycle for renewal to be even longer. While it is sometimes possible to add a last-minute module of current science in such an exhibit, a new system for developing current research offerings with greater *speed* is needed to address the issue overall. Things simply are not very "current" if they have been in development for four years.
- To stay current in this sense also requires the development of new offerings regularly at a *rate* that is much faster than is typical of our usual exhibit or program development patterns.
- This rate of new development also means that total *volume* of material to be researched and developed into exhibits or programs in the course of a year is much greater than we are used to, and we may not have sufficient staff resources to do all the work needed.
- Programming around current research may require more of a *journalistic* approach than science centers are familiar with. Many, if not most, do not have the staff resources with the different skills needed to develop exhibits and programs in a journalistic style.
- Current research topics may not lend themselves to typical hands-on learning approaches and in fact may involve topics that are very *difficult* for visitors to understand. In this sense, making them interesting to visitors and educationally successful may take resources of time and skills that many science centers do not currently have.
- Acquiring *access* to experts, images, objects, and materials that could be employed in a current research exhibit or program is difficult and time consuming, and such materials may not be made available to a science center requesting it.
- Science centers do not have sufficient *income* to take on significant amounts of new work that provides no source of new income.
- Additional *funding* for public understanding of research is limited and will likely favor proposals that have broad geographic impact and support efforts in a variety of institutions.

ADVANTAGES OF COLLABORATION AMONG MUSEUMS

The challenges of building public understanding of research led participants at the PUR conference to consider several advantages of sharing the workload. The sheer volume of material and the rate at which it needs to be produced can be addressed by sharing the work among several institutions. The skills needed to implement a speedier, journalistic approach could be developed in a few key producing institutions, with others utilizing the material without having to develop it. The variety of skills and experiences of a network of collaborators could help find the best solutions to difficult educational problems. A well-organized and effective consortium would likely have access to a greater range of intellectual resources, materials, and funding than an individual science center would.

Furthermore, in the realm of public understanding of research, museums are not in competition with each other for visitor attendance. Our iconic exhibits, like the Coal Mine at the Museum of Science and Industry in Chicago, or blockbuster traveling exhibits may be specific elements that attract visitors to one museum over another and may even attract tourists. But conference participants felt that specific short-lived, changing exhibits and programs on current research, with very few exceptions, are not likely to draw visitors from one science center's market area to another. The idea that there is something relevant and interesting to adults who visit with their children may be a positive factor in the overall visitor experience, but this is something we can all share in.

POSSIBILITIES FOR COLLABORATION WITH OTHER FIELDS

While collaboration among science centers raises a number of interesting possibilities, collaborations between science centers and educational television, radio, or print media raise even more interesting possibilities. Section 4 of this volume offers a collection of projects that are currently under way in print, radio, and television that are useful and instructive for those interested in pursuing these connections. In addition, collaborations with universities and other research organizations add further richness to the mix. These collaborations between dissimilar organizations raise different kinds of issues and potential difficulties that are treated elsewhere in this volume; this chapter focuses on science and technology center collaborations.

SPECIFIC THOUGHTS ABOUT COLLABORATION AMONG SCIENCE CENTERS

Some of the things that science centers could share among each other in support of PUR include the following:

- Audience research: what visitors are interested in, what they know and do not know about a topic, and what misperceptions they have
- Evaluation data: reports on what we have tried and what has been successful and what has not
- Background research on specific topics or areas of research
- Specific material that can go into an exhibit, program, or presentation: scripts, transcripts of interviews, images, audio, video footage, animations, 3-D models, artifacts, objects from collections, music (with licensing) and Web links
- Contacts, outreach partners, scientists' names, academic connections, and people who can serve as spokespersons
- Sample press releases
- Scripts for live theater presentations and a pool of scientists and writers with experience writing for science theater

All these possibilities led participants in the PUR conference at the Science Museum of Minnesota to suggest some specific vehicles for collaboration, including the following:

1. A central database model: a repository of information on scientific research that all have access to, developed by a collaboration of museums and including many if not all of the previously listed items. Such a database would also need the following:

   - Staff dedicated to sharing the database
   - An agreement on standards for content, format, rights, union fees, scientific oversight to ensure accuracy, and so forth
   - Special-purpose National Science Foundation (NSF) supplements to support sharing of data and other resources

2. A subscription model: various kinds of materials outlined previously would be delivered to participating institutions in one or two formats

to allow quick updating and customizing. This might include the following:

- Creation of consistent templates so that material can be updated quickly in both physical and digital formats
- Digital automatic loading platform for high-speed updating
- Kit of materials, including artifacts and hands-on activities
- Videoconferencing of research activities or expert speakers
- Staff training/swapping

3. Codesign and coproduction model: one or more science centers work together to produce exhibits and programs in support of PUR

Regardless of which models are used, the act of collaboration will bring some additional benefits to participants:

- Skill building among collaborating institutions
- A wide range of experience and expertise that could facilitate rapid improvements to exhibits and programs developed in haste to meet the goal of timeliness
- Broader impact of educational efforts as producing institutions deliver information and materials to exhibiting institutions

A number of efforts are currently under way to develop collaborations among science centers in support of PUR. They will explore the infrastructure for collaboration and test models that can be implemented broadly.

BARRIERS AND BENEFITS OF BROAD-BASED COLLABORATIONS AMONG SCIENCE CENTERS, NEWS AND MEDIA ORGANIZATIONS, AND ACADEMIC INSTITUTIONS

Collaboration among a broader range of institutions opens up additional possibilities but also raises additional questions. Past experiences suggest a range of difficulties in collaboration efforts between or among unlike institutions, such as between science centers and television stations. For example, science centers have sometimes found it difficult to get images and videos from media outlets. In addition, public television stations have national audiences through the Public Broadcasting Service (PBS) network and are much more competitive about programming than are science centers. Some feel that this competitiveness creates stumbling blocks for collaborative efforts in the peer review process for grants. In collaborative funding efforts, issues are raised about who will be the primary grantee. Some institutions feel a competitiveness in this area. Some cite that NSF Informal Science Education funds cannot be used to support collaboration with formal educational partners. While such barriers currently exist, it is hoped that there will be many opportunities to overcome them in the future.

Collaborations that include science centers, media, and academic institutions, however, also suggest a variety of potential benefits:

1. Such collaborations would give participants an even wider range of contacts and resources to support their work.
2. They provide sufficient resources to conduct a project with a scope or cost too large for a single institution to manage.
3. Media need locations, visuals, expert advisers, and people to interview and could make use of science center resources to meet these needs.
4. Science centers could make use of archived images and video material developed by media.
5. A science center can serve as local resource to add context, reinforce or expand a news story, and, with local media, tie the local community to the larger story.
6. Archival news media resources can be used by science centers to relate science center exhibits and programs to real-world issues and science in the news.
7. Collaborations of museums and media can add to public trust and believability, especially with activities coordinated around controversial issues and employing an approach that reinforces a methodology for examining such issues—what we know, what we do not know, and the unanswered questions and the uncertainty.
8. Using the different advantages of each medium, collaborations could tackle difficult educational issues, such as helping the public understand and accept uncertainty or the fundamental nature of research.
9. Graduate students from colleges and universities can practice their skill at communicating with the public while supporting science centers' PUR efforts.

10. Science centers and media organizations could collaborate in outreach programs for the public and for each other. We can learn from each other.
11. A collection of demonstrations that help people understand the fundamentals of an issue can be developed and a menu created so that both science centers and media can tap into this expertise in developing stories, programs, demonstrations, and exhibits.
12. Funding guidelines could encourage collaborations among museums, media, and academic researchers. Collaborating institutions could develop guidelines that encourage further collaboration, such as requiring researchers to allocate a portion of their team's time to PUR efforts.

Since the benefits of this kind of cross-institutional collaboration appear to be many, it is likely worthwhile to explore solutions to the issues that seem to be barriers. Science centers, of course, have had various kinds of relationships with formal educational institutions and with media, and new relationships to support PUR are currently being developed and tested. We need models to overcome the issues of proprietary copyright, competition, and funding. We should evaluate the applicability of corporate models that work, international models, clearinghouses that are successful, and various central server and database models. These kinds of collaborations are beyond the experience of the author and not in the scope of this discussion. They remain to be explored by those working to set up a new kind of collaborative effort.

Next, this chapter examines some successful collaboration efforts among science centers and identifies the characteristics of those efforts that have contributed to its success.

THE MOST IMPORTANT CHARACTERISTICS OF A SUCCESSFUL COLLABORATION

What follows are personal reflections by the author on several collaborative efforts with which he is familiar. They do not constitute scientific evidence or consensus within the field, but may be useful nonetheless in thinking about how to set up future collaborations.

The Science Museum Exhibit Collaborative is one of the most stable and long-lived collaborations among science centers today. It was started in 1983 and is still working energetically. Its membership has remained fairly stable with science centers in Boston, Philadelphia, Columbus, St. Paul, Los Angeles, and Fort Worth as ongoing members throughout the Collaborative's history. Founding members in Chicago and Charlotte dropped out, and a new member in Portland, Oregon, was added. The Collaborative's focus has been around the development of temporary exhibitions.

What are the salient characteristics of that collaboration that have made it successful, and can we apply those in some way to a collaboration around the public understanding of research?

1. *The collaboration addresses a common need.* I think that the first and foremost factor in the successful development of the Science Museum Exhibit Collaborative is that it was a solution to a real problem that its members had and addressed a need common to all of us. We needed good traveling exhibits on appropriate science topics presented in an interactive style with sufficient impact to draw repeat visitors and new audiences to our institutions. Such exhibits were few and far between in 1983. It was hard for any one of us to generate a sufficient supply of such exhibits, but by pooling resources and sharing, we might be able to get what we need.

2. *The collaboration is perceived as fair and equitable to all members.* The second most important factor in the establishment of the Collaborative was a combination of strength and humility in its leadership. Roger Nichols enlisted Vic Danilov, director of the Museum of Science and Industry in Chicago (the largest of all science centers), to work with him in trying to pull the Collaborative together. But Roger quickly put forward the notion that all the possible members should be seen as equal. "We all develop some good exhibits and some not-so-good exhibits." This sense of equality permeated the operating procedures of the Collaborative and has reemerged over and over again throughout 20 years of work together.

3. *The members have commitment to the collaboration.* A third important factor in the success of the Collaborative was the willingness of people to commit the time to make the collaboration work. The Collaborative developed bylaws and exhibit design guidelines right from the start. When issues and problems arose, it took several days of meetings and deliberations and the development of new ways of working together to move the Collaborative forward. These major efforts have occurred periodically over two decades, but significant work is needed just to prepare for annual meetings.

A NUMBER OF OTHER PRACTICAL CONSIDERATIONS IMPORTANT FOR COLLABORATION

Beyond the three top-level characteristics of successful collaboration identified in the previous list, there are a number of other practical considerations that are important:

1. *Everyone understands the rules and the game plan.* While it probably did not really need to, the Collaborative incorporated a not-for-profit corporation. This required the development of bylaws. The Museum of Science worked with its legal counsel to develop bylaws for the Collaborative. The bylaws focused mostly on what rights members had, how decisions would be made, what powers the officers would have, what happens when things go wrong, and how the bylaws could be changed. Beyond the bylaws, but written in the same legal style, we developed some general guidelines for the Collaborative. The idea was to get in writing what we were all agreeing to. These documents were like contracts in that they spelled out our common agreement and each member institution did indeed sign them.

2. *There are funds to support critical collaborative activities.* All the members contributed dues annually to the Collaborative, so the organization had funds to carry out its work. But the Collaborative kept administrative costs to a minimum. Members volunteered their labor and the labor of members of their staff as needed. The funds from annual dues went almost totally into exhibit development. But a portion of these funds was used to ensure that certain activities deemed crucial to successful collaboration would be funded. This allowed equal participation by all members in decision-making and collaborative activities and provided immunity from travel restrictions and other financial controls that an individual member may be experiencing because of economic difficulties.

3. *There are funds to support quality projects.* The one thing that volunteer labor never obtained for the Collaborative was jointly raised funds. When it came to raising funds to be split among eight members versus raising funds for our individual institutions, we had to give priority to our individual institutional fundraising needs. Over the years, the rules of the game changed so that individual members had to raise funds to supplement the Collaborative's contribution to exhibit development. Each institution became responsible for raising funds to support the exhibit that it was developing. By

making better exhibits possible, these funds benefited the entire Collaborative. After the Collaborative tour, each Collaborative exhibit belongs to the producing member, and that member can rent it to others or install it as a "permanent" exhibit. So, the additional funds raised have an additional benefit to the member that raises the funds and produces the exhibit. This provides each member with the incentive to raise money to improve the quality of Collaborative exhibits.

4. *A significant commitment of time is made for working together.* Sufficient contact time to solve problems has been an important factor in maintaining the Collaborative for 20 years. Initially, the directors had two meetings per year, each lasting a little more than an hour. When it became clear that further work was needed, an Exhibit Production Committee was formed of staff reporting directly to the directors in each member institution. This committee scheduled three-hour meetings twice a year and multiple-day workshops on each new exhibit being developed. Now the Collaborative has an Education Committee and a Marketing Committee aimed at strengthening the programmatic and marketability aspects of the exhibits being developed. These meetings have increased the administrative costs of running the Collaborative, but the directors saw how beneficial it was to the professional development of Production Committee members to meet regularly with their peers and so have encouraged similar meetings among Education and Marketing Committee staffs. This evolution of the Collaborative's efforts is still new, and its benefits are not yet proven, but it already seems to have strengthened working relationships within museums as well as between them.

To recap, most of the failures that occur in collaborative efforts result from the absence of one or more of the following seven characteristics or considerations:

- The collaboration addresses a common need.
- The collaboration is perceived as fair and equitable to all members.
- The members are committed to the collaboration.
- Everyone understands the rules and the game plan.
- There are funds to support critical collaborative activities.
- There are funds to support quality projects.
- A significant commitment of time is made for working together.

WHY SOME COLLABORATIVE EFFORTS ENDED

Science Center Exhibit Consortium

The Science Center Exhibit Consortium was formed in the mid-1980s among six science centers in the eastern half of the United States to make animated dinosaur exhibits more affordable. Its members included science centers in Boston, Hartford, Baltimore, Charlotte, Columbus, Louisville, and later Dallas. That consortium initially purchased a group of robotic dinosaurs to avoid high rental costs. It adapted the bylaws of the Science Museum Exhibit Collaborative to serve its own purposes so that everyone understood the terms of the collaboration. It also adopted the model of equality of all participants. The Consortium met a common need and functioned successfully for nearly ten years.

Its members were sufficiently pleased with the spirit of collaboration within the organization that its name was changed from the Dinosaur Consortium to the Science Center Exhibit Consortium to suggest that it might collaborate on a number of other projects.

After several years, some members got tired of the same old dinosaur group owned by the Consortium. The Consortium's dinosaur group would return to each member institution every 18 months. The initial investment that each member made was paid back within three years. The next six years represented dinosaur exhibits with no rental fees. But in the meantime, the range of robotic dinosaurs available for rental grew and diversified. Robotic dinosaurs were successful at attracting repeat visitors, but it became important to have a new twist each time to market them every 18 months. Some members found it more desirable to rent new creatures than to exhibit the same old dinosaur models for free.

In the 1990s, the Consortium no longer addressed a common need. It still provided an exhibit at low cost but not with the attraction power that was present at the beginning. The Consortium admitted a new member and sold it a one-seventh share of ownership in the dinosaurs. This strategy provided the Consortium with funds for upkeep at no cost to the other members. This was enough to keep the Consortium alive until 1996 as it explored the possibility of buying a new set of robotic creatures. But the manufacturers were no longer willing to sell robotic dinosaurs, as the finances of their business were based on lease fees.

While some members found that the ten-year-old robots still met their needs, others did not. The Consortium sold the dinosaurs to one of its members and dispersed the funds from the sale to the others, following the rules for this in its bylaws. Given the absence of a common need, the collaboration ended. The notion that we might collaborate in a number of other areas did not turn into any real projects. Having a real need that all members shared was a key factor in the success of this consortium. None of the other factors that may have contributed to its success were sufficient to advance further collaborative efforts when that need went away.

National Health Science Consortium

The National Health Science Consortium was originally founded in 1991 as the National AIDS Exhibit Consortium. The Museum of Science and Industry in Chicago first called the group together around an exhibition it was developing. Other original members included science centers in Boston, New York, Baltimore, Washington, D.C., Philadelphia, San Francisco, and Los Angeles. Its membership formed around the importance of creating AIDS exhibits and programs in our institutions. It provided support for individuals in dealing with a delicate and controversial topic in a straightforward and bold way. It also provided its members with access to a funding source that was not otherwise available to the members individually. Through congressional lobbying efforts, grant funds were generated to support a collaborative effort to provide AIDS education in science museums.

After the AIDS project, the directors of the member institutions decided that the collaboration had been a beneficial one and should be continued as the National Health Science Consortium. The AIDS project money had provided substantial funding to cover the costs of Consortium meetings and coordination. Staff were hired to operate the Consortium. But after the AIDS project was completed, there were no funds to continue the collaborative efforts. The Consortium staff were eliminated.

A new project was proposed and driven forward by one member of the Consortium. The subject was women's health. Carrying out this project as a collaborative effort was challenging. The collaborators, who had rallied around AIDS education, were not uniformly committed to women's health as a topic. This project did not seem to meet a common need. The directors changed the rules from consensus decision making to home rule for the producing institution. This left many participating institutions uncertain about their role. Feeling an absence of equity, some members showed little commitment to the project. The staff of the lead institution created an alternative structure that gave everyone a role. Time had to be spent detailing the new rules for the collaboration and getting member buy-in. Because there was sufficient commitment to the collaboration itself, the group stayed together for this project. A significant factor for that continued collaboration was the presence of sufficient funds for carrying out a quality project and for paying for meetings and other efforts critical to the collaboration. An excellent exhibit resulted from this effort.

After the Women's Health project, the Consortium engaged in a successful project that brought about its demise. Both the AIDS project and the Women's Health project were funded through lobbying and congressional action. For its third project, the Consortium applied its collaborative efforts to lobbying Congress for the funds necessary to set up an ongoing program within the National Institutes of Health (NIH) to fund informal educational activities, similar to the Informal Science Education program at NSF. While there had been some funds for this for some time, they were very meager, and through lobbying efforts a substantial funding program was created. All science centers now have a mechanism for getting funds from the NIH for health-related informal science education.

The Consortium did not officially dissolve, but it has not met in several years. The need for which it was formed—getting funds not otherwise available—has gone away because through its actions funds became regularly available to its members individually. With no funds for activities critical to supporting the collaboration, an unclear sense of what need it could address today, dissatisfaction with the inequities in the current model, and no active consortium governance structure, the Consortium simply stopped meeting.

A FEW OTHER SCIENCE MUSEUM COLLABORATIONS

There were very few collaborations among science centers before Roger Nichols and Vic Danilov started the Science Museum Exhibit Collaborative in 1983. But that event precipitated a flood of collaborative activities. Three additional collaborative efforts that I will mention here are the Museum Film Network, the Exhibit Research Collaborative, and the Interactive Videodisk Science Consortium.

Nichols was instrumental in the formation of the Museum Film Network, a worldwide collaboration of science centers with Imax and Omnimax theaters formed around the need for high-quality, educational, and attractive large-format films. The membership of this collaboration is larger and more complex than that of the other collaborations discussed earlier. The Museum Film Network even has a media member, WGBH *Nova*, that has different expertise from the rest of the members and often with the responsibility for film production that none of the other members have. Bylaws detail the rules and roles in this collaboration, which continues more than 15 years beyond its founding. There is still a significant need for high-quality educational science-oriented large-format films.

When the Science Museum Exhibit Collaborative was founded, several interested science centers that had participated in the formative discussions established the Exhibit Research Collaborative. This collaboration was designed to create smaller exhibits than those of the Science Museum Exhibit Collaborative and required smaller annual dues. In fact, this collaboration was based on the idea of getting grant money to train staff at its eight member institutions to use formative evaluation techniques in the development of exhibits. The grant money would also pay for the creation of the exhibits. So, the work of this collaborative was totally funded by grants. Successful in creating two rounds of exhibitions, the Exhibit Research Collaborative disbanded when funding for a third fell through.

The Interactive Videodisk Science Consortium was also formed in the 1980s by Roger Nichols and Inabeth Miller. Like the Museum Film Network, this collaboration was built around a particular presentation technology. Videodisk technology was very short lived in the public marketplace. But science centers found videodisks a maintenance-saving substitute for videotape in installations that required playing segments over and over again many times or even continuously. In addition, videodisks lent themselves to "random access" applications. It was possible to create a computer program that controlled an interaction between visitors and the images stored on the disk. Interactive multimedia is so commonplace today that it is hard to appreciate the excitement for science center exhibit developers to have this capability 20 years ago. The Consortium created three interactive videodisks before the costs for creating this kind of interaction came within the range of individual members. Unlike Imax films, videodisks were not a real need. They were a solution to a need: high-quality images in interactive exhibits. Even then, they were more "nice to have" than a necessity. The Consortium really explored the potential of a new technology. Eventually, the time, effort, and funds needed to continue a truly collaborative exploration of this potential did not seem to be merited by the benefits. The technology changed. Computer technology became cheaper, and pooling resources was no longer necessary.

AVOIDING A COMMON FALLACY THAT STANDS IN THE WAY OF COLLABORATION

Twenty years ago, my boss used to say that "the difficulty of a project goes up as the cube of the number of collaborators." If his math was correct, having one collaborator made the project eight times as difficult as doing it alone, and having ten collaborators made is 1,000 times as difficult. Given this view, why would anyone collaborate? Indeed, 20 years ago, almost no one did in the science center world.

I think that this pessimistic view of collaboration comes from trying to establish collaborative activities with partners that do not share common goals. When individual collaborators have very different goals, they can generate conflict throughout the collaborative process. It is important in setting up a collaborative effort to find partners with common goals. The fallacy to be avoided is that you must craft a collaboration to meet *everyone's* needs. Everyone does not need to be involved, and involving everyone can lead to getting nowhere.

If you are going to put the work and energy into starting a collaborative effort, you need to be sure that it will meet your needs. Do you know how to flip a coin so that it randomly comes up heads five times in a row? Flip a lot of coins once. Eliminate those that do not come up heads. Flip those that came up heads again. Eliminate the tails again. Do this over and over until you have flipped coins five times. If you start out with enough coins, one or more will come up heads in five flips. The question is how many coins you have to start with to be successful.

You can apply a similar strategy to setting up a collaborative effort. Instead of starting with the group you will collaborate with and then designing the collaboration, start by designing the collaboration, present it to many possible collaborators, and eliminate those for whom it is not a good fit. Of course, you can design a collaboration that no one wants in on in this way. So you do not want to design the collaboration in isolation. It would be better to have a partner or two with common needs who would form the core of the planning team.

The core planning team works out some general ideas about the collaboration and plans an agenda for discussing those ideas with a large group of potential collaborators. Draft a document that has enough detail to give an idea of what you are thinking about but that is open enough to allow for shaping the collaboration. Invite many more organizations to consider your collaboration than you need to operate (but not more than you can handle). Meet to brainstorm ideas. Have the core team draw from the brainstormed ideas a collaborative model that will work *for you*. Figure out how many collaborators you need. Send your new specific proposal out to all and ask who wants to be in on the specific collaboration your core team is now proposing.

If you find collaborators who share common goals, the collaboration will not be effortless, but it will also not be as difficult as the cube of the number of collaborators.

HOW CAN WE APPLY ANY OF THESE LESSONS TO FUTURE PUR COLLABORATIONS?

The lessons learned from past collaborative efforts are by no means scientifically proven. They are not the product of consensus among experts in the field. They are just personal observations. But I believe that there is some value in considering them when setting up new collaborative efforts. Here are some thoughts on how to do that:

- Clarity of goals for the collaborative activity is essential. It is important for each participant in the collaboration to understand what needs the collaboration must meet for each of the other participants. The group needs to determine if those needs are in conflict or are different enough that they are likely to produce conflicts during the course of the collaboration. Seriously consider a smaller group of collaborators if goals are in conflict.
- Design the collaboration so that participants feel that they have a voice in the decision-making processes and that their benefits are commensurate with their contributions. Discuss the nature of the collaboration with all involved with sufficient time allowed for discussion of this point. Proceed only when all report that they feel the plan is fair and equitable.
- Be sure that everyone understands their roles and what level of effort it will take to meet their commitments to the group and to each other. The organizers should be ready to put in the work necessary to facilitate discussion

and decision making. People are busy with many projects, often working with very limited resources and their own time overcommitted. Facilitation will be necessary to get participants to exercise the rights they demand.

- Produce written documents that describe how decisions will be made, what is expected of participants, what benefits participants will get, how conflicts will be resolved, how finances will be handled, and as many other details as necessary so that everyone feels that they understand the rules and the game plan. Add to these documents and modify them constantly to represent joint decisions that are made during the course of the collaboration. Be sure everyone has a copy and gets updates regularly. New people at participating institutions will become involved as the collaboration moves along. They, too, need to know the rules and expectations.

- Figure out what activities are essential to supporting the collaboration and how those activities will be funded. These include administrative costs, meeting costs, reports, and communication. Figure out which of these activities members are willing to take on at their own expense and which will require special funding. Build that funding into grants, dues, or some other mechanism that will ensure its availability.

- Figure out how the substantial funds for carrying out the work of the collaboration will be acquired. Who will do the work to get them?

- Plan enough time together with other participants in the collaborative effort so that you can both deal with specific project work and address how the process is going. It is very helpful as well to have time to get to know the people representing the organizations that are collaborating. It is important to build trust to facilitate future conflict resolution.

This, not surprisingly, looks like a list of tasks that might best be achieved through the auspices of a good manager. Indeed, the concept of dedicated administrative leadership has not been explored here, but under the best circumstances, a person who is free to focus on group integration in all these areas could make a significant difference in at least the pace of collaboration.

EXAMPLES OF SOME NEW COLLABORATIONS CURRENTLY UNDER WAY
New collaborations among science centers, media, and researchers will undoubtedly vary from the proposed "ideal" characteristics described in this chapter. The Current Science & Technology Center at the Museum of Science

in Boston has a wide range of new partnerships with research and media organizations; some are described next.

The Health Science Education Partnership, funded by NIH-NCRR's Science Education Partnership Award, links the Museum of Science with the Harvard Medical School, the Harvard School of Public Health, the Harvard-MIT Division of Health Science Technology, the Whitehead Institute for Biomedical Research, Massachusetts General Hospital, the Dana-Farber Cancer Center, and McLean Hospital. These research institutions help the Museum by providing content, expertise, and guest speakers for the Museum's programs, and the Museum provides these organizations a means of presenting their work to the public.

In a relationship with New England Cable News (NECN), the Current Science & Technology Center will provide NECN with content for programming while the Museum gets exposure in people's homes throughout New England, providing the Museum with marketing and educational outreach benefits. Cameras in the Museum connected to NECN via fiber-optic lines will allow the cable news station to cover presentations at the Museum from their studios in the suburbs of Boston.

The Museum has a relationship with *Nature* magazine, similar to the one pioneered by the Science Museum in London, that allows the Museum to receive embargoed early notice of important stories that will appear in the journal. The staff of the Current Science & Technology Center are able to interview researchers and develop presentation materials ahead of time to be able to make a relatively in-depth presentation at the time the news embargo is lifted. When an article on the Chad skull (a significant new evolutionary find) was published in 2002, the Museum was able to put a well-developed presentation on the floor midday within minutes after the embargo was lifted. New England Cable News covered the story from the Museum of Science and ran the story hourly the day before it appeared on the front page of the *Boston Globe* and the *New York Times*. *Nature* magazine got additional attention in the Boston area because of the Museum's activities. The Museum got to be the site of the news story in Boston, and NECN got to be on the air with a detailed story before other major media.

Another type of collaboration that may have broad applicability is one in which science centers provide public education and outreach opportunities for research organizations that have federal grants mandating that their research projects include such activities. The Museum of Science has a subaward as part of the NSF-funded Nanoscale Science and Engineering Center at Harvard that includes a partnership with Harvard University, MIT, and the University of California, Santa Barbara. Through this partnership, the Museum receives funding for a staff member to focus on presentations about nanoscale research, and the university researchers have a public educational outreach program.

These are just a few of a long list of new collaborative efforts that are currently being developed in Boston and throughout the world. They create exciting new opportunities for institutions to work together to advance PUR while also strengthening the individual institutions.

11

Funding and Institutional Issues Related to Public Understanding of Research

Laura Martin, Rob Semper, and Sally Duensing

As science centers consider extending their work into the domain of public understanding of research (PUR), there are a number of institutional issues that they need to consider if they are to successfully sustain their efforts. Recent work on developing PUR initiatives at the Exploratorium and other science centers has shown to us that engaging in this work has involved much more than program development. Issues such as *fit to mission, adoption of new delivery models, institutional capacity, partnerships with research and funding agencies*, and *audience development* all need to be considered carefully when embarking on this path.

FIT TO MISSION
Science centers can have many different missions. These include: developing basic science understanding for children and youth, the support of school science activities, providing up-to-date science information to an informed public, addressing science and society issues, providing entertaining science experiences to families, and supporting natural history research.

Museums are unique institutions with a specific environment, culture, audience, and expertise. The PUR program needs to fit directly into the institutional context if it is to thrive. How topics are presented to the public and the place they hold in the institution's portfolio of projects are part of the context and the fit to mission. As with any effort we undertake, we have to be very clear about why a new direction is going to make a difference in people's lives, not just why *they* might care but why it is important from the point of view of the institution's mission. When we know that, it becomes easier to understand how much of our resources should be dedicated to it.

To illustrate some of the points we are making about institutional mission, we briefly describe some projects undertaken by the Exploratorium. In their case, public understanding of current science research has a long history as part of a general theme of providing the public with experiences of genuine scientific inquiry: its very mission is to create a culture of learning through innovative environments, programs, and tools that help people nurture their curiosity about the world around them. Founded by individuals with a strong connection to scientific research, the original exhibits included apparatus from the Stanford Linear Accelerator, Lawrence Berkeley Lab, and Bell Laboratories. The museum also showed the first live images of Jupiter taken by the *Pioneer 10* spacecraft in 1973.

Main exhibit floor, Exploratorium. Photo courtesy of the Exploratorium

Recent efforts along these lines are the *Live@Exploratorium: Origins* and *The Global Climate Change Research Explorer.* These projects use the Web and webcasting to connect a broad distant public with the ongoing, authentic process of science using the museum as an interpretive mediator. They are designed to provide the public a window into the world of current research by connecting people to labs, field sites, and tools of scientists through a field trip metaphor.

In addition to designing online activities, the Exploratorium decided to feature webcasting from the exhibit floor of the museum as a major part of their program. In this way, it hoped to explicitly connect the museum with science on the one hand and with the public audience on the other. The *Origins* and *Research Explorer* projects each have staff consisting of science journalists, media developers and producers, writers and designers, webcast and Web site developers, as well as a Web site operations group. A webcast studio was constructed on the exhibit floor of the museum and staffing developed specifically to focus on program development for these PUR activities. The museum added media production facilities to allow for rapid development of material and created a team to support the Web site

Solar eclipse, 2001, live at the Exploratorium. Photo courtesy of the Exploratorium

infrastructure needed for media streaming. The team also has remote production and communication capabilities to develop stories worldwide. All this has required dedication of resources that would not have made sense if the fit to mission were not strong.

The current focus on PUR at the Exploratorium is an example of continuity in this particular institution at the same time that it opens a new set of undertakings. Centers with less of a history directly tied to scientific research need to decide if presenting research along with more basic content is part of their mandate. We would argue, of course, that PUR is part of the basic mission of all science centers, although choices about scale and allocation of resources are always present. For instance, museums have certainly felt the need to address recent dramatic events in the public spotlight, such as bioterrorism, infectious disease, and buildups of nuclear weapons. Addressing these issues for our public is a responsibility and suggests that all of us need to plan, if not exhibits or installations, then perhaps relevant discussions or programs.

ADOPTION OF NEW DELIVERY MODELS

Because of the nature of the material, PUR programs often fall between traditional museum activities and a journalistic or public forum approach. The fact that much of the content is topical requires the use of more journalistic techniques of communication. Yet the museum is a place where people can get background information and contextual experiences that go beyond standard news sources. Thinking about new information delivery modes, however, means thinking about the fact that the museum is a place that is not generally used to operating in a news time frame: it is a place with a local as well as, in some cases, distant audience; it is a place that uses different media to offer a variety of experiences; and it has a program development time measured in months, not days. Alternatively, it could be argued that since the lines between public institutions are blurring, museums may want to set up news centers, as some of our colleagues have done.

In thinking about how to support PUR in a museum, it is important to match the potential of each medium with the desired outcomes of the work. The PUR projects have developed using different museum media forms, such as public presentations, rapidly changing exhibit capabilities, public forums and media productions, and Internet distribution. But there are difficulties in doing this: exhibits may not be the best way to show the process of research, video may be not very interactive in a museum setting and may duplicate what is already available on television, museums may not be seen as serious public forums for adults, and the Internet does not support the social experience that museums offer so beautifully. As work in educational computing technology has shown, it is a challenge to use a medium to its unique advantage rather than merely importing the functions from one medium into another. To ensure success, it is useful to choose a delivery model that fits the organization's mission and its potential for obtaining supportive resources.

For example, the *Origins* project is a hybrid journalistic–educational approach that concentrates on developing background material and connections to current events in science that are in the news in one form or another. The team realized that one of the best ways to do this was to get the public to the real places and data of active research projects. This suggested using a Web and webcasting approach, connecting the public directly with a remote, live experience. The museum staff tried to apply their design sensibilities in this medium to create these opportunities for the public to interact directly with the process of scientific research.

As we experiment with new delivery mechanisms, we must also consider how to choose new research topics to present in such a way that it captures public imagination. If visitors do not care about the issue or are not drawn by the delivery format, they will not invest time and energy in the exhibit. Since most members of a museum's core audience are not highly technically oriented, it is useful to think about ways to attract them to what they might feel is esoteric. The Field Museum's *Sue the T. Rex* exhibit is an example of a striking artifact and a timely research story that reached a broad audience. The exhibit can be considered to have a PUR message and is a good example of an audience-friendly project.

INSTITUTIONAL CAPABILITY

Stimulating the public to think about current developments in research frontiers is clearly a complicated proposition to undertake, as we have seen. It is important, then, to think about ways in which institutional capabilities can be leveraged to accomplish this kind of work.

Basic Capability

Some museums are equipped to tackle ambitious content delivery by live broadcasts, changing exhibits, and changing interactive exhibits. Others with this goal need to think about developing specialized facilities, such as presentation theaters, demonstration spaces, and media production facilities. This requires a strategic commitment from management and from the development department to secure funding to support the efforts. New technologies might need to be integrated into operations and new operational expertise demanded.

The development of a successful PUR program can often require not just building new kinds of facilities and the addition of staff with new professional capabilities, but even creating additional organizational units given the nature of the subject matter and the currency of the material. The speed of development and the interest in serving new and core audiences could argue for the creation of independently functioning operating units.

Finally, an institution has to consider its basic portfolio of projects and its exhibit change-out schedule in relationship to its resources. Since PUR displays or activities need to change just as others do, their scale of change is also dictated by an institution's resources.

Marketing

Because science museums have the mission of informing and educating the public, they can market on the strength of a PUR program. Marketing should be brought into the process in early phases since it is important to clarify the purpose of the exhibit for the topic and pick topics that speak to issues important to the audience.

Marketing professionals, whose role is to speak for the audience, need to focus their finite resources on core audiences for very practical reasons. From this perspective, risks and resources for PUR can be taken only if the core audience is first secured. Presenting PUR in a lively manner, however, can be part of a marketing strategy.

Because museums depend on return visitors to a great degree, they try to have an array of offerings, a certain percentage of which change in only minor ways over time. Changing PUR presentations can help pique people's interest and get patrons to come back again. However, pointing out what is new to nonmembers and regular patrons on what might be a small exhibition scale is a challenge that needs to be considered if PUR efforts are used to reinforce the perception of change that brings in visitors.

Marketing issues related to PUR are, for the most part, the same as those related to any exhibit or program we may undertake. PUR is good science, so it can work to build a museum's brand.

Funding

Having adequate resources allows museums to be able to take more risks in using new formats and in presenting current research. Agencies that traditionally provide funding for science center activities need to be educated about the changing needs of institutions related to PUR program demands. Fast turnaround on grants for exhibits, for example, may be important because of the need for timeliness in the content. Requests for funds for technological equipment and capacity that allow for timely adaptation and change is an expensive investment for museums, but one that needs to be expressed to funders.

Funders should also be encouraged to consider proposals that are not completely specified, but that promise to respond to topics as their importance emerges. The Arizona Science Center, for example, received a four-year grant from the Howard Hughes Medical Institution to develop four sets of multimedia activities around current topics in bioengineering. While specific examples were discussed in the proposal, the topics were not fixed. Rather, in this rapidly changing domain of research, topics are being selected at the beginning of each development cycle in order to include the most up-to-date work and findings.

An important challenge will be to ensure that PUR activities are a sustained undertaking in science centers. If the PUR effort is grant driven and you have a long-term grant, you have a better chance of being able to make changes within your halls around research topics on a regular basis. On a more limited, short-term budget, it is harder to do, partly because a museum's core budget usually cannot be diverted to a new, sometimes risky undertaking.

Another challenge is that endangering the relationship with a sponsor or a donor because of a topic you would like to address is a real possibility. In that situation, of course, the institution must obviously weigh the trade-offs.

Happily, as more museums experiment with different models, there will be a firmer base and a larger network with potential for partnerships. New sources of support for programs can also open up if a museum is committed to bringing current research to the public. First, sponsors may want to support projects related to their work since an informed public helps their work. An agency like NASA is always a helpful partner in such efforts, but private companies are also willing to support activities with little promotional gain. Honeywell and other companies, for example, have supported JASON Project activities in museums in different communities where they are located primarily because they believe in encouraging students in general.

The cost of introducing advanced technologies to offer experiences and programs will always be challenging to address. However, science centers have priceless resources that cannot be duplicated by more commercial enterprises, including the trust of the public, content expertise, and educational dedication.

Building on Current Capabilities

Capital-intensive and high-tech efforts are not the only option for PUR efforts. Museums have also developed effective low-tech strategies to reach their audiences. Some of the low-tech approaches to public understanding of science that we have encountered are described here. In our desire to deepen the level of discussion about science, we can overlook simple, appealing devices that are familiar to our visiting public.

Lecture series. Local scientists, researchers, and industry representatives are invited to present and discuss their work with the general public, with teachers, and with students. One advantage of this format is it can help the museum develop close connections with some of the leading edge work being done locally. These relationships can lead to support for programs, volunteer assistance, and special events.

Bulletin boards. Many museums post newspaper articles in galleries for the public to read. The Arizona Science Center experimented successfully with a white board in the lobby announcing the science news of the day as an extended headline. Staff members rotated responsibility for posting this information. Racks for flyers from public health agencies and utilities and so on are also an easy way to get new information to the public or to pique interest.

Newscasts. With the help of the marketing department, weather reports and other science news bulletins are broadcast from the museum. Local stations are usually very happy to cooperate and take advantage of the setting. The Arizona Science Center piped in the radio program *Science Friday* weekly in one gallery and organized hands-on activities related to the show theme for visitors.

Current events. Local, up-to-the-minute expertise can be organized and brought to the public through themed events on weekends or at other times. These can feature tables with presenters, materials and models, demonstrations, lectures, and handouts. Responding quickly to items covered in the news is an easy way to make sure the theme is relevant. Researchers are beginning to see that working with a science center is an efficient and enjoyable way for them to bring awareness to their work. Certainly, public agencies, such as health departments and the Federal Emergency Management Administration are always willing to help.

Movies. While hardly inexpensive, if the museum has a theater, it has budgeted for film rentals. Good films illustrating scientists at work, such as *Tropical Rainforest* and *Çatalhöyük*, can be featured with related programming.

Visiting scientists. The local university and even industry labs are easy to mobilize. Their scientists can address headline topics or talk about new developments related to the permanent exhibits.

Dialogue about Research

Many of the low-tech techniques mentioned in the previous list also offer the opportunity to encourage dialogue and debate among research and nonresearch communities, very much a part of public understanding. These exchanges of information can enable everyone to get a broader understanding about concerns, issues, and perspectives from diverse communities that often do not have access to each other's ways of thinking. In addition to conversations and other exchanges at lectures and other public programs, exhibits themselves can offer this opportunity. For example, bulletin boards of current research news stories could include a space for visitors to write and post their opinions, questions, and concerns. A science museum in Amsterdam developed a low-tech, easy-to-update exhibit at which a different news story on science research was posted each week and space was provided for visitors' comments on the research. Science center staff in Amsterdam and at other centers who have set up this form of visitor dialogue have noted that not only do visitors take time to write thoughtful opinions, but they often spend as much time or more reading what others have posted. Science centers are highly social places, and people have strong interest not only in their own responses and interactions at exhibits, but also in seeing what others do, say, and think.

Sharing Resources between Museums

Most museums are small to midsize. Staff are generally overworked, having many different responsibilities as part of their jobs. Most museum staff members do not have time to be involved in collaborations outside their communities. Collaborations with other institutions for up-to-date science programming, then, have to be designed to be efficient, economical, and turnkey.

One example of such a collaboration was undertaken by the Tech Museum of Innovation and the Arizona Science Center under a planning grant from the National Science Foundation to the Boston Museum of Science. The Tech has an ongoing program called Curiosity Counters, where they present new technological devices to the public at stations in their galleries. They use a format that includes a graphic style for displaying the object and for labeling, an "engineer's log" that gives visitors background information on the process by which the device was conceived and designed, and a FAQ (frequently asked questions) sheet for the gallery staff to enable them to answer visitors' questions about the device. The Arizona Science Center, meanwhile, had access to a few interesting new devices from manufacturers located in their community. After agreeing on what might be mutually interesting for San José and Phoenix audiences and which fit best with the centers' respective themes, Arizona procured hydrogen fuel cell models and surgical implant devices for delivering electrical stimulation to the spinal cord. The two museums shared responsibility for writing the print material, the Tech built the displays, and each museum got two new and timely demonstrations at low cost.

This kind of sharing of ideas and objects is a very simple way for museums to act quickly to bring the products of new research to the public. An additional benefit is that the activity allows centers a chance to form a relationship with local companies, who are usually more than eager to cooperate by supplying engineers' or scientists' time as well as material. Companies can even be persuaded to share ideas that are not yet on the market.

Research through Museum Exhibits

Sharing of resources and the acquisition—if temporarily—of technology can also result when researchers and museums team together. Some science centers have developed unique collaborations with researchers from local institutions to create exhibits in which the exhibit itself is an actual research experiment. Working with scientists to set up experiments on the museum floor allows the researcher to collect data and, at the same time, provides the public with the opportunity to learn about current questions and methods of scientific research. Some projects take the form of stand-alone exhibits, while others need to be run or monitored by the researcher, graduate students, or research assistants.

One example of an exhibit experiment was part of an exhibition on cognition and memory at the Exploratorium set up as a working experiment/exhibit with Dr. Elizabeth Loftus on eyewitness testimony. Data were collected about visitors' recollections of an event that they had watched on a video screen at the entrance of the museum. Visitors were shown how their responses compared with all previous responses, as well as a brief text on the rationale for the study. Results were also published.

In addition to providing the researcher with a large and diverse database of responses, the "research exhibits" can help visitors learn more about their own and others' ways of thinking and learning. Thus, museums can get access to experimental equipment and demonstrate current research efficiently as they fulfill their mission to raise visitor awareness of local scientific undertakings.

Note that while museums do not have human subjects committees to screen the ethical aspects of research, all universities do. These documents and the research protocols themselves should be reviewed by museum staff. It is important that exhibit experiments be initially reviewed and approved by staff so that they are:

- an interesting activity to do or are interesting as a result of implications,
- relatively brief (less than 30 minutes),
- explicit in being a "real" experiment, and
- explicit in methodology and question(s) of the study.

PARTNERSHIPS WITH RESEARCH AND FUNDING AGENCIES

A critical point in PUR development is the need to develop relations and partnerships with science-producing agencies. Given the rapid development time line and the need for firsthand information, props, and media, it is helpful to develop long-term relations with individual scientists, scientific institutions, and science journalists. In many cases, the mission of the science museum to provide access to the scientists' work fits synergistically with the desire of the science agency to help the public understand what they are doing. One way to facilitate this is to have on-staff scientists, educators, and journalists who can easily communicate with the scientific staff at research agencies.

As part of the Exploratorium's PUR projects, the staff developed and maintained relationships with scientists and public information staff in many different scientific agencies and major research labs, individual scientists, and scientific associations, such as the American Association for the Advancement of Science. These relationships, like all good partnerships, have taken time to develop.

Agencies that support the research itself, such as National Science Foundation science directorates, the National Institutes of Health, and others have an interest in seeing their work reach the public and often support PUR activities. Local universities that apply for grants for scientific research are often happy to partner with science centers to carry out that part of their grant obligation since it is a very meaningful and broad-reaching way to educate the public: science centers have the expertise to communicate to a lay audience and be educationally effective. Locally, industry is often willing to display prototypes or give presentations on their work for the public, representing a not insignificant in-kind source of support.

Forming alliances with local broadcasters who might stage a newscast using museum staff expertise or a weather story from the museum is also a potentially important investment. These collaborations have the added benefit of reinforcing the institution's image as a source of current information to the community. At the very least, preparing the staff to respond to questions on

current science research events and press releases about responsive programming is a function that can be usefully integrated into the ongoing work of a
museum.

AUDIENCE DEVELOPMENT

The natural audience for PUR often can be more specialized than the general
museum audience. This audience is typically adult, attentive, and well read
though not necessarily science center patrons. Thus, it may require additional
marketing activities to reach them. Some topics, too, have special interest to
specific audience segments. Targeted marketing, through professional associations, hobbyist groups, and specialized mailing lists can help develop new audiences for this work.

One of the audiences most in need of PUR experiences is teachers, especially those teaching elementary- and middle-school grades. These teachers
have less experience with science and less professional time to devote to it
overall. With few exceptions, teachers have trouble conveying the nature of research practices and current content to their students, yet our national standards require that students develop such understandings. Museum PUR
efforts can have a strong role to play here, developing the means to reach
teachers and cultivate their awareness. The Arizona Science Center project on
bioengineering, for example, created a design team of middle- and high-
school science teachers from three districts, industry representatives, and university scientists. They developed and delivered 12-hour staff development
experiences for middle-school teachers on current topics, taping the training
in order to offer streaming video off the Web site for those who could not attend in person. The video includes updates from pioneer researchers in related fields, such as genetic cancer research, plant engineering, and enzyme
manufacturing.

At the Exploratorium, the staff view PUR initiatives as a way to reach an extended audience beyond just those who visit the facility in San Francisco. This
approach allows the results of the extensive development and production
work to be distributed to more people, as well as to extend the presence of the
Exploratorium to new and distant audiences via the Internet. Since national
marketing is an expensive proposition, programming was developed specifically tied to newsworthy events in order to foster program mention in news
stories. Part of that effort involved developing targeted Internet marketing to

specific special interests groups associated with the topics at hand. These groups then spread the word in a classic viral marketing effort.

CONCLUSION

Museums are ideally situated to support the PUR. The PUR programs can reach core audiences as well as specialized niches and serve the mission of the institution. Developing a successful PUR initiative at a museum, however, can require a substantial review of the museum's role and operation. Only through a clear examination of the institutional issues will it be possible to develop successful and sustained efforts.

NOTE

Many thanks to Sylvia Crannell, Education Division promotions, publications, and grants manager, and Jane Eastwood, director of marketing, at the Science Museum of Minnesota for their material from a recent interview on PUR from a marketing perspective.

Section 3

SOME EMERGING PUBLIC UNDERSTANDING OF RESEARCH STRATEGIES AND APPROACHES

So how can museums effectively bring current research to their visitors? We present eight examples, from three continents, of how leading practitioners have addressed the key challenges with considerable success while learning lessons that they reveal here.

12

Understanding the Process of Research

Rick Bonney

Scientific findings have unquestionable impacts on people's daily lives, and the public needs scientific information to make both personal and societal decisions. Unfortunately, many citizens view scientific results and the processes that produced them as precise, linear, and correct. The reality, of course, is that scientific findings are usually tentative and constantly changing because the research process involves conflicting observations, complex experimentation, and cautious conclusions, all shaped by both collaboration and competition within the scientific community. One result is public confusion, even mistrust, as researchers hedge their bets, change their minds, and call for further study. One solution: develop public understanding of research (PUR) programs that help the public understand not only current research findings but also the realities of the research that produced them—its ups and downs, twists and turns, foibles and faux pas. Then, perhaps, citizens would be better able to keep appropriate perspective as they evaluate scientific information and how it affects their lives.

Alan Leshner, chief executive officer of the American Association for the Advancement of Science (AAAS) and formerly a senior executive at the U.S. National Institutes of Health, concurs with this idea (2002). He points out that Project 2061, in *Science for All Americans* (Rutherford and Ahlgren 1990), defined a science-literate person as "one who is aware that science, mathematics, and technology are interdependent human enterprises with strengths and limitations; understands key concepts and principles of science; is familiar with the natural world and recognizes both its diversity and unity; and uses scientific knowledge and scientific ways of thinking for individual and social purposes."

"During 14 years at NIH," Leshner says, "I was repeatedly confronted with how many people have genuinely no idea about the what, why, or how of research. Educated, literate people. Often these were people looking for help with dire health problems, and they wanted to know what the latest research was showing and what had or hadn't been scientifically tested—that means through research. But too often they didn't know what they (or we) meant by research."

The outcome of public education about research, Leshner believes, should be a far greater understanding of what constitutes science-based evidence and what types of evidence should be used to make critical life decisions.

Some might argue that such in-depth discovery should be left to the formal education system. After all, according to the National Research Council (1996), "Students at all grade levels and in every domain of science should have the opportunity to use scientific inquiry and develop the ability to think and act in ways associated with inquiry, including asking questions, planning and conducting investigations, using appropriate tools and techniques to gather data, thinking critically and logically about relationships between evidence and explanations, constructing and analyzing alternative explanations, and communicating scientific arguments." The truth is, however, that most formal curricula still teach science as a rhetoric of conclusions, and the current craze for standardized testing is squelching most opportunity for original investigation. Can informal science education help fill this gap by focusing on "public understanding of research"?

One step in this direction is to develop programs and exhibits that go beyond simply presenting scientific findings—that explain how those findings were made, show the twists and turns that were taken along the way, and present the scientists who made the findings as mortal humans. Many institutions have successfully employed this approach using various subjects and techniques, and their cases are described elsewhere in this volume.

But it is possible to go beyond illustrating the process in exhibits and demonstrations. The public can actually become engaged in science. In fact, some institutions, such as AAAS, are creating formal programs called "public engagement in science." However, "engagement" means different things to different people, as Bruce Lewenstein and I discuss in chapter 3. At its most powerful, public engagement means public involvement in determining the actual directions of scientific research. Indeed, says François Vescia (2002), Web chief editor at La Cité des Sciences et de l'Industrie in Paris, "publics are not only expecting to be attendees and to get a better explanation of what research is producing . . . they want involvement in the choices of developing research. Science centers can help to build a new participatory relationship between research and the public. This new relationship requires involvement . . . because science and research issues are too serious to be left only to scientists. In a way, we are tackling the issue of democracy itself!"

This political perspective on public engagement is demonstrated in museum-based consensus conferences and other participatory activities. For example, the Deutsches Hygiene-Museum Dresden sponsored a 16-month "Citizens' Conference on Genetic Testing" starting in October 2000 (Naumann 2002). Conference goals included promoting open discussion of a controversial issue and creating awareness of the initiative's results among decision makers. The museum chose to focus on genetic testing for several reasons, including the fact that many people feel powerless around the issue because of a lack of public information and understanding. The conference was shown to encourage dialogue on the issue between the public and the scientific community and to expand the original, expert-dominated discussion through citizen participation. Other projects designed to address similar feelings of political powerlessness around scientific issues have shown similar results (Einsiedel and Eastlick 2001).

Another method of engaging the public in research is to involve individuals in actual scientific studies, either by providing opportunities for people to serve as research assistants or by enabling them to conduct their own original investigations. Astronomy, for example, has long relied on amateur stargazers to identify comets and other astronomical phenomena. A vigorous set of activities in many areas of science is listed at the Web site of the Society for Amateur Scientists (www.sas.org). In the remainder of this chapter, I want to highlight my own experience with this approach to addressing the *process* of research.

Having the public participate in real research is sometimes known as "student-scientist partnerships," which were a focus at the U.S. National

Science Foundation (NSF) in the mid-1990s (Barstow, Tinker, and Doubler 1997; Cohen 1997). Because this approach is not limited to schools, I prefer to call it "citizen science," defined as a partnership between laypeople and professional scientists to study scientifically significant questions (Bonney 1996). At the Cornell Lab of Ornithology, where I am director of education, we take citizen science very seriously. In fact, the Lab's mission is to "interpret and conserve the earth's biodiversity through research, education, and citizen science focused on birds." The goal of our Citizen Science Program is to engage the public in professional research with two objectives: 1) to collect and analyze data that can answer large-scale scientific questions and that can be used for habitat conservation and 2) to increase environmental awareness and science literacy among the public.

Citizen science enjoys a long tradition at the Lab, starting in 1929, when our founder, Arthur A. Allen, began soliciting bird-watchers' sightings to construct a comprehensive database of the birds of central New York's Cayuga Lake basin. In 1965, our Nest Record Program became one of the first modern North American projects to seek volunteer-collected biological data in an organized fashion. However, the Lab's citizen science program began in earnest in 1987 with the start of Project FeederWatch, which at that time was a joint project of the Lab and the Long Point Bird Observatory (now Bird Studies Canada). FeederWatch is an annual survey of winter bird populations for which participants count the kinds and numbers of birds that visit their backyard feeders on one or two days each week.

Unlike earlier Lab projects—which supplied rudimentary instructions, used data forms that had to be keypunched by project staff, and provided limited feedback to participants—FeederWatch was the first project to employ a "research kit." This included a written project rationale, complete instructions for setting up an observation area and collecting data, computer-scannable data forms, and a project newsletter providing detailed feedback on Feeder-Watch data analyses. FeederWatch soon proved to be a treasure trove of data for population biologists at the Lab and has now become the best available database on the abundance and distribution of winter bird populations across North America (Bonney and Dhondt 1997).

Citizen science reached another milestone in 1992, when the Lab received a grant from NSF's Informal Science Education program for a project called Public Participation in Ornithology. Until this point, we had considered our citizen-science projects—at that time called "cooperative research projects"—to be primarily scientific endeavors. But the NSF award acknowledged the extensive educational opportunities afforded by participation in organized research. Through this grant, we expanded the research kit concept and developed a series of projects providing explicitly educational experiences. Each project still included comprehensive instruction booklets, but they were expanded to explain how the project was developed, to describe the scientific process, and to show how project data would be analyzed. Research kits also included other educational aids, such as bird identification posters, tapes and CDs of birdsongs and calls, and project reference guides.

By 2003, the Lab's Citizen-Science Program had grown to include eight projects designed to answer a range of scientific questions and to allow participation by individuals in all locations at all times of year (www.birds.cornell.edu/citsci). The projects vary in complexity, from simply counting backyard birds over one weekend in February (Great Backyard Bird Count [GBBC]), to periodically counting the numbers of different-colored pigeons in urban pigeon flocks (Project PigeonWatch), to selecting count sites, describing site habitats, and using timed bird counts and playbacks of recorded songs and calls (Birds in Forested Landscapes). Each project follows the same general structure: participants follow specific protocols, collect data about birds and their environments, and send the information to the Lab. There scientists organize and analyze the data and publish the results not only in the scientific literature but also, with the help of Lab education and publications staff, in a variety of more accessible venues, ranging from project Web sites to newsletters. Participants are thus able to see how their observations compare with those of other observers across the continent and to learn how their data are put to use for purposes of both science and conservation. A significant number of participants are now recruited through museums or through partnerships between museums and local community groups; thus, museums have become a critical component of this approach to PUR.

By 2003, most of the projects also had migrated to the Internet, which has been a boon to citizen science. Data submitted online can be edited in real time (for example, if a participant enters a bird count that seems suspicious for his or her reporting location, a message asks for verification, allowing many errors to be caught before the data enter the database). In addition, online data retrieval enables project participants to receive project results rapidly. For example, during the weekend of the GBBC, counts are updated hourly. Participants can even download data to conduct their own analyses, pursuing research questions independently of the Lab's professional ornithologists.

At this point in our program development, we believe that citizen science is proving useful as a tool for research, conservation, and education. Scientifically, benefits are easily measured by the large number of peer-reviewed journal articles published each year that make exclusive use of citizen-generated data. In fact, many questions about North American bird populations could not be answered by any other method. As examples, recent publications have examined how bird populations change in distribution over time and space (Hochachka et al. 1999; Wells et al. 1998), how the breeding success of certain species is affected by environmental change (Rosenberg, Lowe, and Dhondt 1999), how emerging infectious diseases spread through wild animal populations (Hartup et al. 2001; Hochachka and Dhondt 2000), and how acid rain may be affecting bird populations (Hames et al. 2002).

Citizen-science data also have been used to develop habitat recommendations for bird conservation. For instance, the booklet *A Land Manager's Guide to Improving Habitat for Scarlet Tanagers and Other Forest-Interior Birds* (Rosenberg et al. 1999) has been distributed to hundreds of private and government land managers involved in developing and implementing the North American Bird Conservation Plan. Over the next few years, we intend to prepare similar guidelines for additional bird species based on results from our Birds in Forested Landscapes project.

But for those of us concerned primarily with education, many questions remain: Are citizen-science participants learning about birds and ecology? Is project participation leading to greater conservation commitment? And are citizen scientists learning about the process of scientific research? We believe the answer to all three questions is yes.

For starters, we know that our projects are popular and enjoyable. Already more than 100,000 citizens of all ages and backgrounds have participated in at least one of them. Furthermore, participants have sent blizzards of notes and e-mails describing the personal benefits derived from carefully observing birds and their surroundings. For example, a FeederWatcher from Atlanta, Georgia, wrote, "I have been a casual bird watcher for many years. By taking a scientific approach, I am learning so much more and enjoying it more. I am starting to keep my own records. I am going to continue to count during the summer and note bird actions for my own records. Thank you again." A participant in Project PigeonWatch, after spending an afternoon counting pigeons with her scout troop, told us, "If I could study birds more, I could become a scientist." And a participant in Birds in Forested Landscapes wrote, "I hope by participating in BFL that I can help prevent the loss of any more ethereal thrush music and maybe even hope for their return."

In addition to tracking anecdotal evidence for learning, over the past few years we have employed several more formal evaluation techniques, including written and telephone surveys, pre- and postproject questionnaires, and analyses of project listservs and unsolicited participant comments. So far, we have learned that many project participants gain knowledge of specific biological information and feel that their observation skills are increased. In some cases, they also appear to think scientifically about the manner in which they are collecting data. For example, participants in our Seed Preference Test generally did not follow our prescribed protocol in a mindless manner. When they encountered problems, they took the project seriously enough to make it work, using their knowledge of birds and bird behavior to adapt the protocols. Many participants made additional observations about the microecology of their feeding sites or about animal behavior. Some formulated and wrote out careful hypotheses, and some made suggestions for modifying the experimental design. Therefore, for many people, the process of participating in this citizen-science project contributed to their thinking about biology and the scientific process (Trumbull et al. 2000).

As another example, consider Project PigeonWatch, which was explicitly designed to appeal to inner-city children. This project is often operated at museums that use it to connect with local communities and to show off their collections of birds and other animals. Qualitative evaluations show that many educators praise PigeonWatch and its effects on attitudes toward science. One leader stated, "The group of citizen scientists that we have created through involvement in this program will be bird enthusiasts for life. I believe that PigeonWatch encourages life skills for observation that can be extended way beyond bird watching. It has been enriching for both the partners and the children, bringing science experiences into their homes and hearts." In addition, quantitative evaluations suggest that some PigeonWatchers change their views about scientists. For example, when asked to draw a scientist before participating in the project, most children drew stereotypical scientists (lab coat, messy hair, male). In contrast, after they had observed and collected data about pigeons, many participants drew scientists who looked less stereotyped and more like themselves (Lewenstein 2001).

Still another project, The Birdhouse Network, studies the biology and breeding success of birds that nest in birdhouses. Most participants are suburban or rural adults or children participating through museums or youth groups such as 4-H. In this case, results from pre- and posttesting project participants show increased knowledge of bird biology and habitat needs but no change in understanding of science process or in attitudes toward science or the environment. The lack of measured change may reflect the fact that many participants already have positive attitudes toward the environment when they enroll in the project, or it may indicate a need for including more explicit information about the scientific process in the project research kits (Brossard, Lewenstein, and Bonney, submitted). Nevertheless, as with our other projects, anecdotal evidence for greater understanding of scientific process is strong. For example, one youth group leader has stated, "It is a great project for all ages. Kids learn about carpentry, nature, and scientific procedures as well as responsibility and stick-to-itiveness."

Our most educationally comprehensive project is Classroom FeederWatch, an inquiry-based middle-school science curriculum. Through this project, students learn to identify birds, collect bird data and send them to the Lab, interpret data to answer questions about birds, ask their own bird questions, design and conduct experiments to answer those questions, and finally publish the results of their research in a newsletter called *Classroom BirdScope*. Here, our evaluations have shown that teachers who use the complete range of project materials clearly engage their students in authentic inquiry. Students use Cornell Lab of Ornithology's online databases to formulate and answer questions and to conduct Web searches to find related data. Furthermore, students interpret their Classroom FeederWatch experiences—both collecting data and designing their own projects—as real scientific investigations, and they apply their knowledge of life sciences to reason through their own research questions (Chakane and Trumbull 2000; Trumbull, Grudens-Schuck, and Scarano 1998; Trumbull, Scarano, and Chakane 1999a, 1999b). Finally, the number of submissions to *Classroom BirdScope* that represent authentic inquiry has increased each year since the project began (1997).

The development and operation of citizen-science projects, at least to the degree that they are developed and maintained at the Lab, is not a casual undertaking. Many staff members are required: scientists to determine the questions to be answered and the data collection protocols to be followed, educators to develop the curriculum and support materials, more scientists to analyze and interpret the overall data set, information technology specialists to develop the databases and interactive Web sites required to handle all the data, and marketers to sell the projects to gain operating revenue. In the case of the Lab, such projects clearly pay off because of the tremendous amount of scientific data generated by the public as well as the educational return to participants.

While institutions with a less rigorous research program might find the development of full-scale citizen-science projects to be unrealistic, most museums can develop local or community-based citizen-science projects. Many interesting topics in biology and natural history can be investigated at the local level. Examples include bird-feeding experiments, water quality in local streams and lakes, or studies of the abundance and distribution of local trees and shrubs.

Furthermore, because the citizen-science movement is growing rapidly, most educators can now hook up with an existing project sponsored by a regional or national institution. Most projects are continuously seeking new participants, and informal science educators, such as museum summer camp staff or other youth group leaders, can easily become local project facilitators. Examples include Monarch Watch (www.monarchwatch.org), the North American Amphibian Monitoring Program (www.pwrc.usgs.gov/naamp), the National Weather Service Cooperative (www.nws.noaa.gov/om/coop/index. htm), and Keeping Track (www.keepingtrackinc.org).

François Vescia (2002) tells this story: "While I was in a shop in Athens, the shopkeeper told me 'Down with the tyrant.' So I asked him 'Where is tyranny nowadays?' He answered 'Tyranny is in ourselves. It is our cowardliness. Our ignorance. The fact that we use tools we do not master. We are surrounded by techniques, but we are giving up our understanding of these. We lose the sense of why we use them.'"

I agree with this shopkeeper, but I would go further. I believe that the tyranny extends to science educators who allow the process of science to remain a mystery to the public. Every citizen relies on science, and everyone must learn that science is less often a field of correct and invariant knowledge and more often a field of dreams. As we consider public understanding of current research, as we help people understand the important issues of the day, we must also help them understand the process by which scientific information unfolds, the fact that knowledge is a moving target, and the idea that what is "fact" today may well be fallacy tomorrow. Only when the public understands how science is conducted can the public become truly scientifically literate.

NOTE

The Citizen Science Program at the Cornell Lab of Ornithology has been generously supported by several grants from the National Science Foundation including "Citizen Science Online" (ESI–0087760; "Parents Involved/Pigeons Everywhere" (ESI–9802248); "Schoolyard Ornithology Resource Project" (ESI–9618945); "Cornell Nest Box Network" (ESI–9627280); "Project BirdWatch" (ESI–9550541); and "Public Participation in Ornithology" (ESI–9155700). The program also has received support from the USDA Forest Service, the U.S. Fish and Wildlife Service, the U.S. Environmental Protection Agency, the National Fish and Wildlife Foundation, the Florence and John Schumann Foundation, and the Wallace Genetic Foundation.

REFERENCES

Barstow, D., R. F. Tinker, and S. J. Doubler. 1997. *National Conference on Student and Scientist Partnerships.* Boston: TERC.

Bonney, R. 1996. Citizen science: A Lab tradition. *Living Bird* 15, no. 4: 7–15.

Bonney, R., and A. A. Dhondt. 1997. FeederWatch: An example of a student–scientist partnership. In *Internet links to science education: Student scientist partnerships,* ed. K. C. Cohen. New York: Plenum Press.

Brossard, D., B. V. Lewenstein, and R. Bonney. Submitted. Scientific knowledge and attitude change: The impact of a citizen science project." *International Journal of Science Education.*

Chakane, M., and D. J. Trumbull. 2000. SORP evaluation: Classroom implementation, teacher workshops, and students' inquiry projects during the 1999/2000 academic year. Department of Education, Cornell University, June 2000.

Cohen, K. C., ed. 1997. *Internet links for science education: Student-scientist partnerships.* New York: Plenum Press.

Einsiedel, E., and D. L. Eastlick. 2001. Consensus conferences as deliberative democracy: A communications perspective. *Science Communication* 21, no. 4: 323–43.

Hames, R. S., K. V. Rosenberg, J. D. Lowe, S. E. Barker, and A. A. Dhondt. 2002. Adverse effects of acid rain on the distribution of the wood thrush *Hylocichla mustelina* in North America. In *Proceedings of the National Academy of Sciences of the United States of America* 99, no. 17: 11235–40.

Hartup, B. K., J. M. Bickal, A. A. Dhondt, D. H. Ley, and G. V. Kollias. 2001. Dynamics of conjunctivitis and *Mycoplasma gallisepticum* infections in house finches. *Auk* 118: 327–33.

Hochachka, W. M., and A. A. Dhondt. 2000. Density-dependent decline of host abundance resulting from a new infectious disease. *Proceedings of the National Academy of Sciences* 97: 5503–6.

Hochachka, W. M., J. V. Wells, K. V. Rosenberg, D. L. Tessaglia-Hymes, and A. A. Dhondt. 1999. Irruptive migration of common redpolls. *Condor* 101: 195–204.

Leshner, A. 2002. Presentation at "Museums, Media, and Public Understanding of Research" conference, St. Paul, Minnesota, September 26–29.

Lewenstein, B. 2001. Parents Involved/Pigeons Everywhere Evaluation Report. Year 2, 1999–2000. Ithaca, N.Y.: Seavoss Associates.

McElroy. 2002. Presentation at "Museums, Media, and Public Understanding of Research" conference, St. Paul, Minnesota, September 26–29.

National Research Council. 1996. National science education standards. Washington, D.C.: National Academy Press.

Naumann, J. 2002. Presentation at "Museums, Media, and Public Understanding of Research" conference, St. Paul, Minnesota, September 26–29.

Rosenberg, K. V., J. D. Lowe, and A. A. Dhondt. 1999. Effects of forest fragmentation on breeding tanagers: A continental perspective. *Conservation Biology* 13: 568–83.

Rosenberg, K. V., R. W. Rohrbaugh Jr., S. E. Barker, R. S. Hames, J. D. Lowe, and A. A Dhondt. 1999. *A land manager's guide to improving habitat for scarlet tanagers and other forest-interior birds.* Ithaca, N.Y.: Cornell Lab of Ornithology.

Rosenthal, B. 2002. Presentation at "Museums, Media, and Public Understanding of Research" conference, St. Paul, Minnesota, September 26–29.

Rutherford, F. J., and A. Ahlgren. 1990. *Science for all Americans.* New York: Oxford University Press.

Trumbull, D. J., R. Bonney, D. Bascom, and A. Cabral. 2000. Thinking scientifically during participation in a citizen-science project. *Science Education* 84: 265–75.

Trumbull, D. J., N. Grudens-Schuck, and G. Scarano. 1998. Evaluation of CFW use in the 1997/98 academic year. Department of Education, Cornell University.

Trumbull, D. J., G. Scarano, and M. Chakane. 1999a. SORP formative evaluation report. Department of Education, Cornell University, January 29.

Trumbull, D. J., G. Scarano, and M. Chakane. 1999b. SORP formative evaluation report #2. Department of Education, Cornell University, July 1.

Vescia, F. 2002. Presentation at "Museums, Media, and Public Understanding of Research" conference, St. Paul, Minnesota, September 26–29.

Wells, J. V., K. V. Rosenberg, E. H. Dunn, D. L. Tessaglia, and A. A. Dhondt. 1998. Feeder counts as indicators of spatial and temporal variation in winter abundance of resident birds. *Journal of Field Ornithology* 69: 577–86.

13

Production Aspects of Promoting Public Understanding of Research

David A. Ucko

The characteristics of scientific research significantly impact the production of exhibitions and programs designed to foster public understanding of research (PUR). As a result, such efforts present museums with special challenges and opportunities. Drawing from PUR conference presentations and discussions, this chapter identifies key production implications of those features and possible ways to address them.

PRODUCTION CHALLENGES

Producing exhibitions and programs for PUR is typically more complex than creating similar products based on more established science and technology. By its very nature, scientific research continually creates new findings. To capture this moving target, the time frames for production may need to be accelerated, and the products likely must include the means for continual updating. In addition, PUR producers can draw from only limited material that has already been translated for the public, and there are certainly no "cookbooks" of tested exhibits. This shortage is intensified by the technical complexity of most research today.

Because the scientific process itself is unfinished and messy, the research path may be difficult to present. Significance may be unclear without the benefit of perspective and hindsight. The relevance of new findings may not be obvious or the implications yet clear. Unlike textbook science, where principles have been more thoroughly tested over time, current research deals with results that are far less certain. Thus, PUR programs must communicate both tentative results and consequences. These uncertainties often fuel controversy within the scientific community and among the general public, leading to issues that are tricky to present because they are politically or emotionally charged.

These challenges also create opportunities, however. Because research deals with the unknown, the search for knowledge can be exciting to portray (though many steps involved may be tedious). The unfolding process lends itself to human-interest stories that capture the creativity of collaborating and competing researchers as well as their human frailties. In addition, because scientific research is an ongoing quest, the public may be able to participate through active supporting roles as well as engage in dialogue around potential implications and consequences.

RESEARCH LITERACY AND PRODUCTION FORMATS

Recognizing these inherent challenges, museums can engage visitors in scientific research through a wide range of formats, each with its own production-related issues. The choice of production format depends on those aspects emphasized. Practitioners can think about enhancing three basic facets of public "research literacy": 1) understanding the content of current scientific research, 2) understanding the nature or process of research, and 3) understanding potential research implications and consequences. For simplification, the discussion that follows is organized into these three categories, recognizing that each aspect is necessary and that any particular project may incorporate more than one. Examples are drawn from the "Museums, Media, and the Public Understanding of Research" conference, held at the Science Museum of Minnesota in September 2002, using case studies, poster sessions, and discussions (Bossert and Ucko 2002; see also the appendix to this volume).

Research Content

Most museum-based PUR efforts have employed exhibitions and programs to communicate, translate, and create context for recent research, as with typical science content. Although the practice of presenting current science and technology findings is now receiving attention, it is certainly not new. Formats in the nineteenth century included international expositions and public lectures. One of my own first projects at Chicago's Museum of Science and Industry several decades ago was the Science Alive changing exhibition. Its goal was to present then-current science topics, such as genetic engineering and alternative energy sources, in forms easy for visitors to grasp through text, graphics, and slides. This modest exhibition was eventually discontinued because of the amount of work required to create what was essentially a three-dimensional science magazine.

Today, computers and digital media allow exhibit developers not only to enhance presentation and add interaction, but also to update content much more readily. For example, ScienceNOW at the California Academy of Sciences in San Francisco interprets headline news in the natural sciences and recent research or expedition activities of its staff scientists.[1] The changeable kiosk includes a touch-screen computer station along with a live animal tank and three vitrines for collections; the cycle time for a complete changeover is one month. According to Carol Tang, senior science educator, this kiosk costs only $10,000 to update annually, including portions of salaries for seven staff, following an initial $35,000 investment for design and fabrication. Despite modest cost, this format requires the efforts of a dedicated interdepartmental team that meets weekly and appears most successful when topics relate to major exhibitions. Their project demonstrates that quick turnaround can be accomplished through strong infrastructure, established graphic and stylistic templates, clear duty assignments, institutional commitment, and organization. Elsewhere, at the American Museum of Natural History in New York, changing video kiosks are used to keep permanent halls up to date. Their *Science Bulletins* are based on high-definition video, which raises cost but also production quality.[2]

ScienceNOW (California Academy of Sciences, San Francisco). The flexible format, along with fixed templates, enables staff to provide research updates monthly at low cost. Courtesy of Dong Lin, California Academy of Sciences

An alternative format can be entirely programmatic, such as the MIT (Massachusetts Institute of Technology) Museum's monthly two-hour FAST (Family Adventures in Science and Technology) program, which highlights new research areas, academic departments, or projects.[3] Museum staff recruit faculty and students from MIT groups and departments who help develop demonstrations to illustrate their research and related activities. This format, which can be programmed to create synergies with permanent or traveling exhibitions, is facilitated by a close relationship between the campus and the museum. The Tech Museum for Innovation in San José does not share that advantage and must recruit scientists from local universities and nearby industry for its Curiosity Counters, which offers a similar type of forum.[4] The Tech also hosts special events for area researchers to showcase their work. On an even larger scale, SWR-ARD public television in Germany has organized "science markets" with local universities where many research institutes display their work, and scientists can meet the public in a popular setting. These types of events, of course, can be staged by museums as well. Purely programmatic formats such as these, often facilitated by partnering with other organizations, can be the most flexible and relatively inexpensive, depending on scale.

Some current science formats focus on specific content areas, such as SpaceLink, which serves as a space science and astronomy update center at the Maryland Science Center.[5] Equipped with many different audiovisual sources that can be displayed on large screens, it is part media center, part newsroom, and part discovery room. According to president Greg Andorfer, its most important resource by far is staff, who include space science educators, amateur astronomers, and community volunteers. In addition to teacher seminars and class programs, SpaceLink hosts events with guest scientists to highlight mission milestones and space-related anniversaries. Based on positive visitor response, this approach is being extended to other content areas with BodyLink and TerraLink.

One of the most ambitious examples is Antenna, a constantly changing exhibition devoted to science and technology news at the Wellcome Wing of the Science Museum, London.[6] Using a flexible exhibit case and graphics, four "rapids" convey "bite-size" news stories, with one renewed each week. A larger-scale "feature" gets changed every four to six months, allowing somewhat more leisurely development and greater depth. Exhibition treatment is consciously "edgy" to attract the greatest amount of public interest and media attention. These exhibits are complemented by *Antenna Live*, a BBC science news feed; *Antenna Events*, featuring scientists behind the headlines; and *Antenna Web*. Collaboration with the scientific journal *Nature*, the first of its kind for a museum, has been critical to obtaining "hot" news early.

The Current Science & Technology Center at Boston's Museum of Science represents a corresponding major investment in the United States (see section 3 of this volume, page 235).[7] This installation uses live presentations supported by a sophisticated system comprising a server and 35 networked computers that control 17 live cameras, 3 news tickers, 18 audio inputs, a satellite feed, 7 touch screens, 6 plasma screens, sound, and lighting. Museum educators, scientists, and multimedia producers write and produce daily updates as well as program the presentations and events. Despite technology and back-of-house support, audience impact still depends heavily on the talent of the presenters and their ability to engage visitors in technical subjects. Few museums can afford such large-scale undertakings; as Tim McElroy (Liberty Science Center) commented at the PUR conference, the staff requirement alone is "humbling to contemplate."

Whether on a small or a grand scale, production of content-oriented PUR exhibit elements can be facilitated through the use of digital media based on templates in which new topics and information can replace previous ones with reduced labor and expense. Similarly, creating larger exhibitions in modules allows elements to be replaced or modified without the need to replace everything. Use of templates and modules also facilitates sharing between institutions and helps mitigate the trade-off of quality reduction inherent in a more rapid production cycle.

The use of digital content and live presentations allows more rapid updating than traditional methods. Yet the key question remains: How current should the "current" science be, and what should be the turnover frequency? Don Pohlman (Science Museum of Minnesota) raised an important point at the St. Paul conference: Is PUR too focused on the news? (See the afterword to this volume page 329.) Museums may be better off presenting topical issues that need refreshing less often than breaking news items, which may require daily change. After all, the core business of museums is interpretation and education, not presentation of the most recent developments, which is the primary province of the media. One possibility, consistent with a longer view, is production of a *Consumer Reports* style of annual review and analysis of scientific research for the public.

Museums must present current research in ways that differ from, complement, and expand on other information sources. Providing "added value" is especially important in the content realm since the Web offers many sites geared toward translating new scientific developments for general audiences. As described in the following sections, it may be in the area of presenting the process and consequences of research that museums have the greatest potential.

Research Process

The research process can be difficult for museums to document and to present. Formal science communication through peer-reviewed journals sanitizes the underlying research, revealing little of the actual day-to-day process or the personal aspects. Nevertheless, several exhibitions have been developed addressing this focus. *Mysteries of Çatalhöyük* by the Science Museum of Minnesota looks at the social interaction among scientists in which ideas get tested through the informal exchange of information. It is based on a Neolithic archaeological excavation in Turkey, where the dig site veranda became a featured exhibit element (see section 3, page 267, of this volume for pictures and description). In addition, a graphic style adapted from cartoons employed word bubbles to convey the conversation and thoughts of archaeologists and other site staff.[8] Earlier examples are *Inquiry* at Chicago's Museum of Science and Industry (Ucko 1985) and *Investigate!* at Boston's Museum of Science.[9] The greatest challenge here is making the abstract and technical process of scientific research relevant and engaging to visitors through the exhibit format.

Museums can learn a great deal from the media, which are well suited to portray the human side of research. As Nancy Linde (*Nova*; see section 4, page 311, of this volume) pointed out at the PUR conference, science makes wonderful drama, and such stories spell success in the television medium. It is hard to tell research-based stories involving dramatic tension in the nonlinear exhibition format; museums can incorporate media techniques to assist. For example, *Windows on Research: Nanotechnology*, a forthcoming exhibition by the Lawrence Hall of Science at the University of California, Berkeley, will make use of interactive stories and multimedia based on scientist interviews to convey the process carried out by teams of researchers. Connections with media are explored further later in this chapter.

Another very different PUR format involves virtual field trips to the laboratories and sites where scientific research actually takes place. Since 1989, the JASON Project has been connecting museums, schools, and other sites via satellite, telephone, and now Internet to an annual expedition led by researcher Robert Ballard in locations around the globe.[10] Their slogan is "Real Science, Real Time, Real Learning." Only live for two weeks each year, the program can be extended over the school year through accompanying classroom curricula. In contrast, the Liberty Science Center stages daily visits to a working surgical suite with *Live from . . . Cardiac Classroom*, in which groups of students communicate with medical staff via two-way videoconferencing.[11] According to director of educational technologies Tim McElroy, taking students into medical and research settings works best as a 1.5- to 3-hour dedicated experience rather than as a brief drop-in component within a larger exhibition.

The Exploratorium in San Francisco has created a program based on scientific research settings worldwide, including Antarctica, Belize, and Geneva (CERN) as well as remote eclipse-viewing sites, which are difficult for the public to access directly. *Live@Exploratorium* offers webcasts mediated by

Live from . . . Cardiac Classroom *(Liberty Science Center, New Jersey). Through two-way videoconferencing, students can interact with medical staff or researchers in action.* Courtesy of Liberty Science Center

studio audiences on the museum floor.[12] The science center serves as an intermediary and interpreter in providing linked visitor and Web experiences. Executive associate director Rob Semper indicated at the conference that the key issue yet to be addressed for this Web-based program, as with many others, is financial self-sustainability. A less costly approach has been taken by Science Center Torino through its *LAB-VR, Virtual Access to Research Labs*, where viewers can "tour" over 30 research labs in Turin, Italy.[13] The lack of any human presence, however, makes this type of online visit less compelling.

Perhaps the most effective way for the public to understand the process of scientific research is to engage in aspects of it themselves. That is the principle behind science fairs (assuming the student, not the parent or adviser, does the work!) and inquiry-based science learning (National Research Council 2000). Inquiry-oriented activities involve visitors in the scientific process through asking questions about aspects of the world around them, planning and conducting simple investigations, using data to construct reasonable explanations, and communicating results. One museum example was Living Labs, a 45-minute research experience for visitors at the Hall of Exploration at the Columbus Center, a research facility of the University of Maryland Center of Marine Biotechnology. Led by graduate student BioGuides, groups of visitors screened actual marine chemicals for their ability to emulsify oil, an activity relevant to the adjacent Chesapeake Bay. Although well received, this program could not sustain sufficient public interest in visiting this working research lab; the science center portion closed after only five months. Former codirector Carol Bossert observed at the PUR conference that tours had not turned out to be practical for providing behind-the-scenes experiences to visitors. This unfortunate outcome supports the case for visitor involvement with research rather than simple observation of others.

Natural history and other museums that carry out their own scientific activities have an advantage in finding ways to involve the public in research programs. Such institutions may offer visitors, students, and volunteers the opportunity to serve as "research assistants" at the museum or through field trips to research sites. Other museums will need to identify area research scientists with whom they can create programs relevant to local interests, such as water quality. Such programs can both provide the means to involve visitors in carrying out meaningful research functions as well as strengthen the museum's civic engagement, supporting a recent call to action by the American Association of Museums (2002).

Involving the community at large in research is the basis for "citizen-science" programs, such as the Colorado Spider Survey of the Denver Museum of Nature and Science.[14] It encourages residents across the state to collect, identify, and systematically report the spiders they find in diverse ecological niches. Or, as an alternative to creating their own programs, museums can consider working with national efforts, such as Project Feeder-Watch of the Cornell Laboratory of Ornithology (see section 3, chapter 12, page 199).[15] Here students collect information about birds and their environments following specific protocols; the data get sent via the Internet to Cornell, where scientists use it to assess changes in bird population distributions and the spread of infectious diseases. Director of education Rick Bonney noted at the conference that their programs have engaged over 100,000 citizens in research on biology, ecology, and animal behavior.

Hands-on research programs, whether organized by museums or other organizations, can help make scientific research relevant to people's lives. They fit extremely well with science center expertise in creating and marketing hands-on activities in general. Successful implementation requires identifying engaging tasks that the public can carry out with limited time and training. Most museums will also need to find appropriate scientific partners for helping guide the research and evaluate the data. These types of programs will have the greatest value when participants can actually contribute in a small way to meaningful research.

Colorado Spider Survey (Denver Museum of Nature and Science). "Citizen science" programs like this one provide the public opportunities to carry out "hands-on research activities. All rights reserved." Courtesy of Image Archives, Denver Museum of Nature and Science

Research Implications

The newest and most challenging role is for museums to serve as places for discussion and debate on the complex issues derived from current research. The critical nature of this task was underlined by Cornelia Dean (*New York Times*): "Today, more and more of the day's political issues involve scientific questions [such as] stem cells, antimissile defense, nuclear waste disposal, and other topics. So, as our job gets more difficult, it gets more important" (see section 4, page 306, of this volume).

For many years, museums have offered talks in which scientists describe their research and its implications. Such presentations, whose impact is highly dependent on the researcher's ability to translate his or her work and its consequences for the public, can now reach much larger audiences at low cost through webcasting. Presentations also may include various degrees of visitor involvement. For example, partnering with Adrian Ivinson from the Harvard Center for Neurodegeneration and Repair, Carol Lynn Alpert at Boston's Current Science & Technology Center created a program on xenotransplantation (moving cells, tissues, or organs across species) based on a dialogue between two speakers, one representing expert opinion and the other acting as devil's advocate. The audience was asked to vote on key issues both before and after the presentation of scientific, medical, and ethical arguments. Ivinson noted at the conference that the topics that work best are those that audiences can identify as relevant to their own lives or communities and those that include significant drama, excitement, controversy, or "yuck factor." He cautioned, however, that this format might not be suitable for all audiences because they must be willing to both think and listen.

Theater provides an excellent format for dealing with the implications of scientific research. The recent popularity of Michael Frayn's play *Copenhagen*, which deals with a World War II meeting between physicists Niels Bohr and Werner Heisenberg, is encouraging. It demonstrates a significant willingness by the theatergoing public to attend dramatic productions based on scientific topics and their consequences. Targeting a younger audience, the Wellcome Trust (United Kingdom) has funded performing arts and interactive children's theater, including a National Festival of Science Drama for secondary schools, to stimulate debate on issues raised by advances in biomedical research.[16] For museums to incorporate theater programs requires skilled actors on staff or contracts to perform on a stage or the exhibit floor. Finding or creating well-written scripts that engage audiences in technical subjects is no easy undertaking, however. Neither is producing these performances on a limited budget. The International Museum Theatre Alliance provides an entry point for exploring this form of emotionally engaging programming.[17]

European science museums have gone farthest in establishing themselves as centers for empowering citizens on issues arising from current research by means of forums, debates, and conferences. François Vescia (La Cité des Sciences et de l'Industrie, Paris) explained at the conference that since science and the public have both changed, the role of mediators, such as museums, must change as well. La Cité has responded by creating Le College, a program of regular debates, conferences on science and society issues, and participative conferences with an emphasis on life sciences, information technology, and the environment.[18] In a similar vein, the Deutsches Hygiene-Museum in Dresden, Germany, organized a nationwide "Citizens' Conference on Genetic Testing."[19] This forum involved 19 citizens randomly selected from a pool of 10,000 who met with scientific experts, formulated recommendations, and discussed them with decision makers.

The Café Scientifique is a more informal format that takes place in bars and restaurants as well as cafés, primarily in the United Kingdom and France.[20] For the price of a cup of coffee or a glass of wine, anyone can join a scientific expert in exploring the latest ideas in science or technology. The goal of these gatherings is to make science accessible and promote public engagement through an appealing forum for debating scientific issues. Whether it occurs in a museum or more casual setting, this aspect of fostering PUR offers an opportunity for many institutions to extend their audiences beyond children and youth to adults.

Compared to several of their overseas counterparts, U.S. museums have limited experience in dealing with controversy, and most have deliberately chosen to stay away from doing so. Yet, much of current research deals with "hot" topics that stimulate debate. They may raise moral issues, particularly among the 59 percent of those in the United States for whom religion "plays a *very* important role" in their lives (Pew Global Attitudes Project 2002). These strong feelings became evident while conducting a front-end study for a new National Academy of Sciences museum being planned to address controversial current issues. A significant number of respondents strongly opposed topics that others had ranked high because they suspected the museum would

present a point of view different from their own. Such topics need to be portrayed in ways that help audiences view science as a necessary but not sufficient tool for guiding personal decisions and national policy; many other
factors typically must be considered as well.

Formats based on the implications of research, such as those described,
provide another way for museums to increase their community involvement,
particularly if they focus on local science- and technology-based concerns.
Raising an institutional public profile in this way entails some risk, but serving as a neutral public forum for engaging and informing citizens on critical
regional issues can only increase the value and importance of museums. In
this way, they can become much more than places to visit occasionally for an
enjoyable educational experience. Museums can transform themselves into
community centers in the truest sense.

In summary, the following list identifies the strengths and challenges associated with each of the main PUR production formats:

Research Content
Exhibitions represent the primary museum medium and strong suit.
- But they require frequent updating that may be staff intensive.
- Digital media and modularity can reduce time and cost.
Examples: ScienceNOW, *Science Bulletins* (kiosk), SpaceLink, Antenna,
Current Science & Technology Center (large)

Programs provide the most flexible format and are relatively inexpensive.
- But they require skilled presenters who may be hard to find and train.
Examples: FAST, Curiosity Counters

Research Process
Exhibitions (see "Research Content")
- But the process may be difficult to portray effectively.
- Using storytelling techniques and media may help.
Examples: *Çatalhöyük, Inquiry, Investigate!*

Virtual field trips make distant research settings accessible.
- But access and interaction may be limited.
- Using live staff to mediate increases impact.
Examples: JASON Project, *Cardiac Classroom, Live@Exploratorium*

Hands-on research engages visitors in inquiry-based learning.
- But finding meaningful activities and partners may be challenging.

Examples: Citizen science (Colorado Spider Survey, Cornell Ornithology programs)

Research Implications
Programs (see "Research Content")

Theater offers an effective format for raising issues.
- But integrating quality art and science is difficult.

Examples: Copenhagen, Wellcome Trust

Forums, debates, and conferences provide important community forums.
- But dealing with charged, controversial topics is challenging.
- United States museums can learn from their European colleagues in this area.

Examples: La Cité College, citizen's conferences, Café Scientifique

Overall, in selecting formats for addressing PUR, museums should assess what their strengths are, where their impact can be greatest, and how their efforts can best complement those of others. Based on these criteria, two directions appear most fruitful. By engaging the public in meaningful hands-on research activities, museums can build on their expertise in hands-on learning and make effective use of inquiry-based learning techniques. By providing forums for discussing research implications, they can build on the community respect their institutions hold and further civic engagement. Both these roles fill important niches not generally filled by other organizations and supplement the PUR programs available through news media, television documentaries, and the Internet.

Of course, such efforts do not occur in isolation. Museum planners would do best by connecting and integrating diverse PUR experiences throughout their facilities. Exhibitions and other types of programs can effectively complement hands-on research and community forums. All these activities can be enhanced through partnering with scientists and the media as described in the following section.

ROLE OF SCIENTISTS AND MEDIA IN PRODUCTION

In addition to the general concerns for staffing and funding, development and implementation of PUR exhibitions and programs, as just noted, carry additional requirements of timeliness and the communication of complex, changing content and issues. By working closely with scientists and the media, museums can find ways to mitigate these complicating factors.

The characteristics of PUR efforts make them nearly impossible to create and deliver without collaboration. Scientists, who conduct the research and produce the ongoing results, are obviously essential as sources for content and process. They are also needed to provide different points of view on research findings, especially since the tentative results have not yet withstood the test of time, nor have the researchers necessarily yet become established.

The media also bring valuable resources that support museum-based PUR efforts. Science news organizations follow the hot areas of research. They offer the potential to access human-interest stories and interviews as well as images, video, and computer graphics having high production value. Partnering with news sources may eliminate or reduce the need to create a separate museum news bureau, an investment few museums should consider. The media offer multiple channels that can complement, reinforce, and potentially cross-promote museum PUR programs. Museum forums and debates, particularly those that focus on community issues, lend themselves to media coverage and partnership.

Most conference participants would agree that the meeting in St. Paul was a step toward breaking down barriers among museums, researchers, and media, but that further efforts are much needed. Mark Shelley (Sea Studios) noted that many of us seem to still be living on "different planets." What is needed is a common mutual understanding of how each field can benefit the others, demonstrating value that aligns with mutual self-interest. As noted by Tobias Wolff, exhibition manager for the Universum Science Center in Bremen, Germany, which is adding a current-science issue area to its new Visionarum wing, the museum, media, and university scientists each can benefit in the following ways:[21]

Benefits for Visionarum: Current science news; newspaper articles, pictures; film material from science programs.

Benefits for media: Forum in a science leisure facility, "playground" for material evaluation, scientist network.

Benefits for scientists and universities: Public understanding of science, presence in the media, reputation.

Further potential benefits provided by museums to the media include added opportunities for dissemination; a setting for focus groups, screenings, and other means for obtaining public input; a venue for events with an opportunity to greet audiences and supporters in person; a source for on-air, issues-based programming; and complementary public programs with local connections that enrich and cross-promote media offerings.

Additional potential benefits to scientists include a vehicle to help recruit undergraduate and graduate students, a source for volunteer research assistants and data through citizen science, the means to satisfy grant requirements for education and public outreach, and further ways to become involved with their communities.

Scientists

Some museums, especially some natural history museums, have an easier time involving scientists in production because they are on staff. In several, staff hold joint appointments as research faculty (such as the Adler Planetarium, where four astronomers are affiliated with the University of Chicago and two with Northwestern University) and, thus, can facilitate contact with other faculty. The small numbers of university-affiliated museums, such as the MIT Museum, obviously have ready access to campus researchers, although only a fraction will be willing and able to become involved. Most museums, however, must seek out and recruit partners from university, corporate, and government research institutions in their communities.

But who should be recruited? If the scientist is to be a content source, this question gets answered on the basis of the importance of her work, potential audience interest in the topic, and a willingness to participate. If the scientist is to play a more visible role, other requirements become paramount. Scientific expertise may not translate into communication skills to lay audiences without training—or at all. Unfortunately, there are few formal programs, such as the Aldo Leopold Leadership Program, for environmental scientists who want to be more effective communicators. Some conference participants made the case for working with mature scientists, who may face less pressure to publish. Others argued for graduate students, who are closer in age to younger audiences and who would benefit by learning early in their careers the value of science communication. The answer ultimately depends on the researcher's priorities and commitments, as well as background, skills, training, and personality.

How to find scientists? The paths from museum to researcher and from researcher to museum are not well defined. The conference revealed the value to museums of university public information officers or press officers, who can serve as guides to university scientists on campus. Aligning that field's Science Communicators conference to coincide with the annual Association of Science-Technology Centers (ASTC) conference was suggested. Some universities, often those with extension services, have excellent science outreach programs already. The University of Wisconsin's Why Files is an outstanding Web-based example.[22] Among the lessons its editor Terry Devitt shared in St. Paul were to 1) pick a niche, 2) keep looking for the edge, 3) take risks, and 4) humor is power. Another route to scientists can be through the local chapters of Sigma Xi, the honorary research society.[23] Although corporations may first come to mind as donors and sponsors, they can also be sources for cutting-edge research scientists as in the biotech and information technology industries; in fact, relationships with research staff are likely to improve long-term funding prospects. Connections can and should also be made at an institutional level nationally, such as by linking content-rich organizations like the National Academies with audience-rich museums (Ucko 2001). One such effort, being led by the emerging National Health Museum in Washington, D.C., is the creation of the National Public Health Partnership,[24] whose goal is to link the resources of the public health community with museums and science centers.

A less obvious possible source of scientists for museums might be the Society for Amateur Scientists, which promotes citizen-science activities.[25] Another nontraditional channel is offered by the new generation of "science shops," more common in Europe, where they are linked to universities.[26] In contrast with academic or corporate research centers, science shops assist or carry out socially oriented, community-based research projects in such fields as environmental issues, energy conservation, and public health. In the United States, the Loka Institute, a nonprofit research and advocacy organization concerned with the social, political, and environmental repercussions of research, science, and technology, has identified approximately 50 community research centers.[27] The potential for this type of partnership will depend on the willingness of a museum to engage in advocacy along with education.

One of the challenges of working with scientists and other content experts raised at the conference by Bronwyn Terrill (Dolan DNA Learning Center, Cold Spring Harbor, New York) is that stakeholders may grossly overestimate the amount of information that an exhibition can actually convey. Thus, establishing realistic expectations up front is critical. Because researchers may not make the best presenters, many museums have instead used staff, actors, and others in that role, choosing to train them in science. Each application must determine whether actual scientific research experience or presentation ability is most critical for a particular program since the combination is uncommon. Finally, nonscientist experts may be essential, especially for programs based on the implications of research, where humanists, social scientists, and clergy become valuable participants.

Media

Despite their differences, print, television, radio, and Internet media share common production characteristics. For most, the time frame is far more rapid than museums. Media channels are proprietary and competitive, seeking to "scoop" their rivals on breaking developments. As emphasized at the conference by Cornelia Dean (*New York Times*), the focus for news media is clearly information, not education. For most publications, "entertainment" value is also a vital factor.

These features complement museum PUR efforts and, as noted, provide resources that can enhance production and reduce cost. But for museums to take advantage of media products, they first need to better understand the media field and potential barriers to working together. As explained to PUR conference participants by Eliene Augenbraun (ScienCentral), corporate and legal issues relating to fees, internal approvals, liability protection, branding, and intellectual property rights can stand in the way of sharing materials and require considerable persistence to overcome. These issues should be addressed early in development of media projects to allow appropriate permissions to be obtained or perhaps even produce museum-based versions at the same time to lessen expenses. Walter Sucher of Germany's SWR public television also pointed out that exploratory discussion between potential partners over "versioning" could ultimately lead to fruitful collaboration.

Some types of media-related museum activities offer fewer constraints, such as building on existing national shows, such as *Nova*, using local researchers to answer questions from the most recent program, to give related demonstrations, to discuss issues raised, and so on. In fact, local PBS stations may be willing to cross-promote these kinds of mutually beneficial educational programs.

In addition to gaining access to science news and research-based resources, museums can learn from media experience. Incorporating an emotional component (a media strength) into museum exhibitions and programs would enhance their impact. The three critical elements, as noted at the conference by *Nova*'s Nancy Linde, are "story, story and story." Although museum visitors do not have a remote control allowing them to instantaneously flip channels as attention wanes, they are certainly free to walk away from less-than-engaging exhibits or activities. Adding the emotional "hook" advocated by Linde reduces that risk.

Museums can also learn from media audience research, marketing studies, and program evaluation. For example, based on a survey of listeners to the 90-second *Earth and Sky* radio segments, Marc Airhart recommended 1) focusing on people and process rather than simply results, 2) explaining the relevance of new scientific findings, and 3) presenting themes rather than simply news. Although not earthshaking, these findings support the knowledge museums have about their audiences from other sources.

Collaboration, termed an "unnatural act" by some, requires overcoming multiple barriers, whether based on working with scientists, media, or other museums. As noted by conference-goer Christine Roman, whose St. Louis Science Center participated in the Mississippi RiverWeb Museum Consortium (along with the University of Illinois National Center for Supercomputing Applications, the Illinois State Museum, and the Science Museum of Minnesota), concerns included a long learning curve (everyone had to become a learner in new areas), cultural differences, the difficulty in creating common understandings of design and production process, and decision-making issues. Had a media partner been included, additional issues undoubtedly would have been raised as well. Training in how to build a collaboration based on best practices would likely have helped.

The ideal relationships with scientists and media are ongoing, institutional, and long term rather than project based. Such interactions naturally take time to develop and nurture. One participant noted that continuity is essential because it takes time to understand audience needs, establish connections, build trust, and just make things happen.

REGIONAL AND NATIONAL PRODUCTION STRATEGIES

In addition to one-on-one partnering, regional and national interactions could significantly enhance PUR production efforts. For example, Susan Norton (Science Channel, *Discovery*) suggested to conference participants that museums could host monthly or quarterly meetings in their communities involving researchers and media representatives, creating forums and networks for sharing information and resources. Regional directories would be beneficial as well.

PUR consortia, like exhibition consortia, could enable participating institutions and organizations to each develop resources for sharing with other members, leveraging individual efforts. Products might include programs, scripts, or changeable exhibit modules, with an opportunity for customizing by each institution. One suggestion was for ten museums to develop and share materials on ten different topics to support presentations by local experts. Agreement on common frameworks and standards would facilitate such exchanges. A series of PUR kits based on a template might even be feasible; kits could include objects, digital media, scripts, contacts for scientists, and promotional materials.

Finding ways to help small museums address PUR is a major need. One idea is that large museums could produce products for dissemination to smaller institutions where they can be tailored to their needs. The creation of national PUR centers with specialties in particular areas, like National Science Foundation–funded scientific research centers, would be another approach for producing materials for wide dissemination.

Another good idea is the formation of "intellectual alliances," suggested to the conference by Rob Semper, which would increase communication and interaction across professions. Such alliances could be furthered through such mechanisms as the following:

- A Web site for posting information, articles, and projects
- Electronic mailing lists and cross-registration on existing lists
- Internet newsgroups

- Printed publications and cross-disciplinary articles in existing ones, such as regular columns in *ASTC Dimensions, Science,* and media publications
- A regular national conference and PUR threads in existing museum, scientific, and media conferences (including the World Congress of Science Producers)
- A national PUR organization and special-interest groups within existing ones, such as the American Association for the Advancement of Science, whose annual conference already includes both scientist and media participation

Through these and other means, each profession could exchange information with those interested in PUR, facilitating resource sharing and collaboration. Another way to encourage cross-fertilization would be through internships or fellowships in which museum staff devote a period of time to working in a research or media setting. Professional development programs could serve a similar function of breaking down barriers. Sharing best practices both within and across fields would also be valuable.

Museums would clearly benefit from the creation of some form of national PUR clearinghouse to enable sharing a wide range of information and resources, such as the following:

- Contacts and interested organizations
- Content, background research, and interviews
- Graphics, photographs, and other images
- Computer animations and simulations
- Audience research and evaluation data
- Audio and video clips
- Exhibition and program information and demonstrations
- Educational curricula

Such a clearinghouse, say in the form of a searchable database or archive, could reduce duplication of efforts, production time, and costs even if only a portion of this "shopping list" were implemented. Its creation raises many questions yet to be answered, however: Who would run it? How would it be funded? How could we deal with competition and intellectual property rights? How does it ensure accuracy and quality? Suggested homes for such an enterprise include the National Science Foundation, the National Institutes of Health, the Association of Science-Technology Centers, or a new organization similar to a news-wire service, ideally international in scope. A peer-to-peer computer file-sharing system, such as Napster or Kazaa, was also proposed as an alternative that would eliminate the need for maintaining a central database.

"Matchmaking" is a related valuable function. It could occur passively, as in the giant-screen film industry, where the status of various projects get regularly communicated, indicating where they are in the production pipeline. Museums, media, and researchers interested in participating in a PUR project could then choose to make contact. More active models are ProfNet (Professors Network),[28] which links reporters with expert sources through university public relations and information officers, and the Sigma Xi Media Resource Service.[29] This kind of approach could be broadened to connect researchers, museums, media, and funders interested in PUR topics or projects. For example, it might match scientists who have education and outreach funds available with potential museum partners.

Involving others in addition to museums, scientists, and media would further enhance the impact of PUR programs. As previously noted, collaboration can be difficult but rewarding. Educators at different levels are essential in creating curricula that relate museum and media PUR programs to classroom activities. Libraries could support local or national themes through complementary programs. Although more limited in number, science writers and their national associations are another possible resource.

In conclusion, this overview has presented a range of measures and strategies for producing exhibitions and programs designed to foster PUR. The following is a summary of key museum recommendations:

- Identify the most appropriate mix of the components of "research literacy" (content, process, implications) based on audience, project, and institutional needs
- Employ digital media, templates, and modularity to facilitate updating and sharing content communicating new research developments
- Present hands-on research through such programs as citizen science to engage the public in meaningful research experiences

- Consider creating forums for discussing the issues raised by current science and technology as a means for civic engagement
- Explore recruiting researchers through diverse channels, including university public information officers and community research centers
- Nurture long-term media partnerships to create synergies, as well as to obtain resources for enhancing production and reducing cost
- Form or join a regional consortium to share material development and production
- Establish connections and communications that break down barriers between organizations and institutions involving scientists, media, educators, and others involved in PUR activities
- Support efforts to create a national clearinghouse and related mechanisms for sharing and disseminating information and resources

Identifying production strategies such as these is just the beginning. Which ones individual institutions and national organizations choose to pursue and ultimately how their audiences respond to those efforts will determine the success of the emerging PUR endeavor.

NOTES

1. www.calacademy.org/science_now (accessed April 3, 2003).

2. www.sciencebulletins.amnh.org (accessed April 3, 2003).

3. http://web.mit.edu/museum/programs/fast-sunday.html (accessed April 3, 2003).

4. www.thetech.org/exhibits/Co_cam.html# (accessed April 3, 2003).

5. www.mdsci.org/exhibits/spacelink/index.cfm (accessed April 3, 2003).

6. www.sciencemuseum.org.uk/wellcome-wing/antenna/index.asp (accessed April 3, 2003).

7. www.mos.org/cst (accessed April 3, 2003).

8. http://catal.arch.cam.ac.uk/catal/smm2001 (accessed April 3, 2003).

9. www.mos.org/exhibits/current_exhibits/investigate.html (accessed April 3, 2003).

10. www.jason.org (accessed April 3, 2003).

11. lsc.org/cardiac/cardiac.html (accessed April 3, 2003).

12. www.exploratorium.org/webcasts/archive.html (accessed April 3, 2003).

13. www.torinoscienza.it/lab-vr (accessed April 3, 2003).

14. www.dmns.org/spiders (accessed April 3, 2003).

15. www.birds.cornell.edu/whatwedo_citizenscience.html (accessed April 3, 2003).

16. www.wellcome.ac.uk/en/scs/activities.html (accessed April 3, 2003).

17. www.mos.org/learn_more/imtal.html (accessed April 3, 2003).

18. www.cite-sciences.fr/francais/ala_cite/college (accessed April 3, 2003).

19. www.buergerkonferenz.de/pages/start_en2.htm.

20. www.cafesci.org (accessed April 3, 2003).

21. www.smm.org/pur/documents/digital_posters/Universum.doc (accessed April 3, 2003).

22. www.whyfiles.org (accessed April 3, 2003).

23. www.sigmaxi.org/chapters/lists/index.shtml (accessed April 3, 2003).

24. www.nationalhealthmuseum.org/initiatives/nphp (accessed April 3, 2003).

25. www.sas.org (accessed April 3, 2003).

26. www.bio.uu.nl/living-knowledge (accessed April 3, 2003).

27. www.loka.org/crn/cbr.htm (accessed April 3, 2003).

28. www2.profnet.com (accessed April 3, 2003).

29. www.mediaresource.org/index.shtml (accessed April 3, 2003).

REFERENCES

American Association of Museums. 2002. *Mastering civic engagement: A challenge to museums.* Washington, D.C.: American Association of Museums.

Bossert, Carol, and David Ucko. 2002. Public Understanding of Research Meeting held in St. Paul. *Informal Learning Review* 57: 22.

National Research Council. 2000. *Inquiry and the National Science Education Standards: A guide for teaching and learning.* Washington, D.C.: National Academy Press (available at www.nap.edu/catalog/9596.html).

Pew Global Attitudes Project. 2002. *United States stands alone in its embrace of religion.* Washington, D.C.: Pew Research Center.

Ucko, David A. 1985. Science literacy and science museum exhibits. *Curator* 28, no. 4: 287.

———. 2001. Science centers and the national academies. *ASTC Dimensions,* September/October, 10.

14

Bridging the Gap: Interpreting Current Research in Museum Settings

Carol Lynn Alpert

It was a bright, cold Saturday morning, and something had gone terribly wrong. The transmission from NASA grew eerily quiet on the large plasma screens in the Current Science & Technology Center (CS&T) at the Museum of Science in Boston as weekend crowds began to flow in. Tania Ruiz had driven down from her home in New Hampshire early that morning in preparation for a big day: after 16 days in low earth orbit, the space shuttle *Columbia* was landing, bringing home its diverse crew and the results of more than 80 science experiments. During the previous month, Tania had devoted considerable effort into reporting on this mission: delivering presentations, creating multimedia, and posting Web stories.

As the devastating truth began to seep in, her voice sometimes quavering, Tania continued doing her job, interpreting earth and space science for the public. We switched the big screens over to CNN and back to NASA as warranted, and over the next seven hours, backed by weekend staff, Tania explained, interpreted the data, offered background, and took questions from the hundreds of Museum visitors who streamed through the Blue Wing as, slowly, NASA pieced together the time line of the disaster. The news media arrived. That evening, Tania was seen on television by thousands, explaining what the shuttle mission had been all about and who and what had been lost.

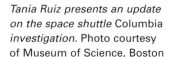

Tania Ruiz presents an update on the space shuttle Columbia *investigation.* Photo courtesy of Museum of Science, Boston

Over the next several days, visitors flocked into CS&T for Tania's multimedia presentations and updates on the progress of the investigation. The exhibits team helped us move the Museum's large shuttle scale models to the CS&T stage, and we put flowers by them, a portrait of the seven lost crew members, and postings of the latest news on the investigation. News media found the models a focal point for their reporter stand-ups. Tania used them to help interpret the latest findings, as new data and analysis accumulated over the next several weeks. The presentation got so big at one point that it lasted nearly an hour, and still our weekend audiences flocked to it and stayed riveted even weeks after the accident, probably learning more about manned space science in one hour than they had absorbed the entire decade preceding, demonstrating once again how a tragic event can stimulate attention and learning. Our producers quickly got an edited version of the presentation up on our Web site. Tania kept her presentation, touchscreen, and Web stories updated throughout the course of the investigation, conveying to all her audiences the process by which conjecture gives way slowly to rigorous, evidence-based analysis.

The morning of February 2, 2003, reminded me of nothing more than the morning of September 11, 2001. That day, a Tuesday, the Museum was nearly empty, but we pulled CNN up on the big plasmas, and Museum staff were thankful to have some place to be together as a community and witness the tragedy. In the next weeks, we chose not to deliver interpretation on the science and technology aspects of September 11—why the steel structure had failed, how the radio frequencies had clashed, or how a jet loaded with fuel for a transcontinental flight made an effective guided missile. Those topics seemed too insensitive to the immensity of the loss.

When the anthrax letter attacks began, however, CS&T's Health Science Program manager, Meena Selvakumar, stepped up to the plate with a series of penetrating presentations on anthrax and its biology and morphology. Meena invited guest speakers in to address public concern: Dr. Ralph Timperi, the state's lab director, came in, and CS&T intern and Harvard Medical School student Liz Hick quickly addressed the threatened run on antibiotics with a presentation and media on the scourge of antibiotic resistance. Soon our attention turned to advanced research on anthrax: the youthful Dr. Michael Mourez, also of Harvard, arrived with a portfolio of stunning electron micrographs. He described to our audiences how the anthrax bacillus produces three perfectly engineered toxins that act as a precision tool kit to enter human cells. CS&T staff continued to leverage public concern with terrorism to refocus our audiences

Meena Selvakumar reports on the etiology of anthrax just after the letter attacks began. Photo courtesy of Museum of Science, Boston

on the logic of epidemiology and public health as well as on the intricate science of microbiology. This line of programming continued to evolve: later we focused on the science and epidemiology of smallpox, and that soon morphed into a discussion of the risks that health care workers would need to weigh as they pondered the government's call to volunteer themselves for vaccination.

Every week now, it seems, the public faces strange new risks, requiring us to digest and weigh current research findings in making everyday choices. To vaccinate or not to vaccinate? To fly or to drive? To take hormones or not to take hormones? To eat beef? Such judgments require more than facts alone: they require some measure of understanding of the process of research, its benefits as well as its limitations, and its role in risk assessment.

In the past two years, CS&T staff have addressed nearly every headline science and technology news issue that has come down the pike: severe acute respiratory syndrome (SARS), stem-cell and cloning research, mammography and hormone replacement therapy, global climate change and energy policy, Internet security, West Nile virus, mad cow disease, foot and mouth disease, genetically modified organisms, antibiotic resistance, bubble fusion, evidence of water on Mars, hominid skull found in Central Africa, black holes, mechanical heart trials, and so forth. The endless flood of new research findings and current events and controversies continuously spark the public imagination and send the news media conjecturing.

In order to take on topics that are controversial and in the news, CS&T staff have had to transform themselves into a new kind of hybrid: scientist–educator–performance artist–journalist–multimedia producer–forum facilitator. Staff had to learn to report, motivate, foster discussion, and provide frameworks for understanding debates on controversial and highly sensitive topics, all without projecting a personal point of view. On the other hand, the very fact that these issues have caught the public's attention, primed their interest, and got them asking questions means that the frontline battle of science educators—getting an attentive audience—has already been won. That in itself would be sufficient reason for covering current science in science centers, but it wasn't the only one, nor indeed the primary one, that helped get the new movement energized.

TACKLING CURRENT SCIENCE IN MUSEUMS

Typically, schools and science centers have shied away from controversial topics. Science education is tough enough; no need to stir up conflict or, worse, the terrible uncertainty that is characteristic of science on the leading edge. Older, already accepted science is much easier to deal with anyway, particularly in museums. The exhibit development process itself is costly and time consuming: from conception, fund-raising, research, design, exhibit prototyping, formative evaluation, redesign, and remedial evaluation to fabrication, installation, and summative evaluation—three to five years is about standard. Given that production cycle, you wouldn't want to take huge risks with newly published research that might be proved wrong in a year or two. Just reprinting and remounting exhibit label copy can be an expensive and time-consuming ordeal, involving research, testing, rights, and permissions.

To some extent, the whole thorny issue of currency and relevancy was neatly trumped by the kind of hands-on, inquiry-based interactive exhibits that have became so popular in science centers over the past few decades. These exhibits concentrate on basic classical principles of scientific practice— observation, experimentation, classification, and so forth through hands-on experiential activities. Specific science content was not necessarily the primary concern. Museums morphed from somewhat somber showcases of objects, notable either for their sheer normality or for their singular oddity, to fun-filled family playgrounds brimming with buttons to press, levers to pull, and wheels to spin. The transformation coincided and, perhaps, fostered an enormous growth spurt in the science center industry. Membership in ASTC, the industry's professional association, grew from less than 50 in the United States and Canada in 1973 to 445 throughout 42 countries in 2002. However, as the Exploratorium's Rob Semper points out, science museums still offer a much better demonstration of the maxims of nineteenth-century science than of the branching inquiries of current research (Semper 2001).

This gap grew more poignant as the pace of research and its application by industry began to accelerate and even to dominate public sensibility in the boom times of the 1980s and 1990s, aided by large infusions of public and private investment. Info-, bio-, and agrotechnology; the Internet; and major advances in genetics, medicine, space science, remote sensing, computing power, and micro- and nanoscale physics and materials science—all sorts of scientific and technological advances permeated the culture and made it to the headlines of the national and business pages, to lifestyle sections, and even to some extent to the arts. However, these advances were less likely to be represented in most science centers, which had made huge investments 5, 10, or even 20 years earlier in permanent exhibits and child-friendly interactives.

The pace of research is certainly outstripping the public's ability to assimilate it—especially now that so much research occurs in realms almost completely inaccessible to human perception, as in the nanorealm, or indirectly deduced through computing and statistics. The pace is also outstripping the capacity of democratic societies to process, debate, formulate policy, and legislate all the boundary-pushing implications of new research. Hence, there is demand not only for a continuing supply of new researchers, but also for continuing adult education and literacy in these rapidly evolving worlds. As Hyman Field of the National Science Foundation (NSF) has noted, the science center industry and the media are, perhaps, best suited to shoulder the task and might even be more effective if they could find new ways to collaborate (Field and Powell 2001).

THE MUSEUM OF SCIENCE CASE

The Museum of Science had wrestled with the challenge of currency for years before I arrived at its door, including an earlier shuttle disaster, a first mammal cloned, a mysterious disease outbreak, and a deadly earthquake. People would stream into the Museum looking for insight on stories being featured in the news and find the usual: permanent exhibits, hands-on experiences in basic science, large-format films, and planetarium shows on the slowly revolving panorama of the skies. Museum directors would ask their vice presidents, "We're getting inquiries, what are we doing about [fill in here any current sci-tech topic in the news]." And museum exhibits and education department heads would consider their options, factor the time and expense, check the day's school bookings and the week's exhibit installation deadlines, and shrug their shoulders, often with deep regret. With regard to the typical exhibit planning cycle, current science means within the past five years, and museum educators are science teachers, not science journalists.

Recognizing a deep-seated need for change and with an eye to developing an experimental model for future Museum development, Museum of Science Director David Ellis, Vice President for Exhibits Larry Bell, Vice President for Programs Cary Sneider, and a group of dedicated overseers and trustees began meeting to formulate a plan. There were few models to go by. The trustees, with experience in media and broadcast, recognized that whatever was to be created had to call into play some of the characteristics of that world—a focus on news, agility, digital video, and commentary. They drew up a plan that called for a current science and technology center, a place that would be devoted to science in the headlines, science behind the headlines, and, if we really cared to go out on a limb, science in the headlines of science journals. The team hired me to lead the effort. The fact that I had a practical background in current science and technology documentary production and an academic background in history and science was helpful.

Shortly after I came aboard, Larry Bell and I toured examples of some of the relevant current practices we could find among our science center brethren: our tour took us to the stunning new Earth Hall at the American Museum of Natural History, where Smokey Forester showed us his HDTV Science Bulletins efforts and, of greater interest to us, an updateable multimedia management and display system; then on to SpaceLink at the Maryland Science Center, where Flavio Mendez emceed a room buzzing with live NASA-TV and computer simulations; to the Monterrey Bay Aquarium, where staff mediated live conversations between visitors and researchers offshore; to the webcast studio at the Exploratorium, where Rob Semper treated us to front-row seats at the Iron Science Teacher Competition webcast; and finally to the massive blue-walled shell of the new Wellcome Wing of the Science Museum of London, where we donned hardhats and followed Graham Farmelo and Janet Carding through a cold and dusty tour of the future Antenna science news exhibit area, then under urgent construction, as the Queen would officially open the new wing in four months.

On our return, in February 2000, Larry Bell and I, with Exhibit Director Larry Ralph, had a month to put together a request for proposal (RFP) in order to meet Museum Director David Ellis's strict deadline for a late September opening, timed to coincide with the Museum's annual meeting. We drew on ideas from the best of what we had seen and added ideas of our own—particularly those emerging out of our Museum's already impressive live presentation culture and those I had brought from my experience in broadcast television and desktop media technologies.

The guiding principal for the design of the CS&T was to provide an infrastructure and tools to facilitate continuous content production and delivery. We were adamantly opposed to making an exhibit about the current or future state of any particular science or technology; instead, we were making a process and a place. As Larry Bell put it in our short video about the project,[1] we weren't going to repeat the mistake others had made, investing significant capital in an exhibit about the future, which would quickly become the past and probably the wrong past.

The Museum gave us a central but very exposed location in which to work: an open atrium-style area in the Blue Wing, taller than its 1,500-square foot-print and bounded on all sides by exhibit halls, escalators, and balconies.

Dr. Jim Morris briefs a CS&T audience on the Human Genome Project. Photo courtesy of Museum of Science, Boston

This space would need to accommodate a presentation stage, audience seating, large display screens, and an exhibit area that would feature rapidly changing displays focused primarily on new technologies. We wanted a full range of live communications links to researchers in the field, plus the ability to instantly call up stored digital images at will or in response to audience questions. We liked the idea of touchscreens that could serve as multimedia exhibit label enhancements and could be updated with news and video overnight. We hoped to come up with a system of interlocking cases and add-on peripherals, such as we had seen plans for in London, that might allow us to quickly configure small, timely showcase exhibits. We took note of the London team's careful advance planning, including staff training exercises, advance partnership agreements with *Nature* and the BBC, and the detailed production time lines they devised to help carry out their intention of staying just a touch ahead of the news curve. Graham Farmelo and Janet Carding warned us of the high cost of currency: it is staff intensive and requires considerable staff training. Larry Bell, David Ellis, and I, in a leap of undying optimism, figured we would wing it somehow.

Our RFP brought forth several entries from teams of architects, exhibit designers, and audiovisual system specialists. A few declined, telling us that our six-month time line would get us only halfway there. We chose Magian Design Studio, an Australian team, won over by their willingness to deal with our content production and updating needs, a recommendation from the American Museum of Natural History, for whom they had devised the updateable touchscreen system, and the visionary drawing they included with their proposal. Their architectural concept shattered the horizontal paradigm of our space by postulating a stage suspended from the beams through the great cubic airspace of the Blue Wing, leaving most of the floor free for audience and exhibits. Cambridge Seven Architects wedded the concepts to reality. Of course, construction got delayed through nobody's fault in particular; there were engineering difficulties, software writing complexities, equipment back-orders, difficult cost-cutting decisions, and, as always, the inflationary influence of Brilliant New Ideas—all of which conspired to push our opening ahead to April 2001, making it exactly the one-year process that saner heads had predicted.

Our program rested on three key pillars: 1) live presentations for Museum audiences—long a staple of Museum of Science programming—but now enhanced with multimedia and live communications tools; 2) short-term, rapidly executable exhibits, relying on flexible exhibit structures that CS&T staff would be able to quickly reconfigure, on their own, without too much help from an already overcommitted exhibits department; and 3) a digital desktop multimedia production studio for creating touchscreen and plasma display content, interpreting exhibits, supplementing presentations, and providing programming for the gaps between presentations. We planned at a later stage to add in cable, webcasting, and programs designed specifically for school groups.

Multimedia touchscreens in CS&T interpret exhibits and provide stories on current research. Photo courtesy of Museum of Science, Boston

We were quite fortunate because the technology of digital cameras and desktop video production had just reached a point where one could produce and edit high-quality digital video for a fraction of the cost that was typical even two years prior. We could skip right over the expensive Avids and all the digitization fuss and leap directly into native digital editing with Final Cut Pro on our Macs.

GARNERING SUPPORT
The Museum made a substantial financial and fund-raising commitment to this project, budgeting a $2.5 million capital campaign to build the architectural and digital infrastructure. Eleven founding sponsors grasped the mission presented by Museum development officer Gene Dubrow and generously supported it. Led by EMC, the group included Boston Scientific, Cabot Corporation Foundation, Compaq Computer (now Hewlett-Packard), Deloitte and Touche, Draper Laboratory, Mercury Computer Systems, Nortel Networks, Teradyne, Tufts Health Plan, and Unisphere Networks. A year later, with the collapse of the technology market, many of these companies suffered down-

sizing; we are grateful that most all of them maintained their commitment to the Museum.

In addition to the capital campaign for CS&T, the Museum also committed a yearly general operating budget of close to $200,000. (By 1999, the Museum had been operating in the black for several years because of Director David Ellis's fiscal discipline and a booming economy.) The operating funds included the commitment to hire, in addition to the manager of the operation (me), a staff of two. I wrote job descriptions for an education associate (content producer and presenter) and a multimedia producer/director. Whoa. Three people were not going to be able to handle the ambitious program we had designed. The problem we had put off addressing returned to stare us in the face.

Skeptics sometimes point to our capital campaign goal of $2.5 million for CS&T and say that it sets a nearly impossible barrier to entry for doing current science in most science centers and thus disqualifies us from ever being a true role model: our data point would be thrown out as an extreme. However, the majority of those funds went to the engineering and construction of our signature live-event stage and winch-rigged plasma screen assembly, both dramatically suspended from the beams of the Blue Wing, whereas, in fact, any old stage equipped with adequate multimedia resources would do. The real barrier to doing current science is its staff-intensive nature. With only two FTEs, I knew I was not going to be able to fulfill the promise. My museum grant-writing career began in earnest.

CS&T's fall 2000 SEPA award from the National Institutes of Health (NIH) allowed us to hire three full-time content producers and also provided exhibit funding and a second desktop multimedia production unit. Best of all was the five-year time line and the commitment to a rigorous evaluation protocol that would help us refine our practices while innovating during our developmental period. We partnered with seven top-quality research institutions, including Harvard Medical School and School of Public Health as well as the Whitehead Institute and Massachusetts General Hospital. SEPA was a tremendous shot in the arm for us, and I am forever indebted to NIH, ASTC, and Congress for working together to make this opportunity available.

Emboldened, we went in on an educational outreach proposal with Harvard, the Massachusetts Institute of Technology, and the University of California, Santa Barbara, for a new Nanoscale Science and Engineering Center. This NSF grant brought us another education associate and more exhibit

funds. Later the Museum partnered with Tufts University in becoming a regional NASA broker–facilitator, and that collaboration helped expand our
space science research partnerships and outreach.

In the meantime, we strove to master new operating systems and technologies that came with their own learning curves and break-in periods. Our
first year was full of emergency patches, frequent breakdowns, and wholesale
data losses. Nevertheless, slowly, steadily, we learned how to wrangle the technology and reinvent ourselves as science communicators. Happily, the team
we hired for CS&T—which, by the spring of 2003, numbered seven full-time
and four part-time staff and interns—proved resilient, resourceful, passionate, and dedicated, and they stuck by each other. It had taken a long time to
recruit and hire the right candidates—there is not a huge pool of people out
there who have practiced advanced research, write compellingly and jargon
free, command an audience's attention with flair, make their own multimedia
graphics, welcome living on an educator's salary in an expensive city, and
allow themselves to be squeezed into a tight windowless office space with
other passionate individuals while constantly problem-solving their way
through situations of urgency with great teamwork but sometimes minimal
outside support—but, thank heaven, we found them. Of course it wasn't all
roses; there were tensions, anxieties, and frustrations, but, for the most part,
sheer pluck and courage and a good dose of humor usually pulled us through.
It helped for us to frame it all within a five-year perspective—five years to
realize the initial vision, develop best practices, work out the kinks, and begin
to realize the full potential of the system we were building, piece by piece.

SOME GOOD NEWS

The interim results are promising. We can cautiously say we have proof of concept. We do, indeed, manage to keep up with the news and sometimes to antici-
pate it. We do, indeed, attract a broad audience—mostly teens and adults of all
ages, though families frequently participate in our offerings. We do maintain a
seven-day-a-week schedule of three to five live presentations per day, updated
weekly, with a couple of whole new ones created each month. Live presentations
are easier to update than exhibits, easier to adapt to the audience du jour and
wonderfully effective with their face-to-face quality of inspiration and discussion.

We carry on a formidable schedule of guest researcher appearances—the
fall of 2002 had us geared up for a Friday afternoon "Chandra X-ray Observatory" guest researcher series, a Friday evening "Astrobiology" guest

researcher series; a Saturday "Harvard Medical School Presents Science in the News" series, a Sunday afternoon "Frontiers of Health Science" guest researcher series, and a twice weekly satellite phone link between museum visitors and members of the International TransAntarctic Scientific Expedition, camped on the West Antarctic ice sheet. We also ran numerous one-off special events in partnership with other organizations: Sun-Earth Day, Assistive Technology Day, International Bird Migration Day, etc.

We run a Web site that features daily science news updates, multimedia feature stories, edited video of our live presentations, links to related research sites, and exhibit and schedule information.[2] We offer a feedback service and have signed up more than 7,000 people to our subscriber list. Cablecasting through New England Cable News began in the spring of 2003. We have also begun an experimental collaboration with the Museum's Science Theater organization, collaborating on new plays that address controversial research, followed by facilitated forumlike audience discussions. With these, we tackle new topics—such as cloning, xenotransplantation, stem cell research, and the psychology of risk perception—every three to four months.

Current Science Theater presents "The Clone Show," by Jon Lipsky with audience discussion to follow. Photo courtesy of Museum of Science, Boston

We are testing other forum-style formats for engaging people in the meatier science and society policy discussions that we believe will play a larger role in the science center of the future. And we are starting to conceive and plan a Web-based kiosk network that will allow us and other content-producing science centers to distribute downloadable multimedia research updates to large and small museums alike to help them keep their exhibits fresh and timely.

The staff's productivity has been enormous: in a nine-month period between May 2002 and January 2003, CS&T staff created over 50 unique and timely presentations, hosted over 40 guest researchers, produced two new Current Science Theater plays, produced more than 20 short video pieces, and provided programming on almost all the top science and technology news stories of the past year. Over 18,000 people attended approximately 900 CS&T live events during these nine months.

The CS&T Web site entertains about 170,000 page hits a week. Web visitors spend an extraordinary average of 18 minutes on the site. By January 2003, the site featured about 60 eight-page multimedia stories and 70 newsbytes on current science and technology research in addition to illustrated descriptions of our exhibits and live events.

It was gratifying to have the hard work recognized: in March 2002, CS&T was named one of the selected "Best Practices for Communicating Science and Technology to the Public" by a peer-review panel[3] assembled by the U.S. Department of Energy, Office of Science, and the National Institute for Standards and Technology (National Institute for Standards and Technology 2002). In May 2002, the American Association of Museums gave CS&T its Gold Muse Award "in Recognition of the Highest Standards of Excellence in the Use of Media and Technology for Interpretation and Education in Science."[4]

Perhaps more significantly, our independent evaluation team, headed by Martin Storksdieck of the Institute of Learning Innovation, conducted formative assessment of our staff presentations first and concluded in January 2003, "Staff presentations at the CS&T multimedia stage have reached a level of mature programming: they seem to attract the target audience, keep the audience interested, successfully convey their messages, and are enjoyable for most visitors. . . . The presentations in their conceptualization and their concrete implementation can be further promoted as successful models for conveying current science and technology issues to [teen and adult] audiences of a science museum or science center" (Storksdieck et al. 2003). A subsequent

analysis of preliminary data on our guest researcher and current science theater presentations offered similar results along with some helpful guidance for
improvement.

One thing I find most striking about our live events is that our audiences
tend to stay for the duration of the presentation or theater piece, and many
hang around for questions and discussion. Getting 20 to 30 minutes of a visitor's attention to the intricacies posed by current research—in the midst of a
busy, distracting environment—is a true coup by science museum standards
and probably by *any* standards in a free-choice science learning environment.

THE POWER OF PARTNERSHIP

The area of partnership—both with research institutions and with other
media—has proved enormously fruitful, and I have already mentioned our
NIH-, NSF-, and NASA-funded research partnerships. There are other more
casual collaborations; for instance, the Woods Hole Oceanographic Institute
has teamed up with us twice for live satellite phone discussions with
researchers aboard the deep-sea submersible *Alvin* during the 2002 expedition
to the Galapagos rift and the 2003 expedition to the New England seamounts.[5]

We have also developed very helpful media and journal partnerships. A
special preembargo relationship with *Nature* allowed us to provide in-depth
coverage on the Chad fossil hominid skull find through Boston television sta-
tions within an hour of the embargo lift. Our agreement with ScienCentral,
Inc., allows us access to almost all the science news segments they produce for
ABC news affiliates in return for our production services on stories shot in the
Boston area. We are developing additional partnerships with the AAAS and
Science Channel, *Nova*, National Geographic Channel, and WCVB-Boston.
NSF's Hyman Field has been especially helpful in getting broadcast media
producers and science center content developers talking with each other, and
I found that my own background in broadcast documentary production
helped bridge the gap between the different institutional worldviews. As we
begin our cablecasting venture with New England Cable News, we will have
the opportunity to reach an additional 2.8 million New England households.

AREAS OF CONCERN: IDENTITY

CS&T is located centrally in the middle of the Museum's large atriumlike Blue
Wing, surrounded by exhibit galleries and balconies. This lends great visibility

and a wonderful "drop-in" spontaneity to the space but makes it a challenge providing spatial identity and sound and traffic insulation for live events. Design and construction funds ran out before we could solve all these challenges and provide an overall unifying "look and feel" to the Center. Even our Times Square–style newsband, which was meant to encircle the perimeter, remains incomplete. Hence, our formative evaluation results show us that most visitors do not even know they are in the Center when they are there, although they understand that the events and exhibits are current.

AREAS OF CONCERN: EXHIBITS

Some of our biggest challenges have been with exhibits. The original concept had been for small showcase exhibits on various subjects: easy in, easy out. We wanted to relieve the exhibits department from having to interrupt major projects to custom design and engineer brief, timely displays. However, our first attempt at engineering easily reconfigurable exhibit showcase structures was unsuccessful, and we didn't have the resources to design and build new ones before our opening.

Nevertheless, wonderful exhibit opportunities came along, and we plunged ahead with a series of themed multiobject displays—energized by sheer gumption, the willingness of research partners to lend us cool stuff, and the good graces of the exhibits department. These weren't necessarily the most aesthetic of exhibit experiences, but they were all really interesting, and our visitors liked them. We started with an exhibit on high-definition television (HDTV) technology and the Federal Communications Commission's controversial broadcast conversion plan, continued with a large exhibit on the latest in music and technology, and added in a progressive exhibit on the building of the International Space Station. We next assembled another large multiobject exhibit on advanced robotics and brought in a popular custom-designed *Virtual Maze* as an example of "smart space" design. In 2003, we launched an astrobiology exhibit and a very ambitious medical technologies exhibit, including everything from an Abiocor® Implantable Heart to a MetiMan Human Patient Simulator®.

Along with the exhibits, we produced associated live presentations, demonstrations, guest researcher appearances, multimedia touchscreen and Web stories, and video loops that we ran on the plasmas between presentations.

The physical aspect of exhibits exhausted us. A six-foot robotic tuna from Draper Labs demanded very different treatment from an endoscopic pill camera. Standardization proved an elusive ideal. In addition, we weren't able to get our heavy touchscreens independently mounted so as to interpret particular exhibits: we resorted to printing and mounting our own labels, rigging up computer displays as needed, and grasping for lighting.

Many new technologies available to us on loan begged to be demonstrated or made interactive in some way. For short-term loans, we couldn't engineer teen-proof interactive solutions: we needed live demonstrators. With a full development and presentation schedule, we couldn't spare staff for those long hours. Volunteers were fabulous, but in short and uneven supply. You get the picture.

It soon became clear that we had to slow down this aspect of the Center until we had the right hardware, more exhibit support, more staff, and independently mobile touchscreen pedestals. We also need better lighting, infrastructure, and storage for exhibit components. In the meantime, rather than planning another stream of large themed exhibitions with definitive openings, we will concentrate on casually staggered, multiple small displays.

AREAS OF CONCERN: SUSTAINABILITY

Coverage of current science and technology is extremely staff intensive. Corporate sponsors like to fund *things*—exhibits and buildings. Foundations will fund portions of staff time on a project basis. However, the commitment to produce continuously updated exhibits and programs requires a team of dedicated and well-trained full-time staff.

Our current experiment is built mostly on the unstable soil of Museum revenue generation and government grant funding, both of which are subject to drought-like conditions. Ideally, museums could make one of their long-term goals the endowment of dedicated staff positions for current science and technology—as a higher priority, perhaps, than the latest domed theater technology. But then again, theaters produce revenue, and what CS&T produces— more thoughtfully informed citizens—cannot pay the utility bills. During the drought-like conditions museums have been experiencing in the wake of September 11 and economic implosion, nonendowed frontline educators have often been the first to be let go.

Smaller museums have an even more difficult task allocating resources to current science efforts. So it behooves those of us working with a greater pool of resources to constantly attend to our larger community and create new mechanisms for sharing what we produce and devising more efficient means of producing it. These are areas I hope to focus on more intensely in the next several years.

AREAS OF CONCERN: MAINTAINING PUBLIC TRUST

One of the biggest challenges museums face as we increase our capacity to interpret current research is maintaining public trust. The public rates museums quite highly on the trust meter, much higher than the print and broadcast media from which they obtain most of their science information. (The public also rates scientists and medical professionals higher on the confidence scale than Supreme Court justices, teachers, and media; see National Science Board 2002.) In addressing current research, however, museums need to adopt some of the characteristics of news media organizations. The caution here is that in order to maintain the high public trust quotient that we have banked and that may be our most valuable asset, it would be wise to ensure adherence to the highest standards of journalistic integrity. Likewise, in our eagerness to seize on mutually beneficial partnerships with research-and-development labs and media, both public and private, we must exercise constant vigilance for any compromise or appearance of compromise of our journalistic or institutional integrity. Partnerships thrive on mutual benefit; each collaborator seeks its own advancement through the process. Some new technologies we would like to display are available only from companies seeking greater market share, and, quite understandably, even our nonprofit research institute partners have interest in the good public relations they receive through their involvement with the Museum.

On the Museum side of the equation, we need constant self-monitoring so that the choices we make are guided by the Museum's fundamental mission—education, engagement, discussion, and insight—and not based primarily on our own or others' marketing and positioning agendas. We would be wise to create funding, sponsorship, and partnership policies that help us maintain integrity and independence in all that we do. While this issue is already on the table throughout the museum world, the trend toward addressing current research brings it remarkably to the fore.

Similarly, current research is often controversial research not only within the scientific community but also socially and politically. Our role is to offer the tools and establish the frameworks for understanding and interpreting the debates and to undertake a critical examination of the issues at hand, clearly separating fact from value or supposition. That's what research is all about.

DISRUPTIVE INNOVATION

A challenge we have faced in Boston that will be faced by other innovative current science and technology teams elsewhere concerns their integration into the larger organizational structure of the Museum. CS&T fits the criteria for what Clayton M. Christensen terms a "disruptive innovation" within a mature industry (Christensen 1997). Museum management teams have developed over time an infrastructure and a culture based on large permanent exhibits, four- to six-month traveling exhibits, large-format films, and slowly evolving programs and presentations. Future growth and revenue-producing efforts center on what Christensen would call "sustaining innovation," that is, marginal improvements to existing products, such as more marketable and more technologically impressive exhibits, better planetarium hardware and software, increased function sales, and a larger share of the standard grant market. By contrast, CS&T tends to exploit new areas of potential growth: grant-funded partnerships with research organizations, short-term opportunities with innovative companies, mutually beneficial partnerships with journals and broadcast media, new digital technologies, broadband and Internet capabilities, new barterable and potential revenue-producing products and services, and a new breed of professional, media-savvy science communicators.

CS&T also quickly attracted its own sources of corporate and grant support outside the Museum's mainstream budgeting process. It formed potent new synergies with nontraditional museum partners, and it provided an unprecedented stream of new content and new forms of exhibits and programs at a pace beyond previous museum experience. Like the successful start-ups that create their own new markets through disruptive innovation, CS&T has thrived on a certain independence from the traditional organizational structure and sometimes presents a challenge to the status quo.

In the traditional museum structure, committees facilitate long, smooth transitions, and planning processes require long lead times. However, timely coverage of current events often requires a SWAT team approach and quick-response infrastructure. CS&T staff has days, sometimes just hours, to respond to news events and to the issues that will be top of mind for our media-savvy audiences. We make decisions quickly and act decisively but must be ready to revise on a moment's notice. We cannot always predict what we will be doing next week or even tomorrow. Content production staff must be well grounded in the fields they cover so that they can quickly assimilate and interpret the latest advanced research findings. Resources must be at the ready for acquiring images, video, graphics, and expert commentary. We put together video and graphics in a flash at our multimedia authoring stations, and we print and mount most of our own labels, signs, and flyers. (The standard turnaround for the Museum's publications department is typically four to six weeks.) There's a sense in which CS&T has become a homunculus, a little museum within the museum, replicating the work of many of its divisions but on an accelerated timescale. We've been managing our own Web site, exhibits area, presentation stage, guest speaker series, video production, editorial functions, partnership and grants procurement and administration, publications, much of our information technology and audiovisual infrastructure, and many marketing functions. In the future, I believe, the current science and technology functions of museums will need to be grouped into a distinct division because the operations timescale issue and the news/journalism ethic frame things so differently; however, at present, the difference poses something of an irritant to the mainstream organization and its well-established procedures, and there is constant pressure to mainstream it once again.

THE FUTURE

Under the leadership of a dynamic new president and director, Iaonnis Miaoulis, the Museum of Science is venturing into other new compelling large-scale initiatives that may alter somewhat the context for this particular innovation. We have been anticipating a five-year development path toward fulfillment of the overall vision for CS&T. On this path, we will have completed our comprehensive summative evaluation and sorted out our better ideas from those of lesser value by 2005. We will have a better understanding of whether we have been able to provide a valuable and resilient model for our own museum's future development, as well as for other science centers seeking to bridge the gap between current research and public engagement. Time will tell. Please stay tuned.

NOTES

1. *Current Science & Technology Center: 2001 Wrap-Up,* 6-min. video, www.mos.org/cst/section/what.html.

2. www.mos.org/cst.

3. Panel Members were Rick Borchelt (chair), U.S. Department of Energy (at the time of the committee's operation, current affiliation, The Whitehead Institute); Debbie Triese (study director), Department of Advertising, University of Florida; Deborah Blum, School of Journalism and Mass Communication, University of Wisconsin, Madison; Lynne Friedmann, Friedmann Communications; Martin Glicksman, Department of Materials Sciences and Engineering, Rensselaer Polytechnic Institute; John M. Horack (ex officio), Space Sciences Laboratory, George C. Marshall Space Flight Center, NASA; Robert Logan, School of Journalism, University of Missouri; Paul Lowenberg, Lowenberg Communications; Charles McGruder III, Department of Physics and Astronomy, Western Kentucky University; Jon D. Miller, Northwestern University Medical School; Gail Porter, National Institute of Standards and Technology; Carol L. Rogers, College of Journalism, University of Maryland; Barbara Valentino, Evolving Communications; Michael Weingold, Department of Advertising, University of Florida; Gregory Wilson (ex officio), SSL, MSFC, NASA; and Kris Wilson, Department of Journalism, University of Texas. The cochairs of the Best Practices conference steering committee, Joann Rodgers of the Johns Hopkins Medical Institutions and Earle Holland of the Ohio State University, served as consultants to the R2 panel.

4. www.mediaandtechnology.org/muse/2002muse_science.html (accessed February 25, 2004).

5. See www.divediscover.whoi.edu (accessed February 25, 2004).

REFERENCES

Christensen, C. 1997. *The innovator's dilemma.* Cambridge, Mass.: Harvard Business School Press.

Field, H., and P. Powell. 2001. Public understanding of science versus public understanding of research. *Public Understanding of Science* 10: 421–26.

National Institute for Standards and Technology. 2002. Communicating the future: Best practices for communication of science and technology to the public. Proceedings of Conference, Gaithersburg, Maryland, March 6–8, 2002. (Available at www.nist.gov/public_affairs/bestpractices/practices.html).

National Science Board. 2002. *Science and engineering indicators.* Arlington, Va.:
National Science Foundation.

Semper, R. 2001. Personal notes from presentation at ECSITE meeting in Luleö,
Sweden, November 2001, and from comments at workshop The Leading Edge:
Enhancing the Public Understanding of Research, Museum of Science, Boston,
February 11–13, 2001.

Storksdieck M., et al. 2003. Museum of Science, Boston, Current Science &
Technology Center Interim Remedial Evaluation Report. Institute for Learning
Innovation, Annapolis, Maryland, January 2003. Unpublished.

At the Cutting Edge: Showcasing Research through a Public Exhibition Center

Christine Cansfield-Smith

Discovery was established by CSIRO (Commonwealth Scientific and Industrial Research Organization), Australia's national science agency. It was opened to the public in August 2000. The award-winning design of the *Discovery* building contains two floors of glass-fronted, state-of-the-art laboratories where scientists and technicians from one of CSIRO's largest divisions undertake field crop research. While the research laboratories are not open to the public, their presence gives visitors to *Discovery* a view of actual science in progress. In *Discovery* there is also a lecture theater, meeting and functions rooms, an exhibition gallery of approximately 2,000 square meters (the main focus for visitors), a science education center, and a cafeteria.

CSIRO, established in 1926, is funded by the Australian government and ranks in the top 1 percent of world scientific institutions in 11 of 22 research fields. Research and development is carried out in fields of economic, social, and environmental importance, including agriculture, communications and information technology, health, manufacturing and construction, minerals and energy, the environment, transport, and infrastructure. Most recently, the organization is tackling Australia's national priority needs through research programs that focus on major scientific resources in areas such as environmental challenges (water, salinity), advanced communications, preventive

health, new energy systems, food innovation, light metals, and ocean resources.

While there are other, smaller Commonwealth science agencies in Australia
and research functions within each Australian university, CSIRO is the only
agency covering such a broad scope of research in areas of economic or social
value to the nation. CSIRO is involved in over 700 current or recently completed research activities, working with leading scientific organizations and
firms in the United States, Japan, and Europe and with developing countries,
especially in Asia. Worldwide, it ranks third in environment/ecology and
fourth in agricultural science.

More than 6,500 people, consisting of research scientists and technical, administrative, and general support staff, are located at 60 CSIRO sites throughout Australia and overseas and within approximately 23 divisions. Of interest
in the context of this chapter is the fact that over 100 CSIRO staff are employed solely for the communication of research aimed at specific stakeholder
audiences. Each research division and even some research projects have dedicated communication staff. Activities are directed to government, industry,
and business stakeholders, as well as to the general public. The divisional communicators are complemented by a corporate team working in education,
publishing, media, and public relations activities.

CSIRO's iconic place in Australian society goes hand in hand with its obli-
gations to explain current research in a clear and concise way. *Discovery*'s raison d'être is to aid the public understanding and appreciation of research.
Discovery has been designed to make CSIRO more accessible, in a physical
sense, to the public. In showcasing CSIRO, *Discovery* communicates how and
why worthwhile scientific research is undertaken in Australia for the benefit of
the nation and its people.

Communication, from a CSIRO perspective, has as its basis the promotion
and perpetuation of goodwill toward its science. If science is to be funded, the
public must be convinced of its value and interest, as well as have an understanding of the essential role of research in collaborative partnerships and networks with business and industry. These principles are extended to the core
mission of *Discovery*, with the challenge to do justice to CSIRO by keeping the
Discovery exhibition informative, educational, authentic, and unbiased. It is a
vehicle for raising general community awareness of the excitement and importance of research and of CSIRO as the leader in Australian science.

Discovery operates like a museum or science center in terms of staffing, opening hours, entrance fees, and various marketing initiatives. In its exhibition design, every effort is made to create a friendly and modern atmosphere. These concepts, along with interactives, are naturally found in many science centers around the globe. But *Discovery*'s design is also intended to be highly sophisticated and elegant, attributes not always associated with the robust displays of more traditional science centers. Maximum visual and aesthetic appeal was employed in the exhibition design with an emphasis on strong and vibrant colors and a large amount of multimedia. *Discovery*'s design is intended to project a particular image for research and to attract a more adult market to the center. In fact, the exhibition provides an overview of CSIRO for high-profile and potentially influential visitors, such as representatives from business and industry, as much as for the public. It is also an information resource center of Australian research where visitors are encouraged to investigate items of interest, specific to CSIRO, on current research or topical issues. In addition, visitors are given access to today's news stories on screen and in a handout and to a hotline to CSIRO *Enquiries*, the organization's national science enquiry and referral service that offers a free mailing of specific information.

The *Discovery* exhibition is the main focus of the complex and dedicated to the presentation of ongoing and completed research and technology. In a relatively small space, only a sampling of CSIRO's research can be showcased. Exhibit topics are always selected for their popular appeal from a diverse range of research possibilities and as a broad sampling of subject matter—climate, the environment, medical advances, new technologies, gene technology, food, and agriculture. Much of the exhibition is about interpretation with very few objects central to the content. One section, however, is dedicated to a display of the Australian national biological collections—the insects, plants, wildlife, and marine collections of which CSIRO is the guardian. Samples from each are displayed, as are explanations about their relevance to research.

The *Discovery* exhibition's text messages are easy to read and understand and concern the initial problem, possible solutions, and the outcomes of research rather than its process. In fact, feedback from visitors and others within the museum industry has been very positive. One visitor remarked that "*Discovery* is the most well-designed exhibition we have seen for a long time. The text is understandable and legible and the design is excellent. It is a credit to CSIRO."

CSIRO Discovery. Photo courtesy of CSIRO *Discovery*

Research is presented as a human-related enterprise and for its national and global benefits. There is a balance between static and interactive components in the exhibition with a significant decision made during development that any interactives should be included only if they complement or at least help interpret the science. Where possible, attempts are made to use actual research tools as interactives and to modify them for public use. One instance is the inclusion of the Haptic workbench, a leading-edge three-dimensional, touch-sensitive computer that is part of CSIRO's ongoing computational work. By applying this method to the exhibition infrastructure, particularly with any computer-based interactives, the exhibits can be updated in line with the research.

What are the challenges of a public exhibition center attached to a research organization? One obvious one is that the core business of the parent organization is not in museums. *Discovery* manages with a relatively small budget and infrastructure. Staff consist of four core, full-time staff and two part-timers, supported by a dozen or so "casuals," the latter mostly doctoral students attached to CSIRO. In terms of its corporate responsibilities, *Discovery* provides as much of a service to CSIRO as to the public. It plays an important role as the host center for any visiting VIPs from government, science, and industry and as a functions and meeting venue for CSIRO. One instance is as the venue for the Industry Link Program, which includes practical workshops and training courses in gene technology for business executives.

The challenge with the *Discovery* model, as with any center charged with creating and maintaining exhibitions, is to keep abreast of changing science and to innovatively find ways to update more quickly and less expensively. This is a challenge still to be resolved.

Discovery has diverted from the standard science center model of exhibition design, particularly from those that have followed the "Exploratorium cookbooks" (Persson 2000, 456). This creates additional pressure to have originality in explaining research problems, solutions, and outcomes while remaining interesting and understandable. A major difference between a science center and the *Discovery* exhibition is that with the former, exhibits have, until recently, been based on the physical sciences and are arranged as isolated, interactive units. In the *Discovery* model, exhibition components and content are linked throughout, with all subject matter on show set within a contextual framework. The aims outlined by Persson (2000) to "deliver depth of understanding in current scientific issues" (457) is therefore satisfied in this model.

The *Discovery* exhibition was put together with a relatively small team of CSIRO staff who selected, researched, wrote, and curated the exhibition content in conjunction with a design firm based in Melbourne, Australia. Prior to contracting the designers, the *Discovery* development staff had met with groups of CSIRO scientists gathered from around Australia to shape the content for each of the exhibit's topics. This information was finalized prior to working with the principal consultant and subconsultants of multimedia and set and graphics specialists.

The question is raised as to the benefits of the *Discovery* model when set alongside the science center model. The latter has indeed proliferated worldwide in recent decades and has played an important role for generations in informing and converting the public to science. However, these efforts to make science "fun" may mean that the public have been misinformed along the way in their understanding and appreciation of the world of real research or, to reiterate Ann M. Muscat's (1993) comment, to see the difference between "science fact or science fiction" (1).

Science centers have added widely to the understanding of basic science concepts. But in so doing, they may have done a disservice to the industry of real scientific research. The concept of relating fun with science has helped turn children around to science, but is a concept avoided at *Discovery*, for while every effort has been made to make the exhibition highly entertaining, stimulating, and interesting, to project an image of fun would be an inaccurate and inappropriate way to depict the challenges, frustrations, and wonder of the world of actual scientific research. It would be an injustice to CSIRO's public image and to research.

There are two strands to the education programs offered through *Discovery*. The Green Machine Science Education Center, located in the *Discovery* complex, is managed by CSIRO Education and belongs to the Australia-wide CSIRO Science Education Centers (CSIROSEC) network. It consists of junior and senior laboratories and structured lab-based experiments and demonstrations for local primary and secondary schools in the region.

Schools throughout Australia can take advantage of the education programs attached to the *Discovery* exhibition. The core program, Discovering Science in Society, is intentionally designed to teach children that applied research involves high-level industry collaborations and widespread networks. Students are required to take on the role of an imaginary company director with an opportunity to provide funding for research. They individually consider and vote for one of three major research topics. Each semester, the topics change and are selected from a range of issues currently being researched by CSIRO scientists. The students investigate and assess the research in the context of the exhibition and decide its value to society and its eligibility for further research funding. Their information about the topics is provided by *Discovery*'s casual staff: doctoral students working as scientists with CSIRO. This program has been extremely well received by teachers and students. Postevaluation reports from each school following the visit prove that the students are taking the lesson and their role playing very seriously and are actually learning about relevant and practical issues in science.

Certainly, schoolchildren are an important target audience for *Discovery*. But adults are also remembered. A cross section of visitors to *Discovery* reveals that adults, an often-forgotten audience with science centers, make up a large proportion of visitors to the exhibition. *Discovery* is intentionally aimed at an audience above 12 years of age. But it is appealing to all members of family groups and even to very young children. These children are catered to with a virtual reality theater; CD-ROMs about insects, rain forests, and other environmental issues; and the Optuslab, a hands-on area for undertaking lab-based experiments in physics and chemistry.

It might be assumed that the public have little interest in complex information and a general disregard for contemporary research. A national opinion survey of Australian science undertaken by CSIRO in 1997 revealed some very interesting statistics. Among the attitudes toward science and technology, 72 percent felt that science makes our lives healthier and easier, 86 percent felt that science research is vital in protecting and restoring the environment, 78 percent felt that it is important to have some knowledge about science in our daily lives, and 70 percent believed that science and technology offer greater opportunities for future generations. Of interest is

Part of the Australian National Fish Collection in Discovery. *Photo courtesy of CsiRO* Discovery

that women seem more interested (39 percent) in science than men (19 percent) (ACB McNair 1997). Positive feedback received from visitors to *Discovery* confirms the need for centers such as this to disseminate the nature and scope of current research. Comments received have included that "it is a truly remarkable education and public outreach center" and, one highly descriptive sentence from a visitor, "leading edge, innovative, intelligent, modern, radical, not nerdy and classy."

But what of the future? James Bradburne (1998) called for "a real transformation of the science center institution." He argued that "the field (science centers) has suffered for decades from the lack of debate, fueled perhaps by the belief that the supporters of the science center movement . . . would withdraw their support if any sign of dissent showed in the ranks of the movement." Bradburne believes that "we are mature enough to encourage a critical look at our institutions, our field, and our performance" (237). Even Persson (2000), in his critique of Bradburne's treatise, agrees about the challenges ahead of the science center industry, particularly in "maintaining scientific integrity, providing a meaningful mission in a changing world, and keeping up with increasing competition in the leisure market" (450).

Scholars argue that visitation to science centers is proof of their popular appeal (Persson 2000, 451). This may have been helped by some science centers having successfully integrated the life sciences and physical sciences with a general move toward more factual content in their exhibitions. But while science centers do a respectable job in providing a basic understanding and appreciation of science, the complete story about real scientific research is not yet communicated fully by them. There might also be an aesthetic and interpretive problem in mixing the look and style of the traditional science center with a new model for communicating scientific research, especially if not set within context.

The *Discovery* model works because it represents an organization that needs to have a tangible expression of the diversity of its research and a venue that is up to date with its science. It is attached to a unique research organization of world renown and attempts to honestly replicate the processes and the appearance of the world it serves. This formula works for the *Discovery* model. This chapter is not proposing the full integration of the *Discovery* model into all science centers. Rather, it is an attempt for those in this area of the museum industry to recognize the risk of the public being never fully informed if the gap between science centers and real research remains as wide as it still appears. The young, in particular, will never have a chance to mature intellectually about topical issues in society and their relevance to research and technology if the messages do not change. Separate centers for the public understanding of research need to be clearly identified and need to pick up where science centers finish, both in Australia and overseas. Their challenge, however, will be to link into actual research organizations for authentic, current content.

CSIRO's *Discovery* is an attempt to fill a niche within the movement for the public understanding of research and the communication of contemporary science. Persson had called for experiencing science at work—to see or experience the "real thing." *Discovery* delivers this promise as well as an opportunity, particularly for schoolchildren, to meet and interact with real scientific staff. These representatives of science are selected for their age and their ability to converse well with students. *Discovery* has satisfactorily provided a meeting place for the public and scientists. But more work is needed if *Discovery* is to involve the public other than just educating and communicating to them. New initiatives and ideas need to be devised to include the public in research, to invite them to formulate their own opinions, to provide feedback about the research on show, and to encourage more discussion, interaction, and debate.

REFERENCES

Beetlestone, John G., Colin H. Johnson, Melanie Quin, and Harry White. 1998. The Science center movement: Contexts, practice, next challenges. *Public Understanding of Science* 7: 5–26.

Bradburne, James M. 1998. Dinosaurs and white elephants: The science center in the twenty-first century. *Public Understanding of Science* 7: 237–53.

CSIRO Snapshot. 2002. October.

Field, Hyman, and Patricia Powell. 2001. Public understanding of science versus public understanding of research. *Public Understanding of Science* 10: 421–26.

ACB McNair. 1997. Survey of public opinion of CSIRO and various science and technology issues. May.

Muscat, Ann M. 1993. Creating a science education center for the 21st century. Article developed for the Japanese publication *Illume*. Semiannual review on science education, November 1993.

Persson, Per-Edvin. 2000. Science centers are thriving and going strong! *Public Understanding of Science* 9.

16

Catching Science in the Act: *Mysteries of Çatalhöyük*

Don Pohlman

Mysteries of Çatalhöyük was a 6,000-square-foot exhibit and website that opened at the Science Museum of Minnesota (SMM) in September 2001. The large exhibit has since closed, but the Web site remains in use. The project was funded by the National Science Foundation's (NSF's) Informal Science Education Program. It focused on science as a social process exemplified by the ongoing archaeological research at Çatalhöyük, a world-famous Neolithic site in central Turkey.

The rationale for our project was that public understanding of science requires opportunities for the public to see science not just as a body of knowledge but as a dynamic social process. As we wrote in our NSF proposal,

> Science exhibits and programs for the general public deliver their messages through specimens, artifacts, and demonstrations of natural phenomena, but they rarely show how science pursues its inquiries and builds its understanding of the world through its communities and ongoing conversations. The fact that science is done by people working together to exchange and critically examine each other's ideas is often obscured or altogether absent in these programs.

It is worth noting that we saw the focus on research or science process not as something outside the public understanding of science but as something integral

Photo courtesy of the Science Museum of Minnesota

to it. It remains a question worth asking as to what extent we should define or pursue public understanding of research (PUR) separately from other efforts to advance the public understanding of science.

As for Çatalhöyük, how we became involved with it, and why we saw it as an opportunity for informal science learning, I'll first describe how our project played out and then ask a few questions it might pose for PUR practitioners.

Çatalhöyük is among the most important archaeological sites in the world. It consists today of two large debris mounds on either side of an ancient river channel. The larger, older mound is primarily of Early Neolithic age with occupation levels that date roughly to between 9,000 and 7,500 years ago. The remains of one of the largest known Neolithic settlements, it holds clues to understanding early agriculture, animal domestication, and the beginnings of urban life.

Photo courtesy of the Science Museum of Minnesota

Çatalhöyük was first excavated in the 1961 by British archaeologist James Mellaart, whose work revealed remnants of what he called a "Neolithic city" with intact mud-brick structures decorated with remarkable murals, plaster reliefs, and sculpture. In part because technology to conserve the exposed murals did not exist at that time, many were lost, and the site was closed in 1965.

In 1993, archaeologist Ian Hodder, then of Cambridge University, assembled an international team of scientists and conservators to reopen and excavate Çatalhöyük using the latest archaeological methods. That effort, which remains active, is expected to take 25 to 30 years to complete and involves researchers from over a dozen countries, including large teams from Cambridge; the University of California, Berkeley; and Stanford, where Hodder is now based.

SMM became involved with the research project through our curator for archaeology, Dr. Orrin Shane, who worked on public interpretation of Çatalhöyük as a member of the research team for several years before this project took shape. But beyond that personal link, what attracted us to the work at Çatalhöyük was an opportunity to explore the workings of science within a rich and supportive context.

There were several aspects of the Çatalhöyük research project that we found attractive. The first was clearly unfinished science. We believed that we needed to catch science in the throes of uncertainty if we wanted to show non-scientists what it is like to do science. Scientists know a lot, but it is what they don't know that drives what they do next. With decades to go and not too many conclusions reached, Çatalhöyük seemed to fit the bill.

The second was access to the research process and to artifacts of that process. The most crucial aspect of our decision to focus this project on Çatal-höyük was the willingness of the research team to work with us. Ian Hodder favors a highly reflexive approach to archaeology with continuous examination of the team's interpretive assumptions throughout the project. Without going into details, this theoretical stance made the research team's social process much easier to discern and encouraged team members to share access to it with us.

Third, we hoped to capture the social phenomena of science in real time. Much of the conversation among scientists is inaccessible or pursued asynchronously through publication. But another useful by-product of Hodder's reflexive approach is a relatively large amount of real-time interaction be-

Photo courtesy of the Science Museum of Minnesota

tween members of the team. The dig site includes a permanent facility with labs and living quarters that encourage the complete team to assemble at once, and both their method and the close quarters encourage lots of conversation. At Çatalhöyük, we were able to capture some of that conversation on the veranda and in the dining hall as well as in the labs and excavation trench.

I should note is that this might be the first archaeology exhibit anywhere without any artifacts. This was not intentional but instead was a result of our failure to get permission from the Turkish government to borrow objects for the exhibit despite nearly two years of trying. The only real material from Çatalhöyük in the exhibit was some charred plant fragments and some prepared thin sections that were part of a microscope activity. This lack of artifacts made us very nervous, but we consoled ourselves with the thought that we were trying to do an exhibit about process.

Another point worth noting is that in pursuit of the archaeological process, the exhibit often left behind the context of the excavation to head into settings more familiar to our visitors. For example, we used the trappings of a dentist's

Photo courtesy of the Science Museum of Minnesota

office to talk about what one's teeth could add to the archaeological record, and we used contemporary dolls and action figures to show the difficulty of inferring the symbolic meaning of artifacts whose makers are no longer around for questioning. Our most extensive use of this technique involved a modern American kitchen as a setting to present what was known about diet and food preparation at Çatalhöyük.

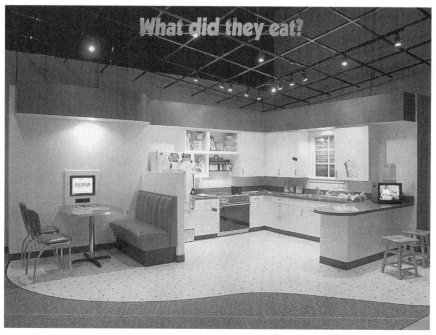

Photo courtesy of the Science Museum of Minnesota

Our intention to uncover the social process of science showed up in several ways within the exhibit. First, we identified researchers as individual characters to make the idea of social process concrete and accessible. We made extensive use of video interviews, drawing on over 100 hours of footage we shot at Çatalhöyük. We also adopted a hybrid graphic style that allowed us to combine photography with the familiar talk and thought bubbles from the comics. This allowed us to show what researchers were saying and thinking without resorting to video exclusively. I can't divulge how we obtained the thoughts of the researchers, but I will say that we took pains to ensure that no one's mental life was misrepresented.

Photo courtesy of the Science Museum of Minnesota

We also tried to model the social process of science with Web and exhibit visitors by asking them to share their own explanations for some of the current questions raised by the research team. An example of this is the mystery trading cards that we created to drive traffic to the Web site and publicize the exhibit. Each of these cards included a photograph of a Çatalhöyük find with a description of its context and a question it raised. Visitors who followed the URL to the Web site could learn more and could post their own interpretations of the evidence, which we shared with other Web and exhibit visitors.

My attempt at a conclusion comes from Aristotle's *Poetics* and the formative years of reality television. Some will remember that in April 1986, Geraldo Rivera aired *The Mystery of Al Capone's Vault,* a live television special that promised to uncover a stash of loot hidden somewhere beneath Chicago. What was remarkable about the show before it aired was that Geraldo promised to find the treasure during a live broadcast rather than roll tape of treasure already safely in hand. What was remarkable about the show after it aired was that it had aired despite the fact that Geraldo and his crew had not found any treasure. It's hard to adjust in real time.

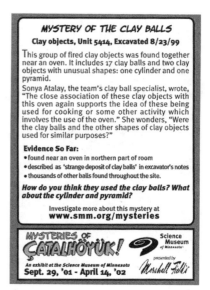

MYSTERY OF THE CLAY BALLS

Clay objects, Unit 5414, Excavated 8/23/99

This group of fired clay objects was found together near an oven. It includes 17 clay balls and two clay objects with unusual shapes: one cylinder and one pyramid.

Sonya Atalay, the team's clay ball specialist, wrote, "The close association of these clay objects with this oven again supports the idea of these being used for cooking or some other activity which involves the use of the oven." She wonders, "Were the clay balls and the other shapes of clay objects used for similar purposes?"

Evidence So Far:
- found near an oven in northern part of room
- described as 'strange deposit of clay balls' in excavator's notes
- thousands of other balls found throughout the site.

How do you think they used the clay balls? What about the cylinder and pyramid?

Investigate more about this mystery at
www.smm.org/mysteries

Photo courtesy of the Science Museum of Minnesota

Which brings me to Aristotle. What Aristotle knew and what Geraldo perhaps forgot was that good stories need a beginning, a middle, and an end. In his groundbreaking foray into reality television, Geraldo nailed the beginning, but he failed to satisfy when he tried to stretch the middle all the way to the credits. If you tell people you're going to find the treasure, you actually do need to find the treasure and to find it on time if you're looking for it on live television.

One of the assumptions we seem to be carrying in PUR is that it must be pursued in the present—that only current research can elicit the public understanding we are seeking. Certainly our project followed that logic, and I'm not claiming in any way that we exhausted its potential. But I am wondering if that is too narrow and demanding a strategy for it to be the only path to our goals.

The *Mysteries of Çatalhöyük* project left me with two strong impressions: one was what a struggle it had been to try telling a current and unfinished story; the other was how little of the results of that struggle showed up in what we finally produced. I think we did do an exhibit about the process of scientific research and one that even captures some of that elusive social process that we sought. But in the end, what worked in the exhibit worked not because the research was still fresh and new but because we managed to connect it to the lives of our audience. To that end, history and analogy were as useful in elucidating the research process as anything that we found in the moment. I'm still wondering how much it mattered that we were working in the present tense and still wondering if PUR is too focused on the news.

The questions that this exhibit poses, then, for PUR practitioners have to do with the necessity of presenting current research instead of using science past to connect the audience to a real understanding of the process. Is this approach still called PUR? What about analogy as a method of eliciting understanding? Can it be used in the service of PUR? It is my opinion that these things should be considered a chance to broaden our outlook and increase our effectiveness in sharpening audience comprehension of the pursuit of science past, present, and future.

17

Public Understanding of Research in a Natural History Museum: The Darwin Centre

Sir Neil Chalmers

Many people today are deeply concerned at the apparent schism that they perceive between the world of science and scientific research on the one hand and the everyday concerns of the general public on the other. To many nonscientists, science is seen as something distant, threatening, and incomprehensible. This perception applies as much to the research carried out in the great natural history museums of the world as to that of any other research institutions. Such museums are centers of excellence for research into the biological and geological diversity of the earth, yet this research is largely hidden away behind locked doors, out of sight and mind to the multitudes of visitors who flock to the museums' exhibitions. The perceived gulf between scientific research and the public understanding of that research is, in the case of natural history museums, quite literally a physical gulf. It has existed for more than 100 years in museums such as the Natural History Museum in London, which in the 1890s separated its research collections on the one hand from its display collections on the other. The former were housed out of public view in large curatorial areas, arrayed, rather like books in a reference library, for rapid access by researchers, annotated solely with technical information and allocated close to laboratory and library facilities. The public collections, by contrast, were far less densely stored, were well displayed, and were accompanied by helpful explanatory labels in everyday language suitable for the general public. However well intentioned this policy was at the time and however right it was at the time, the gulf that it has created is today profoundly damaging and cannot be allowed to continue. The Natural History Museum in London took an important step to bridge this gulf when it opened the first phase of its new Darwin Centre in the autumn of 2002.

The Darwin Centre is, I believe, a unique initiative in the public understanding of research. To explain what it is trying to achieve, it is first necessary to explain something about the Natural History Museum as it is now, at the beginning of the twenty-first century, and also something about the way it has changed over the 250 years of its existence leading up to the institution in its present form. Today the Museum is one of Britain's most visited attractions, with nearly three million people coming to see its exhibitions each year in London and more than one million seeing its exhibitions on tour in Britain and around the world. We know from their reactions that they enjoy seeing and learning about the main ingredients of natural history, namely, the diversity of life on earth, about planet earth itself, and about the solar system. We also know, even though the Museum's exhibitions and educational programs are underpinned by the earth and life sciences, that they are given very little chance to understand either the nature or the intensity of the scientific endeavor generating the information they see on display.

Behind the scenes, like the other great natural history museums of the world, the Natural History Museum is a major scientific research organization. Some 300 scientists care for and research the collections of 70 million animals, plants, rocks, minerals, and fossils and publish their work in peer-reviewed science journals, just as in any other research organization. This very important part of the Museum's work is largely hidden from the public, yet when I have taken visitors behind the scenes to see something of what we do, they have been enthralled.

The aim of the Darwin Centre is to bring out into the open what was previously hidden. This is important for a number of reasons. First, we need to demystify science. People need to be able to see science in action, to talk to scientists engaged in the process of science, and to debate and discuss with them what they are doing, how they are doing it, and why. People need to be able to see that science is an understandable, reasonable, and worthwhile activity carried out by understandable, reasonable, and worthwhile people—by real human beings just like themselves. There is considerable public skepticism toward science in Britain at present, even hostility, much of it fueled by crises such as the foot-and-mouth epidemic of 2001 or the implication of bovine spongiform encephalitis in Creutzfeldt–Jakob disease, where many sectors of the public see science as having played a sinister role. Science has a tough job on its hands in cleaning up its public image. Second, and on an altogether more positive note, we need to get across the wonder and creativity of science and of the natural world that it reveals. We need to enthuse the next generation of scientists and embed science in our popular culture as strongly as art, literature, or sport.

The Darwin Centre aims to achieve these goals. Before describing how it does so, however, it is worth reflecting on how the relationship between scientific research and the public face of the Museum has changed since it was founded in 1753. Animals, plants, rocks, minerals, and fossils have been collected as individual items of curiosity, beauty, or practical value since the earliest times, but the habit of organizing them into special collections, or Cabinets of Curiosities, did not begin in Europe until the sixteenth and seventeenth centuries. It was in the 1650s, for example, that the Danish medical professor Olaus Worm created a private collection for his students of natural philosophy, thus founding one of the earliest natural history museums in Europe. However, the notion of a natural history collection simply as curiosities was soon superseded. Collections came to have two functions, both of which have a very modern ring. The first was to support what we would now call blue-sky or curiosity-driven research. This is simply the pursuit of knowledge for its own sake and, in this case, knowledge about our natural world. The second function was to enable people to use this increased knowledge for practical benefit.

The collections of Sir Hans Sloane provide a good example of these two functions. Sloane was the founder of the British Museum in 1753, of which the Natural History Museum formed a major part. From 1687 to 1689, Sloane had been the physician to the Duke of Albermarle, who was the British governor of Jamaica. While he was in the Caribbean, Sloane collected many local mammals, fish, and plants. One kind of plant that particularly caught his attention was sugarcane, *Saccharum officinarum*. He collected specimens, chose one as an exemplar (type specimen), described it meticulously, preserved it so that it is to this day housed in the Museum's collections, and published a fine illustration of it as well. His study of Caribbean sugarcane, as well as sugarcane from other parts of the world, led him to conclude that the Caribbean

Photo courtesy of Darwin Centre, the Natural History Museum, London

cane was originally from the Pacific and so had been introduced only later into the area. In this way, Sloane carried out fundamental, curiosity-driven research in the biological disciplines that today we would call morphology, systematics, and biogeography. Not content with this, Sloane became intensely interested in and wrote extensively about the production of granular sugar from cane, an area of great practical importance given the economic significance of sugarcane as a crop. The notion that his collections should exist in isolation from the practical concerns of the real world would have been alien to Sloane. Given that the collections that he amassed during his life became the foundation of the great collections of the Natural History Museum in London, his breadth of vision was extremely important.

It was in these early days of exploration that natural history museums became great research centers. As voyagers sailed around the world discovering new lands, they marveled at the host of unknown animals, plants, fossils, and minerals that they encountered, and they brought them back to the museums of western Europe for scientific study. As discovery continued, Cook, Banks, Solander, the artist Sydney Parkinson, Darwin, Wallace, and many others all contributed to the museums' scientific coffers. These museums have been eclipsed only during the twentieth century, as the "big sciences" of particle physics, astronomy, and molecular biology have become major industries. But, as we will see, the need for natural history museums in their leading-research role is now greater than ever before.

In the nineteenth century, the natural history departments of the British Museum separated from their parent body and were established on a site in South Kensington in London as the institution now known as the Natural History Museum. When the Museum opened in 1881, Superintendent Richard Owen wanted its displays to reflect the latest scientific thought (in truth, his own latest scientific thought) on the characteristics and relationships of the major groups of organisms. The exhibitions on display thus functioned as an index of life and were, in fact, overtly referred to as an Index Museum. Owen took it for granted that the fruits of the latest scientific research should be on display and saw no need to create boundaries between the two.

It is, therefore, a paradox that one of the Natural History Museum's greatest directors, Sir William Flower (1884–1898), should have created a highly significant boundary that persists to this day in nearly all the great natural history museums around the world. He divided the Museum's collections into two distinct parts: the display collections for the edification of the visiting public and the study collections for scientific research. The study collections and the scientific staff who used them—quietly, intensely, and privately—became hidden from public view. No doubt this was the right decision at the time, but its long-term consequence was that the practice of scientific research in natural history museums became divorced from public display.

In the years since, the separation of the Museum's scientific research from its public programs has become increasingly pronounced. The design and production of exhibitions rightly became recognized as a specialized activity requiring different professional skills from those possessed by research curators. Moreover, the kind of science carried out by research curators remained focused on or close to the disciplines of systematic biology and geology, whereas the public programs ranged over a wide array of biological and geological topics as their horizons expanded. By the end of the twentieth century, when the need for science within the United Kingdom to be out in the public arena was particularly pressing, the gulf between the Museum's highly specialized and technical scientific research on the one hand and its more wide-ranging, popular programs for the public on the other had become immense.

The Museum's answer to this situation is the Darwin Centre. It is both a building and a concept. The concept has three strands. The first is to create a top-class environment within which the Museum's science can flourish—to provide state-of-the-art storage facilities for the Museum's magnificent collections and good laboratory, communications, and office facilities for the scientists who study them. The second is to display the collections and facilities in such a way that the Museum's visitors can see both. We want visitors to see something of the sheer size and variety of the collections, to understand why such extraordinarily rich and enormous collections are needed, and to realize that they are actively used. The third strand is to show science in action—to enable visitors to meet the people who do the science, to see what their research involves, and to discuss it with them, whether in terms of the science itself or in terms of how it relates to contemporary topics of public concern.

The Darwin Centre is really a principle perhaps most easily summarized as "Open Up Your Science." But it is still also a building—the focus within the Natural History Museum where this principle is being realized. For purely local reasons of logistics, the building is being constructed in two phases. It is the first phase, which provides a home for some 22 million animals pickled in alcohol and research facilities for some 100 scientists, that was opened to the public in the autumn of 2002. The second phase, which is currently in an advanced stage of planning, will house some 30 million insects, six million plants, and 160 scientists.

It may be helpful to describe how the first phase of the Darwin Centre achieves, through its design, the previously mentioned goals. In museum terms, it is quite large: eight stories high and 100,000 square feet (10,000 square meters) of floor space. Visitors enter through an atrium running down the center of the building that splits it like a wedge from the main floor to the translucent roof far above. On one side of the atrium lie the collections, visible through special fire-resistant windows and protruding out into the atrium in floor-to-ceiling cases. Seeing the collections area towering up to the roof, visitors experience something of their size and diversity. The aim is not for people to see and study each specimen, which is plainly an impossible task. Instead, we provide them with information on the groups of animals found in the collections—fish, amphibians, reptiles, numerous groups of invertebrates, and even an unfortunate rat that was found dead on the building site when it was under construction. We explain that we collect around the world, from tropical forests to the Antarctic, from high mountains to the ocean depths. And we explain that we collect in order to discover more about life on earth so that we can use it wisely and sustainably, that we still know less than 20 percent of the species of life on this planet, and that ignorance of such extent is shocking. We explain why we must collect several specimens of each species to discover the full range of variation found within any one species. And we explain, above all, that collections are a starting point for scientific research, whether it be research into blue-sky subjects, like the evolution of life on earth, or into subjects of great practical value, like control of the malarial parasite and the mosquitoes that are its carriers.

These explanations are made partly in conventional museum format, with captions on display panels, but depth is provided through touchscreens. Visitors can explore their individual concerns for themselves, whether environmental conservation or the significance of the work of Charles Darwin. Given the international composition of the Museum's audience, the touchscreens operate in 12 languages.

If visitors wish to see the collections in more detail, they can go on guided tours behind the scenes every 30 minutes during the Museum's opening hours, seven days a week. They can book for these either on the spot or before their visit using the Museum's Web site. Visitors are issued white laboratory coats for their tours, a practice that simultaneously serves several functions: it protects visitors' clothing from the remote risk of alcohol spillage (used to preserve the collections and on tap within the collections area), it readily identifies visitor parties so that the tour guides can keep track of their party members, and it seems to please the visitors themselves. It also helps keep visitors warm since the collections areas are chilled to 13 degrees centigrade to reduce the fire risk from the alcohol and to reduce the evaporation rate from the glass storage bottles. (There are, in fact, some 450,000 such bottles stacked in 25 kilometers of shelving. The storage area of the predecessor building was not chilled, and it took curators some two years to go around the collections topping up the evaporated alcohol just in time to start all over again.) The tour guides are mostly young science graduates recruited not only for their scientific knowledge but also for their ability to interact well with a great variety of visitors. Others have been selected from among the Museum's existing guides working in the Museum's main galleries, again for their interpersonal skills and, in some cases, for their linguistic abilities.

When they are on the tours, visitors can come up close to fish, mollusks, and other animals collected by Darwin himself or to the huge range of animals collected during the great Challenger and Discovery maritime expeditions of the nineteenth and early twentieth centuries. They can see the giant and mysterious oar fish, pickled pythons, and a shark's head donated by Harrods's food hall. Ascending the atrium in a glass lift, they can see on the one side the collections area and on the other the laboratories, libraries, and offices of the scientists. While tours do not usually go into the laboratory area, in order to allow the scientists to carry on with their work uninterrupted, for many people this is their first sight of laboratories, and it comes as a revelation that such a major scientific activity is going on in the Museum. The tours are proving so popular that at many times of the week the staff cannot cope with demand.

Whether or not visitors go on guided tours, they have the opportunity to take part in what is perhaps the most exciting feature of the Darwin Centre. Twice a day, seven days a weeks, they can join in a discussion with one or more of the Museum's scientists about his or her science. The event takes place in a special demonstration area in the heart of the atrium on the main floor. It looks a bit like a seminar room and a bit like a broadcasting studio, and it holds approximately 70 people at a time. This is not so big as to be intimidating, not too formal, but it is big enough to cope with a good number of people over a period of time. Our aim is to have a scientist bring along some specimens from his or her area of special knowledge and talk with our visitors about them in such a way as will respond to the visitors' interests and, if at all possible, to subjects of contemporary concern. Elaborate audiovisual facilities help things along, projecting on a series of screens anything from minute organisms on microscope slides to the latest news footage of, say, an erupting volcano. Where objects are too large or remote to be brought into the demonstration area, we link up by computer to anywhere else in the building or by satellite to anywhere else in the world. The subject of the talk on Halloween, topically enough, was bats, and the presenter of the day linked up by satellite with the Museum's field station in Belize in Central America to show living bats flying around and being collected at the station. Another discussion, led by one of the Museum's fish experts, linked up to the Museum's gigantic tank room to show the investigation of the first barracuda ever caught off the southwest coast of England. Since barracuda are normally found only in much warmer waters, was this just one very lost fish, or was it evidence of global warming? The ensuing discussion with a very informed audience probed deeply, not only issues of global warming, but also the nature of scientific evidence.

There are several key features of these *Darwin Live* sessions, as we call them. First, they feature the real experts with their real specimens, and they have revealed considerable and sometimes unexpected performance skills among our scientists. Many were at the outset somewhat apprehensive about going on a show like this, but their sheer level of knowledge and enthusiasm has been able to carry the day. Some, in fact, are developing into real stars. Interestingly enough, audiences really like the fact that the scientists are so obviously the genuine article and are not highly polished, artificially groomed media presenters.

Photo courtesy of Darwin Centre, the Natural History Museum, London

Second, the presentations are discussions or dialogues and not lectures. To achieve this end, each presentation has a host. Hosts, like guides, are specially recruited science graduates who are good with people. Their job is to help scientists put together the material for their presentations and to help the sessions along. The host introduces the scientist of the day, gets the discussion going by throwing questions to the speaker if audience members have not already done so unaided, hands around microphones among the audience, and eventually rounds things off. Visitors are free to come and go during the discussion if they wish, but the great majority stay to the end—indeed, I have seen some audiences cheering enthusiastically for more if the host incautiously suggests that it is time to stop.

The topics so far covered in the *Darwin Live* sessions have been varied and have included Desert Tomatoes—wild relatives of cultivated tomatoes that flourish in arid condition; Life in the Dark—the exotic communities of creatures found in the ocean depths; and London's Air: How Close Are We to Suffocating?—a discussion of how lichens can tell us about the levels of air pollution experienced in industrial countries over the past hundred years. It is important to emphasize, however, that the *Darwin Live* presentations are not simply expositions of scientific fact. They explore how scientists work, collecting plants while wading up tributaries of the Amazon River or collecting fish from the ocean depths; how they interpret what they find; and how they themselves first became interested in science. In one such discussion, a member of the audience asked this question of a Museum beetle expert who was giving the presentation. The expert's mother was in the audience and jumped in to say, "Oh, he's been collecting beetles since he was a little boy!" Such human-interest stories have proved particularly popular, and while several of our scientists initially adopted a fairly orthodox research/seminar style of delivery, they readily adapted to the new format and, indeed, have started to explore for themselves the new possibilities offered by the Darwin Centre.

There were perhaps three main difficulties we had to overcome as we created the Darwin Centre. The first was how to enable the public to come close to the Museum's collections without putting either the collections or themselves in jeopardy. The collections are, of course, a treasure of incomparable value and so must be protected from accidental damage from visitors walking by. They are also stored in highly flammable alcohol, which poses a fire risk and hence a risk to the safety of both the public and the Museum's staff. Both of these issues mean that the collections are, in truth, less accessible than we would wish. The collections are housed in a highly specified fire-resistant area that is chilled to reduce the fire risk. While many of the first-phase collections can be seen through fire-resistant windows from the main public atrium, sheer cost prevents this from being possible on all floors. The collections are also protected by ensuring that visitors are escorted through the collections areas in small groups, although this necessarily limits the overall number of tour visitors. In the second phase of the Darwin Centre, where the Museum's insect and plant collections will not present such extreme challenges, we plan to enable visitors to move at will along set routes through the collections so that much larger numbers can gain access than is possible in the first phase.

A second and more predictable problem is the cost. It is only human nature for one's ambitions to exceed one's budget, and we had to make some painful decisions as we balanced the competing claims of laboratories, collections areas, and public areas. The budget for the project had an absolute ceiling of £30 million, representing the amount that the Museum had been able to accrue from its own income-generating activities over a number of years in addition to a small amount of government money allocated specifically to the project. (This is not a strategy we will be repeating for the second phase of the Darwin Centre. At £65 million, the second phase is simply too expensive to be funded in this way, and we are resorting to the more conventional strategy of fundraising. At the time of this writing, we have raised approximately £31 million toward this total.)

Some of the fiercest arguments that took place during the planning phase centered on the provision of a common room. Should a room for tea and coffee for our staff have precedence over more space for collections, laboratories, or our visitors? The answer was that it should, and although I had doubts at the time, I am sure now that it was the right decision. This is because of the third big issue that we had to face when planning the Darwin Centre, namely, how to involve and gain the support of our staff and particularly our scientific staff. Many of them were initially apprehensive, some because they foresaw a possibly unwelcome interruption to their research and curatorial duties, some because they were not used to coming face to face with the general public. We sought to overcome these apprehensions in a number of ways. First, we involved those scientists whose laboratories, collections, and offices were going to be in the Darwin Centre in the design of their own facilities. If they judged that a common room, for example, where they could meet colleagues informally to discuss their work, was more important than an extra laboratory, then it was important that they should have the opportunity to make that argument. Second, we involved a number of our scientists in planning how to engage the public. The scientists worked with our exhibitions and communications staff to develop the components of the public experience that I described earlier.

Finally, we made it clear that we wanted all our scientists at the Museum to contribute in one way or another to the Darwin Centre's public programs. We decided early on that no individual should be required to devote more than two days a year giving *Darwin Live* sessions. This in itself provided reassurance that, however important, the sessions in public were not going to intrude too much into scientists' normal programs of work. We then provided training so that they would feel comfortable about performing in public in a situation closer to an informal workshop than a formal lecture. Many of our staff were and are, of course, experienced and accomplished lecturers, but others are not. Regardless of their level of experience, we emphasized that the sessions are not lectures but genuinely interactive discussions. Many of our scientists have since agreed that such training was valuable.

As time has gone by since the opening of the Darwin Centre, the commitment and enthusiasm of our scientists to the Darwin has grown to gratifying levels. Many of them find it rewarding to discover that their own professional knowledge and passions are interesting to the public at large. Most of them love talking about their work, especially when they have their favorite specimens on hand. In short, almost all their initial reservations have vanished.

The *Darwin Live* presentations are designed first and foremost for more adult audiences than those who typically visit the Museum's main galleries; the latter are especially favored by families with younger children, and we want this to continue. But we do see a strong need to bring serious science and serious issues of the day to people of all ages, and we are trying to make the Darwin Centre particularly attractive to older visitors. These are still early days, of course, and my belief is that we are only just beginning to re-alize the Darwin Centre's potential. This is particularly true of the *Darwin Live* space, where the opportunity to bring science into the world of current affairs is the greatest. I believe that in the coming years we will discover still better and more compelling ways to marry the skills of our scientists and the wonder of our collections with the potential provided by new media. I hope very much that the Darwin Centre will provide a starting point for a new voyage of discovery.

WHAT MUSEUMS CAN LEARN FROM MEDIA PUBLIC UNDERSTANDING OF RESEARCH INITIATIVES

Public understanding of research is relatively new to most museums but has a long history in most other media. So what can other media teach museums about bringing current research to wide audiences? In this section, we learn from experts in mass-circulation newspapers, television, and radio.

Emerging Best Practices at Research-Performing Institutions

Rick Borchelt

With the fall of the Berlin Wall in 1989, the historic justification for federal investment in science and technology—Cold War superiority on all military, economic, and technical fronts—evaporated overnight. The Russian threat diminished, the United States was clearly established as the dominant world leader, and scientists returned to long-unused arguments about scientific literacy and public good to justify programs that had been rationalized with little more than Cold War rhetoric since World War II.

The decade since has seen a tremendous surge in science communication programs ostensibly aimed at retaining or increasing public support for science in the absence of the Cold War threat. From federal science agencies like the National Science Foundation (NSF) and the Department of Energy (DOE) to research universities and institutes, the push has been to explain what the nation gets for its substantial investment in research and development. This has not been solely a U.S. problem, either—other countries, particularly in the Western world, have faced similar crises of confidence in support for science and technology. The current grim world economic picture promises to increase the scramble for dwindling public support for research worldwide.

Against this backdrop, I was charged by the National Aeronautics and Space Administration (NASA) in 1998 to initiate a review of "best practices" in public communication of science and technology in use at research-performing and research-funding organizations. With the assistance of a blue-ribbon panel of academicians, journalists, public affairs practitioners, and other science communicators, I spent the next three years identifying and evaluating candidate programs. In early 2002, we convened an international public conference to review these communications initiatives and share the techniques that made them successful.

We were looking for hallmarks of good communication: the targeting and understanding of the needs of a discrete audience, a good match between the medium (mass media, direct mail, Web based) and the information being conveyed, content that illustrates both the process and the products of science and that ideally involves the scientist in telling the story, and rigorous forma-tive and evaluative research to make certain that public understanding mate-rially improved.

INSTITUTIONAL ADVANCEMENT OR SCIENTIFIC UNDERSTANDING?
Most of the programs we reviewed, quite frankly, were institutional advance-ment programs masquerading as science communication. While it is true that some science gets communicated as a by-product of institutional press re-leases, house organs, and glitzy advertising campaigns, this communication seldom reaches the appropriate target audiences with the right messages to be effective as science communication.

This unfortunate conflation of communication goals is exemplified by many of the federal agencies that fund research. There were few examples of scientific communication conducted with the explicit goal of increasing pub-lic understanding of research rather than public support for research con-ducted by the agency in particular. Most communications were aimed either exclusively at congressional budget makers or, alternatively, at a constituent base so broad as to be meaningless. To a large extent, this approach pervades even well-respected communications powerhouses like NASA, which enjoys broad, if shallow, public support for space travel and space science. Similarly, the National Institutes of Health conducts prodigious research on how best to communicate the consequences of health decisions to the public, but its own institutional communication can best be described as self-referential. This was equally true of public agencies in other countries that we examined.

Notwithstanding this emphasis on corporate communications by federal research agencies, we did note two emergent trends that argue for an improvement in how the public might come to learn about science and technology apart from institutional advancement.

At NASA, for example, major federal grants given to principal investigators in most space and earth science programs have for some years now carried a "set-aside" of around 2 percent for education and public outreach related to the grant. The NSF also is exploring the set-aside concept, and some grants now have reserved funding for outreach purposes. While there is great potential for this approach to empower bench scientists and grantee institutions to engage in robust programs of public understanding of science, the effectiveness of this alternative to traditional communications funding has not been evaluated.

We learned anecdotally that a thriving cottage industry has emerged among freelance communications firms and agency public information offices to help scientists spend their set-aside dollars, and not surprisingly these are seldom coordinated with overall agency goals. This system of funding, for example, has led to a confusing welter of "education" Web sites under the NASA umbrella, few of which pass muster as effective communication tools. Alternatively, many researchers simply use their dollars to support page charges for publication or student travel to present papers at academic conferences. Perhaps the most telling indicator of the regard with which the agencies view these set-aside programs is that we could not identify a single instance in which the education and public outreach component was the final determinant of a grantee receiving an award or in which a grantee was admonished for ineffective use of these dollars.

On the other hand, some programs that benefit from these set-asides were identified as model practices. At NASA's Marshall Space Flight Center, for example, core funding from the Center and from headquarters mingled with set-aside dollars funds an excellent Web site, Science@NASA, that provides well-written, substantive space and earth science articles aimed at an adult science-attentive audience.[1] At the time it was reviewed, the site also was paired with educational units aimed at elementary and junior high students; unfortunately this companion site has not received continuing support from NASA. The Science@NASA team regularly reviews Web statistics on this site and other NASA sites to determine audience interests and information-seeking behavior and modifies the site to match.

Similarly, a suite of products called Passport to Knowledge (P2K) uses NASA, NSF, National Oceanic and Atmospheric Administration, and other funding to integrate research and education and outreach.[2] With programs aimed at educators, students, and broadcasters, the P2K materials allow audience-specific messages from a single-site source. It is not inexpensive to maintain, however—from 1994 to 2002, P2K expended some $6 million on its programming.

Moreover, it must be kept in mind that many of the effective programs we reviewed and selected for presentation at the 2002 conference are otherwise funded in whole or in part with federal dollars, so it cannot be said that the government fails its communication responsibilities completely.

DRIVEN BY NEW TECHNOLOGY

Many of the programs we selected are not "new" in the sense that they had not been tried before, successfully or not. But what merited attention was their use of new technologies, such as the Internet, to target different discrete audiences (such as specialized media) or aggregate content from multiple sources.

One area where we saw such new tricks for old dogs consisted of special news services distributing science and technical materials to the press. At first glance, this hardly seems innovative, but some of these programs could not have existed prior to the rise of the World Wide Web. EurekAlert!, for example, a Web site hosted by the American Association for the Advancement of Science, offers a one-stop shop for reporters, providing embargoed journal articles, news releases, and backgrounders that have become a staple for reporters covering science.[3] At present, more than 3,000 reporters in the United States and abroad regularly use the site to find material for their stories. It has truly become a "must-use" resource for science reportage. Such a program depends utterly on the Internet technology behind it, and that characterizes a number of similar programs we identified as emerging best practices.

Similar in intent, but much simpler in execution, is a news-release distribution system operated by Steven Maran on behalf of the American

Astronomical Society. Maran serves as a central distribution point for astronomy, astrophysics, and space science stories from many research institutions that he then redistributes to a confidential list of space and physics reporters. In a sense, he serves as the "honest broker" who quickly reviews the content for credibility before sending it along to the press while making no claims about the research itself. This model could be easily adapted to other disciplines, such as ecology, biomedicine, or agriculture. It offers a "push" technology in real time for niche reporters currently unavailable on sites like EurekAlert!

Where the World Wide Web also offers a new approach to existing initiatives is as an adjunct to classroom learning for students. An exemplar of this approach is the Dolan DNA Learning Center at Cold Spring Harbor.[4] The learning center actually is a suite of Web sites dedicated to genetic education at all levels, from K–12 to adult learners and the press. At $500,000 a year, however, it is unlikely to be replicated by any but the most dedicated or well-funded programs.

Another elegant use of Web sites to supplement traditional classroom education consists of the biointeractive virtual labs and knowledge environments hosted by Howard Hughes Medical Institute.[5] In addition to offering an extensive collection of animations illustrating key concepts in molecular biology, the site offers virtual laboratory experiences that can be used in lieu of or to reinforce wet-lab experiences in the classroom. The animation console element of the program is most easily adaptable and could be used by museums, universities, or other institutions to organize and deliver science education materials.

LOCATION, LOCATION, LOCATION

Some of the best programs we selected will not be easy to modify for general use because they are oriented around natural or topographic features. Among the best we saw was the Ashkui Project of Environment Canada.[6] Observing that native peoples in northern Canada gather in special geographic areas for sharing information about the natural world and natural resources, the Ashkui staff trek themselves to these areas for the consultation and information gathering that informs their conservation efforts.

Similarly, the Murray-Darling Basin Commission[7] in Australia takes advantage of the innate interest of Australian schoolchildren in a large riverine system to spark creation of knowledge units and classroom plans developed in conjunction with the Primary Teaching Association.[8] The collaboration provides an effective template for public–private partnerships in scientific communication.

The panel also identified a very useful Web site hosted by the DOE at the University of New Mexico that provides a clearinghouse for policymakers and affected stakeholders interested in transportation of radioactive materials across the nation's highways and other transportation modes. Positioned as a public interface for public outreach, the site (dubbed T-REX) is critically dependent on the usability of its several online searchable databases to access material for a variety of patrons.[9] Of all the programs we studied, the T-REX team arguably did the best job of advance research to guide the development of the Web site.

DIRECT-TO-CONSUMER PROGRAMMING

We frankly were disappointed at the few successful attempts we reviewed at reaching adult audiences directly rather than through educators, reporters, or other information mediators. One such program was an outreach effort by the Kansas Geological Survey to directly reach policymakers about critical issues in geologic resource management in Kansas. Their Annual Field Conference attracts legislators, government agency staff, business leaders, environmental leaders, and others who need natural-resource information to make policy decisions.[10] These discussions take place in the field with people who use or are affected by geological resources.

For a more generalized audience of science attentives, the National Academies of Sciences Beyond Discovery project is a Web- and print-based publication series aimed at illuminating the role of basic research that underpins well-known or well-publicized medical or scientific breakthroughs.[11] It is an effective tool, meticulously audience tested, and translated into foreign languages for overseas audiences as well.

In this last respect, Beyond Discovery was atypical of most of the programs we reviewed and even some we eventually selected. Formative and evaluative research was one of the most prominent missing elements of public communications programs, and this was true even of Web sites where it is relatively easy to generate usage and usability data. Most of the program administrators we talked with were apologetic, but expressed that they get no support from program or agency managers who see dollars wasted on evaluation when they could be used to support more programming. This was as true, incidentally, of communicators in museum settings as it was of public information officials in traditional academic and corporate settings.

This is a false dichotomy, of course, and ultimately erodes the success and credibility of programs aimed at public understanding of research. Every poorly planned program competes for the attention of consumers already overwhelmed with communication of all sorts and from all media; both the achievement of a specific communication goal of the institution and science communication as an enterprise are diminished.

In many ways, this conference celebrates the diversity of communication efforts across a wide variety of institutional settings. While on a conceptual level it seems easy to justify "letting a thousand flowers bloom," we run the risk of sabotaging the effectiveness of the communications we undertake unless we exercise restraint and discretion in science communication to the public. We have an obligation as a professional community to promulgate and enforce "best practice" approaches to develop not only good programs, but also the formative and evaluative tools to benchmark these programs.

NOTES

1. www.science.nasa.gov (accessed February 25, 2004).

2. www.passporttoknowledge.com (accessed February 25, 2004).

3. www.eurekalert.org (accessed February 25, 2004).

4. www.dnalc.org (accessed February 25, 2004).

5. www.hhmi.org/biointeractive/ (accessed February 25, 2004).

6. www.stmarys.ca/administration/gorsebrook/ashkui.htm (accessed February 25, 2004).

7. Murray-Darling Basin Commission, www.mdbc.gov.au.

8. Primary Teaching Association, www.peta.edu.au/project/project.htm (accessed February 25, 2004).

9. www.trex-center.org (accessed February 25, 2004).

10. www.kgs.ukans.edu (accessed February 25, 2004).

11. www.BeyondDiscovery.org (accessed February 25, 2004).

19

It's the Way You Tell 'Em

Tim Radford

One of the more common fantasies within science is that the public is potentially interested in research, or would be if only broadcasters and newspapermen were doing their jobs properly. In fact, people are usually interested more in *what science can do* than in *how science is done*. The payoff matters; the process can be left to the professionals. Such an attitude should not be a surprise: even scientists are naturally interested in their life insurance premiums but hardly ever in the wretched minutiae of how actuaries and accountants arrive at them.

So the hard-won advances of modern research—how a drug interferes with the spread of a virus, how a cell picks the moment to divide, what it takes to trigger totipotency in a stem cell, and so on—do not get detailed attention in the popular media. New vaccines and cures, cancer treatments, and cloned sheep, however, do. The triumphs of the kind of physics that deal in electron capture, Bose–Einstein condensates, or atomic array tend to get lost in stories about quantum computing or the miracles of some future nanotechnology. The language of the press—which is the language of the populace—should be a guide to these matters. A widespread interest in science would be matched by the frequency of correct use of a number of key words coined and widely used by scientists.

Since 1985, according to a computer search, the word *phenotype* has appeared in the British national press 54 times, the word *phylum* has appeared only 25 times (11 of them in my own paper, the *Guardian*), the word *albedo* 18 times, and the word *mitochondrion* 17 times. The geological term *isostasy* has, according to admittedly haphazard newspaper databases, never appeared at all.

Yet, all British newspapers have science reporters or commentators of one kind or another. You would know this just by searching for the word *Franken-stein*, which appears at least 4,226 times in the same 17-year database, quite often in connection with cloning or genetic engineering. The phrase *Pandora's box* also occurs 1,227 times, and the description *playing God* pops up 1,606 times. Sometimes all three occur in the same article. The other useful cliché, *Faustian bargain*, disappointingly, has been used only 189 times.

What could you conclude from these things? You could conclude that the British press does not report science as such, that instead it prefers to dismiss science in terms of loaded imagery, hand-me-down metaphors, and cheap clichés culled from the humanities. You could also conclude that very few journalists know their Marlowe, Gounod, or Goethe. These conclusions, however, are based on a misunderstanding. On the whole, there are always exceptions—science reporters in Britain and in the United States do not even try to report science, not in the sense of science as a series of systematic, one-step-at-a-time advances in knowledge on a huge front. They look instead for stories within the field of science, rather in the way that sports reporters look for stories in the world of sport. In a daily paper, science reporters compete with other reporters not just for space but, more important, for readers.

Consider the problem. The total number of words in a newspaper is huge—the equivalent of *Dombey and Son* or *A Tale of Two Cities* every day— but the time devoted to reading a newspaper is brief: half an hour or so at breakfast, or during the journey to work. So a morning newspaper should be regarded not as a full bacon-and-egg breakfast of sensible nourishment to be consumed in an orderly and sustained manner, but rather as a huge smorgas-bord table from which a million or so readers may snack, pausing to select this or that tempting morsel before moving on to another delight. Readers will choose those stories that thrill, shock, or amuse; that appeal to a sense of delight, humor, piquancy, prurience, fear, or horror; stories that are sensational in that they appeal to one of those senses.

They are also less likely to read stories that kick off with baffling or alienating words such as *phenotyope, mitochondrion, isostasy,* or *phylum.* Why should anybody be surprised at that? Experts may feel compelled to reveal, and journalists may claim a mission to explain, but readers have never felt obliged to read something that mystified or bored them.

Journalists and scientists have a lot in common: both are driven by curiosity; both regard the phrase "I don't know" as an interesting starting point, not an admission of defeat; both frame hypotheses, do literature searches, systematically gather evidence, write their results, and submit their articles to peer review before publication. There the likeness ends. Scientists take as long as they need to complete a paper; daily newspapermen do what they have to do inside a day. But that is not the important difference. A scientific publication matters even if hardly anybody ever reads it: it exists as a marker, as a record to be accepted or challenged, as a claim to priority. A newspaper story that was read by nobody would have been a complete waste of time. Newspapermen and women have more in common with Queen Sheherezade, who for 1,001 nights skillfully spun stories—we tell them still, of Sinbad the sailor and Aladdin and his magic lamp and Ali Baba and the 40 thieves—for the benefit of a delighted caliph. Had Sheherezade lost the ruler's attention just for one night, she would have been beheaded like all the other wives. And when they lose the attention of their readers, newspapers, too, also die.

So scientists and journalists are, at bottom, looking for two different things. Both are concerned to find the truth. But the scientist wants an answer, however dull. The journalist would rather find a story. Both findings have to withstand the test of time, but the time in each case is different. That is why scientists spend five years or five months on a complex and profound piece of research that then takes five weeks to write up and another five months to finesse through the editorial board of a learned journal. And then journalists come along the next morning, ring them up, and spend five minutes asking them what the hell it means. What journalists write goes into a newspaper five hours later, and the next morning a reader picks it up, comes across a term like *mitochondrion* or *functional genomics*, and stops reading, all in a fifth of a second, to go on to something else, perhaps something enjoyably disgraceful involving a politician and a call girl or a famous footballer and a fracas with the police. There is, technically, no reason why a newspaper should not use a word like *phylum*. It is only likely to do so, however, when it occurs in a good story.

A story is paradoxically difficult to define but easy to recognize. Here is an account about one golden day in the life of a science writer. It began with a visit in 1997 to a university far from London on behalf of the British Association for the Advancement of Science, ostensibly to talk about the media and its obsessions to a party of physicists, chemists, biochemists, zoologists, geographers, geophysicists, and so on. It was also, of course, an excuse to get out of the office and find some stories. In the course of an afternoon and the next morning, I managed five encounters and found four stories. One involved the provocative subject of science and religion; the second, a challenging piece of genetic engineering of potentially huge importance to the developing world. At the third laboratory, someone cheerfully announced that his laboratory had just built a transistor so small that it could be hidden underneath a common cold virus. At the fourth, a professor began to tell me about the design of a life-size robot iguanadon designed to stroll around the corridors of European museums. His role was to confront some immediate zoological puzzles: Did the iguanadon snort, or hiss, or roar, or just moo? Was it mottled, or blotched, or mamba green, or elephant gray? Was its skin taut, or was it a bit baggy?

With four stories in the bag already, I was frankly relieved when the fifth encounter turned out to be instructive rather than compelling. It was about how polymer scientists could alter the characteristics of a compound by changing the shape of the molecule without changing its chemistry. There were some practical payoffs involving bone repair, hair shampoos, and so on. But it didn't seem to me that I had a story.

I then delivered a talk to the assembly of scientists about what the media wanted, mostly by giving examples of other good stories that had emerged on laboratory visits, during conferences, and so on, and by showing how quite often just one good sentence, delivered in plain English, could turn a complex piece of scientific research into that magic thing: a story that everybody would read. At the end of it, my polymer scientist came up to me and said pleasantly, "I did that all wrong, didn't I?" I assured him that he had not. It had been a most interesting briefing and fascinating as well, only I wasn't quite sure yet how I was going to. . . .

He cut me short. "What I should have said to you was that we can take supermarket shopping bags and turn them into a bullet-proof vest strong enough to stop a bullet from a magnum .44 pistol," he said. He then led me to a secure corner of his laboratory, and there, on a tripod, was a .44 magnum. Three meters from it, on a tailor's dummy, were 40 layers of polyethylene, dented but not pierced by a bullet fired at a muzzle velocity of 400 meters per second. He had, of course, also hit the spot in a reporter's heart.

There are three great stories in science: where the universe came from, where life came from, where we came from. Reporters have no trouble writing stories about the Big Bang, the beginning of time and space, the condensation of matter from some expanding fireball of energy, the search for the evidence 15 billion years later in the cold darkness of the space between the stars. They don't have much difficulty writing about dinosaurs in the Cretaceous, or of Neanderthals in the Paleolithic. Dendrochronology is a breeze, especially when it evokes the Bronze Age of King Midas or the Dark Ages of Europe after the fall of the Roman Empire.

These are, of course, parallel or updated versions of the same great stories told by the Greek myths, by the Bible or the Koran, or by Homer and Malory. Such stories deal not just with the visible and the imaginable; they deal with things that people have been trying to figure out for the whole of recorded history. On the other hand, it is quite a challenge to write about solid-state physics, nanotechnology, molecular biology, quantum mechanics, and other invisible science.

The paradox is that research that makes no practical difference whatever to modern human life can be compellingly interesting, while technologies that profoundly change the way we live and work remain simply things in black boxes. There are exceptions: reporters and readers are liable to become quite excited about antimatter, teleportation, and manifestations that seem to exceed the speed of light. The arrival of Dolly the cloned sheep caused worldwide uproar. But these stories "work" because the ground has been prepared by nonscience, that is, by the fiction of the television series *Star Trek* or Ira Levin's novel *The Boys from Brazil*. Clones and teleportation were, therefore, already "old" stories when they happened. Humans are remarkably eager to hear familiar stories and surprisingly unwillingly to make the effort to assimilate the new. In theory, science reporters should be the lucky ones, with something new to say every day. In practice, science reporters have to write the same story a number of times before anybody notices the science at all. When it does begin to make headlines, human drama tends to take over from science. The Human Genome Project, for instance, remained off the news pages until it turned into a race between charismatic figures and until the researchers themselves started taking crash courses in metaphor manufacture and hyperbole handling. Reporters had been blithely describing genetic experiments with crops for a decade before genetically modified food became part of the political debate.

There are plausible reasons why much science remains unreported, under-reported, or poorly reported. One reason is that all news requires a touch of fanfare, but science reporters, on behalf of the public, tend after a while to become wary of hailing revolutions, breakthroughs, and dramatic advances in science, largely because of the decades-long gap between the initial promise of a piece of research and the final delivery of, say, a treatment for cancer, heart disease, or cystic fibrosis. Another reason is that science is hard to explain, especially in the 400 or 500 words of a newspaper story. Why should it not be? It is performed by Ph.D.s rather than dilettantes. Of course it would be hard to explain. A third has been the refusal of many academic scientists to engage with the rest of the human race in clear, simple, and vivid language. A fourth is the persistent set of snobbish attitudes, in Britain at least, that have tended to rate science, engineering, and technology as somehow less glamorous or less important than, for example, conceptual art or merchant banking and that have made the profession of ignorance of science into a kind of badge of respectability. These last two factors mean that any dialogue between scientists and the public is in danger of becoming an encounter between the effectively mute and the selectively deaf.

And then there is the lexicon problem: science is the discovery of the new, and new things have to be named. There are clumsy circumlocutions for *phenotype, mitochondrion, albedo, isostasy,* and *phylum,* but there are neither simple analogies nor simple alternative words. So the coinages must be used, but in conditions of circumspection. The word *mitochondrion,* dropped carelessly, could send 100,000 readers skipping to the racing page. So reporters with an ambition to be right, but with an even greater ambition to be read, will cheat. They will aim to leave the reader with the illusion that something has been explained (using a sophisticated technique called PCR, or politically correct rhetoric) and get on with the main point of the story: that forensic scientists could identify a suspect from the DNA on the stem of a wine glass. To get back to the list of words with which we began: *phenotype* tends to appear in newspaper columns actually written by scientists. *Albedo* occasionally pops up in climate science news, but Albedo is also the name of a publisher and a theater company. *Mitochondria* are most likely to be mentioned in a story about kinship and DNA. The word *phylum* achieved fleeting worldwide currency from a report in the journal *Nature* some years ago. *Symbiont Pandora* was announced as the only specimen of not just a new species, not just a new genus or family, but a whole new phylum. It was a mysterious little beast that seemed (in the published drawing at least) to be blessed with two penises and a marvelously mysterious asexual route to reproduction as well in which the little creature dispatched its teenage phase to the wider world with no brain at all. This alone would have struck a sympathetic chord with any parent or anybody who could remember having been a teenager.

But *Symbiont Pandora* had even more going for it. It had been discovered, purely by accident, sitting "like an animated cold sore" (said *Nature*'s own press release) on the lips of a Norway lobster also known as nephrops or Dublin Bay prawn. It was the story of chance discovery involving food, sex, and strange sea creatures, and it had everything. It also, of course, gave science reporters a chance to introduce the idea of the phylum to a million readers at a time, confident for once that they would see the word and go on reading anyway. That, in the end, is all science reporters can do: introduce difficult ideas, a bit at a time, and go on reintroducing them, but always under cover of a good story, until these ideas start to become part of the intellectual currency of a democracy. Next challenge: to get the word *isostasy* into a 400-word news story. But that step will have to wait on a piece of research appetizing enough to make the idea worth explaining. The public understanding of research for its own sake is a great idea. And yes, the popular media could—and one day may—do more to advance it. But don't hold your breath.

20

Covering Science at the *New York Times*

Cornelia Dean

This chapter discusses the coverage of science at the *New York Times*—what we do, who does it, and the problems we face in the process. The Science Department at the *Times* provides science and medical and health coverage for the daily and weekend papers, and we also produce the weekly Science Times section. We have what is probably the largest science staff of any daily newspaper in the world: 14 full-time staff writers and another 8 regular contributors on contract with us, most of them former *Times* staffers. We usually file two or three news stories a day to the paper—often more—and have a good share of space on page 1, which has a huge readership.

Many readers know us best, though, as the people who produce Science Times, the regular weekly section on science and health. This section was established in 1978, when the newspaper expanded to four sections (today we have many more). The added sections covered sports, food, home decor, and entertainment, and the executive editor at the time, Abe Rosenthal, thought the fifth daily section should have some intellectual bite. He chose science as its topic, and the result has been a big success. More copies of the *New York Times* are sold on Tuesdays, the day Science Times comes out, than on any other day of the week. We typically have about 40 columns of news space in Science Times, more if we treat special issues like the ones we have done recently on the Genome Project, the stem-cell policy debate, and the arguments over cancer screening. Ordinarily, each section will have 15 or so major articles, with photos and graphics, and a number of smaller pieces.

Most of our coverage, in the section and out, is produced by staff members of the *Times*. We use relatively little freelance work, and most of that comes from former *Times* staffers. About half of us have science training of some kind. One of our medical writers is a physician, for example. One of our writers has a Ph.D. in physics, and another stopped just before completing his dissertation. One has a master's degree in the history of science, and another trained as an engineer. Our behavior writer has a master's in social psychology. Two of our regular contributors are physicians. The rest of us—the other writers, five editors, a graphics coordinator, an art director, and a photo editor—have no formal science training, though most of us have been involved in science news for a while. Even so, we struggle to keep up with the news of science, medicine, and health.

The demands of the job are huge. We cover everything from anthropology to astrophysics. We advise other departments when a ballplayer is injured, say, or a court overturns a pollution regulation. And our purview extends into areas that might not at first glance look much like science. We did quite a lot of the newspaper's coverage of the September 11 tragedy/terrorist atrocity and its aftermath, including the engineering of ground zero, the anthrax attacks, and the vulnerabilities of the nation's infrastructure. We write regularly on topics like antimissile defense, crime, and advertising practices of the pharmaceutical industry, to name just a few subjects.

People often ask how we decide what to write about. These decisions come out of the constant conversations among reporters, their news sources, and editors. All of us look regularly at major scientific publications for reports that look important. The science editors and reporters converse early in the day to decide how much space we will need in the next day's paper for the spot news and enterprise we hope to produce. Usually we get what we need. And when our stories do not get the play we think they deserve, it is often because we have done a poor job communicating, clearly and quickly, why they are important. (This is a problem we share with scientists who complain that their work does not get the attention it deserves.)

We are guaranteed a fixed amount of space in the weekly Science Times section, and space configurations on some of its inside pages are also guaranteed so that we can plan art and photo layouts in advance. But the job of deciding what to put into the space is becoming harder and harder as science becomes increasingly specialized. Even journalists with advanced training can have trouble determining what is and what is not important. Not too long ago, an eminent physics journal decided to cope with this specialization problem by issuing new instructions for would-be contributors, advising them that the first three paragraphs of all submissions must be readily understandable by any garden-variety Ph.D. physicist. From the journalist's perspective, this requirement does not set the clarity bar very high.

This specialization is more or less apparent across the board. Another complication of relatively recent origin is the intense, widespread commercialization of research, particularly medical research. Not so long ago, scientists who reported their findings in the journals of their fields could be relied on to play it relatively straight. The journalist could usually be confident that the scientist would make a good-faith effort to put the findings in their rightful scientific context. Now, as more and more researchers turn their labs into test beds for their own companies, have grants from major commercial concerns, or seek venture capital, they have powerful motives for making the most of their results and playing down anything that might challenge them. This kind of conflict of interest is now so widespread in science that even some government agencies have given up regulations that once prevented people from serving on advisory panels for subjects in which they have a financial stake. It was becoming apparent that in many areas, no one who was knowledgeable was free of commercial ties.

Scientific publications are making the same choices when it comes to choosing reviewers or authors of editorials and commentaries. But though they may instruct contributors to disclose potential financial conflicts, these instructions are not always honored. Even research journals themselves, eager to attract attention, subscribers, and advertisers, tout forthcoming reports in press releases that sometimes go significantly further than the research they purport to describe. So journalists are left with another layer of confusion to work through. If we are insufficiently vigilant, we can be sold on something whose true significance is far from clear. Or we may be so cautious that we miss truly important developments or muffle them in a blanket of cautionary caveats.

These are not problems that can be solved by journalists, even journalists with the considerable resources of the *New York Times* behind them. For journalists at most news outlets—many of which are fortunate enough to have one or two full-time science or medical writers—the problems are insurmountable. They can be addressed only by scientists committed to explaining their work to the lay public in clear and dispassionate terms. But while some researchers are all too eager to discuss the importance of their own work, others are unwilling to talk at all. This reticence is beginning to give way, and it is less a problem for those of us at major news organizations like the *Times*, but it still exists and for reasons that are easy to understand. For most scientists, talking to the press is still a no-win proposition. Reputable scientists do not normally communicate their findings in the lay press; they report them in scientific journals or at scientific meetings. Newspaper articles do not necessarily help them in tenure decisions or grant applications. In addition, if their work is described inaccurately—and often it is—it reflects badly on them. Finally, even if everything works perfectly and their research is described clearly, their colleagues may dismiss them as publicity hounds. The result is that scientists have little incentive to speak to the press, and their inexperience shows. Often, they are shocked and dismayed that reporters are not already up to speed on their research. When they are asked to explain their work in simple terms, they are at a loss.

Scientists need to realize that even specialist science journalists cannot possibly stay on top of every field they might be called on to cover. If scientists want science reporting to be clear and accurate, they must help make it so. When I speak to scientists, I tell them they should prepare for a press interview the way they would prepare for a professional presentation: they should know what their most important points are, and they should know how to convey them clearly and simply. They should have graphs, charts, photos, maps, or whatever other material helps explain their work. As anyone who reads Science Times knows (I hope!) that the section stands or falls on the quality of its photos, graphics, maps, and charts. They are crucial to telling our stories, and we devote considerable attention to them.

Finally, scientists should also encourage reporters to ask questions, even if the questions are ill informed or silly. More and more of the day's political issues involve scientific questions, like stem cells, antimissile defense, and nuclear waste disposal; they are all issues voters can expect to confront in the polling place. So as the science reporter's job gets more difficult, it also gets more important as the public responds to news of science that plays an ever-larger part in their daily lives.

21

Nova: The Leading Edge

Nancy Linde

Nova is widely recognized as the flagship television science news program in the United States, and I was not surprised to be invited to the recent "Museums, Media, and the Public Understanding of Research" conference held at the Science Museum of Minnesota in September 2002. I was surprised, however, when I was told that conference organizers were not particularly interested in the successes we have had at *Nova*. Instead, they wanted to hear about the challenges and problems of our public understanding of research (PUR) projects; they wanted "the seamy underbelly."

Of course, the first problem is that we don't actually *have* a PUR project; all we've done so far is submit a proposal for such a project. The reader is warned that what may sound like fait accompli in this chapter should be qualified with "if we get funded" in his or her mind.

What is our PUR project? We call it *Leading Edge*, a title we stole directly from Hyman Field of the National Science Foundation, a leading enthusiast of bringing cutting-edge research to wider audiences, in his earlier writings about the importance of a PUR initiative. *Leading Edge* is a magazine-format program that focuses on current and emerging scientific research. It will be broadcast in the *Nova* time slot approximately quarterly, with a special fifth program we're calling *The Science Year in Review*, which will air around the turn of each year. Unlike *Nova*, *Leading Edge* will use on-air correspondents and a series anchorperson. We will seek individuals who have both strong backgrounds in science and/or science journalism and the talent to tell compelling and entertaining science stories.

Since it's in magazine format, the stories within the series are very flexible in content, length, and production style. We plan to start each program with a news update exploring the science behind the most recent headlines. The backbone of each program will be the feature stories, which will run about 12 minutes long so that each hour-long program will usually contain three feature stories. There will also be short features that will run about three minutes in duration and "Science Moments" that will use from 30 to 90 seconds.

Now, to get back to that seamy underbelly: since our PUR project is in such an early stage and I can't fulfill the request to examine the problems we've encountered with it, I thought the best approach I can take is to tell you what makes a "perfect" *Nova* and then talk about the challenges we are facing with *Leading Edge*.

There are three critically important elements in creating the perfect *Nova*:

- story,
- story,
- and story.

Story is where television succeeds. While television does not do detail very well and is not particularly good for exposition, a rollicking good story will bring viewers to the program—which is not an easy task. A museum audience, on the other hand, makes the enormous commitment to drive to a facility, pay for parking (at least that's true in Boston), and plop down the entrance fee (which for a family of four is no small potatoes), and then they belong to the museum—for a couple of hours at least. Of course, if they are not entertained and engaged, it's not likely they will return.

But there are other differences between museum and television audiences as well. Museum exhibits are not temporal and often not linear. If someone has to visit the bathroom, they can usually come back to the exhibit and pick up where they left off. That's not true for us. The story continues on whether a viewer is watching or not. Second, while I haven't made a study of this, I'm guessing that there aren't several science museums next door and across the street competing for patrons' attention. Again not true for television. We are in competition with 60, 80, or 100 or more channels. And our competition might be no less than the latest Steven Spielberg movie or a blockbuster show like *American Idol, Survivor, Sex in the City, West Wing, South Park, The Simpsons,* or *Friends.* All our viewers have to do is push a button, and they're gone. So the perfect *Nova* has to first attract an audience and then somehow keep them in their seats for an entire hour. The best way to do that is to involve them in a story where they just have to find out what happens next.

What makes a good story? At the risk of oversimplification, I think there are four basic elements that must be considered when embarking on a *Nova*:

1. *The narrative.* That's just another word for the story itself. It has to be entertaining, stimulating, and enlightening. Viewers have to walk away knowing more than they knew before they watched.
2. *Characters.* Good characters are critical. They have to be appealing, concise, articulate, and interesting.
3. *Dramatic arc.* A story has to build and release tension—not only over the course of an hour, but each sequence must experience conflict and go through a process of change.
4. *Visuals.* Television is a visual medium. The pictures must move. There must be action. Filming something in process is key.

Where does science fit in? Science can be wonderfully dramatic—people working at the limits of human knowledge on things that can profoundly change our lives, our health, our environment, and our basic understanding of how the world works; it's the very stuff of drama. But the story must be told correctly. You can have tons of science in an hour-long program, but you must include it only on a need-to-know basis. Even at a series such as *Nova*, with its long-term commitment to tackling difficult subjects, we recognize that science must be in service to the story. Clearly, the perfect *Nova* requires courage: the courage to reject an important subject because the story just isn't there, the courage to reject an important scientist because he or she cannot communicate research in an effective way (at least on television to a general audience), the courage to choose the elements of the story that will keep a viewer on the edge of his or her seat, and the courage to find new and compelling ways to visualize complex or abstract ideas.

Those are some of the elements that go into making the perfect *Nova*. So what are the challenges of *Leading Edge*? Since we haven't actually made any programs, the best thing I can do is to talk about the challenges we envision. After spending an enormous amount of energy on this in writing the proposal and learning a great deal in making the test video, I could probably list a hundred questions that we explored: What is our target audience? How can we attract new viewers—especially younger viewers, women, and minorities who don't traditionally watch science television—without alienating the traditional *Nova* viewer? We wondered what the show should look like. Should it have a home base (a studio set)? Should it just cut from story to story? What should the set look like? What about the packaging elements like music and graphics—what should they look like? How many different elements should we have in a single program? Should the programs be completely flexible, or should we establish a format and style that is consistent and that will become more comfortable and familiar to a viewer? Who should work on this project? *Nova* is connected in one way or another with just about everybody who makes science television—a large community of talented people. But which handful of producers are the best at making short-form, quick-turnaround science stories that inform and entertain? Who should be the "face" of *Leading Edge*, the on-air reporters that are critically important in making that personal connection to the viewing audience?

The main challenge we face is similar to the challenges faced in museum work. What subjects do we cover? What stories do we tell? And what are the differences between the perfect *Leading Edge* story and the perfect *Nova*?

While the main requirement is precisely the same—story, story, and story—there's a problem with *Leading Edge*. In a *Nova*, each story has three acts: Act 1—the setup; act 2—the conflict; and act 3—the resolution. But what do you do when there is no resolution? For example, if telling a story about research on fuel cells, you can't conclude with an ending that says, "After we found a cheap and abundant source of hydrogen, the United States converted to fuel cells, and the air cleared up. We were no longer dependent on foreign oil, and everyone lived happily ever after." It's a real dilemma. Surely, we won't get very far if we end *every* story with something like "This might reduce our dependence on foreign oil someday, if it works," or "This might cure cancer, someday, if it works," or "This might reverse the degradation of the Everglades, someday, if it works."

It will be our challenge to craft *Leading Edge* stories in such a way that leaves the viewer satisfied at the end—even though we are covering emerging and ongoing research that doesn't necessarily have an immediate application, that hasn't entirely been solved, or that doesn't exactly have an ending.

So character, dramatic tension, and visual treatment are all equally important to *Nova* and to *Leading Edge*. But *Leading Edge* will have some distinct advantages over *Nova* as well:

1. *On-air correspondents.* It will be wonderful to have lively, engaging, on-air correspondents with whom we can work on these stories. And it will be equally wonderful to put a human face to science reporting, people whom viewers will come to know and trust to explain the ever-changing world around them.

2. *Shorter stories.* It's surprisingly hard to find good science stories with strong characters that sustain for an hour of television. We believe that a wider world of stories will open up to us with *Leading Edge*. Every *Nova* producer—probably without exception—has researched a story and rejected it because there's not enough there for an hour. *Leading Edge* will lap up those ideas.

3. *Flexibility.* The *Leading Edge* format allows more room to experiment with subject, style, and production techniques to create a unique and memorable series.

4. *Pictures.* Television does something else very well in addition to story, and that's pictures. Like *Life* magazine used to do in the 1940s, 1950s, and 1960s, we can bring fascinating scientific visualizations to our audience. And they don't necessarily have to fit into a feature story. In *Leading Edge*, we can show a scientific visual just because it's a fascinating thing to watch.

For example, my most recent *Nova*, called "Cancer Warrior," was about angiogenesis—the subject. The main character was Dr. Judah Folkman, and the story was how he risked his career and reputation following an unpopular idea for 40 years. During the course of research, I found two amazing videos recently taken by researchers. The quality was not good (oh, how I wish scientists had high-resolution, even high-definition, video equipment). Nonetheless, the visuals I looked at were as dramatic as I've ever seen. In one of them, there was a small tumor. Pull wider, and you could see the blood vessels that nourished it. Zoom in, and there was an amazing moment. You could actually see a single cell squeeze through the wall of a blood vessel and enter the bloodstream. It was the first moment of metastasis—the scariest moment in cancer growth. The second video showed a cancer cell halting its travel through the bloodstream to squeeze through a blood vessel and settle in a new area of the body. The cancer had just spread from one organ to another. These films were both fascinating and terrifying at the same time. Amazingly, there was no spot for these visuals in the program (remember, have courage to reject), but there is no question that they could have had a prominent place in *Leading Edge*.

These are the things we obsess about. If we are all going to find ways to work together to share resources, then we need to understand each other's unique needs and problems. In a nutshell, the most important decisions we'll make in *Leading Edge* are the subjects we choose—the stories we decide to tell. And these are the questions we will ask:

- What's the story?
- Who is the main character?
- Who are the minor characters?
- What's the conflict? What are the twists and turns in the story?
- What's the resolution?

Every one of those questions must have a good answer before we will even consider going forward.

Having said that, we are indeed eager to collaborate with other members of the PUR community. As I have learned a lot about the challenges of putting together museum exhibits—particularly on current scientific research—at the recent conference, museum practitioners should know about the trials and tribulations of making science television. By way of preparing for collaboration, our PUR proposal budgeted enough money to clear footage rights for Internet and museum use as well as other public forums. In most cases, our footage will be available for use in exhibits. While we will need to design a mechanism to do this, we are eager to create intellectual alliances to work together to share topics, resources, background research, contacts, and whatever else we can.

We can provide national exposure to a subject. If *Leading Edge* attracts anything like the *Nova* audiences, we should get about six million viewers. We believe that *Leading Edge* will succeed if it draws people into the story and makes them curious to find out more: to read more about a subject, to surf the Web for more information, or to go to the local science museum.

We also think that our on-air reporters can be a real plus. Beyond the actual on-air program, these people (along with producers, executives, contributors to stories, and others) can participate in joint promotional and/or educational events at museums and other locations.

Ideas for other areas of collaboration are welcome. How do you think we can share resources and plans to enhance the public understanding of science and meet the needs of our own unique audiences?

22

Earth and Sky: Some Challenges of Communicating Scientific Research on the Radio

Marc Airhart

Earth and Sky is a 90-second radio show heard every day on 650 stations and another 300 or so translators and sister stations in the United States. Our shows are heard on the new XM Satellite Radio network as well as overseas on Voice of America, World Radio Network, American Forces Radio and Television Service, and Radio for Peace International. In any given week, we have 3.6 million unique U.S. listeners.

In 1999, we created a new subseries of shows within the larger *Earth and Sky* radio series. Out of 365 productions each year, 75 are what we call "Edge of Discovery" shows. These shows are currently sponsored by the National Science Foundation (NSF) under its public understanding of research (PUR) initiative. The shows feature the voices of scientists talking about their work. Instead of reporting on "science news," the idea is to catch scientists in the process of doing groundbreaking work that might lead to big discoveries in the coming months or years. We're trying to find out how science is done.

For producers, there are three major challenges in working on PUR.

CHALLENGE 1: TOPIC SELECTION

Doing short radio shows in the PUR spirit is much harder than the usual science reporting done on radio today. That is to say, we aren't covering news. News stories come about when someone publishes an article in a journal, or puts out a press release, or holds a press conference or makes an announcement at a scientific meeting. We, on the other hand, have to somehow magically know what things people are working on today that might eventually become news.

So how have we met that challenge? First, we polled our science advisers, a group of about 300 scientists with whom we have developed relationships (sometimes for more than ten years; that's one advantage to being a long-lived show). We asked them, "What is the most interesting work going on in your field?" We were surprised—although we shouldn't have been—that most responded by telling us about their own work. That was fine in a few cases where there were interesting stories, but many were too arcane. So last year, we tried a different tack. We asked them, "What will be the hottest science stories in your field in the coming year?" We got some great responses and months worth of story ideas.

So topic selection is a challenge, but it helps to ask the right people the right questions. We also try to think about things that aren't in the news right now. For example, recently we were sitting around talking about how you never hear about the environmental impacts of war in the news. We started making phone calls, and sure enough, there is a whole division in the United Nations devoted to assessing how war affects the natural world, and it is now a new story line. It didn't come from a press release, and there was no press conference or published paper. So, in a way, we're focusing on themes rather than on news.

CHALLENGE 2: THE INTERVIEW

Interviews are more difficult. The usual who, what, when, where, and why questions that can get you by if you're covering an announcement of science news will not do. You have to ask different kinds of questions.

And how have we met that challenge? All writers and producers at *Earth and Sky* have had to reevaluate our interview methods. We've had to learn to focus not just on an announcement or an explanation of a scientific concept, but also on the person doing the science, on his or her motivations and history, and on that scientist's process—what is it that they're trying to do, and why are they trying to do it? We work with a lot of stringers. And even as we've grappled in the office with our concept for these shows, at the same time we've had to give some guidance to our freelancers. Several got the idea right away, while others just can't seem to get away from the old routine of presenting science as a collection of "results."

Personally, one of the most exciting parts of our current PUR project is a series of monthly scientist profiles on our Web site. These allow us to stretch out and present much more than is possible in a 90-second radio show. We interview scientists about how they got into their field, what their fears are, why they do what they do, what obstacles they've had to overcome, and so on. We were really gratified when one scientist we profiled—jellyfish expert Jack Costello from Providence College in Rhode Island—later wrote to us, "You caught my experiences of science even better than I knew about them." I think this is strong evidence that the PUR initiative is having a positive effect, not just on listeners, but also on the scientists who contribute.

CHALLENGE 3: ACCURACY VERSUS REALITY

One of the themes for the PUR conference session on production issues was "balancing accuracy with reality, especially when science is not dramatic on a daily basis." I take that to mean, How do you accurately paint a portrait of what science is without boring people with details that only scientists would find interesting?

One of our writers recently produced a script about an upcoming space mission. A main focus of the script was how the principal investigator was worried that a certain instrument he needed would be manufactured on time by a contractor. The instrument is so unique and difficult to make that it takes months under ideal circumstances, and the manufacturing technique is still a bit "iffy" so that sometimes it takes several more months to sort out mysterious problems. In the end, we felt that while this was probably a common concern in science, it was too mundane to emphasize. The focus of the show shifted to other challenges associated with the search for extrasolar planets. We are not obligated to present the most boring parts of science. Listeners are savvy enough to know that in any field—even an action-packed field like sports—you are going to find boring details that can be left out while still painting an accurate picture.

For example, I could set out to tell you about how a football team works, about how players get drafted, about special training regimens, about how Nike chooses who to sponsor, or about how players memorize their plays. But I'm not obligated to go into all the details of how many jerseys a player goes through in training or how much money the person who mows the field makes. We have to overcome our temptation to do a story simply because we feel that it represents some real aspect of science. Each show has to be interesting, important, and thought provoking—in other words, what we call "good radio."

CONCLUSION

These are some of the challenges of producing PUR programs and how we've tried to meet them. In some ways, it fits our format very well. One advantage we have in doing PUR is that we do a new show every day of the year. This allows us to follow a theme over time. In the coming months, we plan to call up the scientists we've interviewed in the past and see how their work has changed since we last talked—what new questions they're trying to solve, what wrong turns they've taken, surprises they've had, and which of their predictions have come true and which haven't.

In a paper published in 2001 titled "Public Understanding of Science vs. Public Understanding of Research," authors Hyman Field and Patricia Powell wrote, "On-going research is not static and new results are constantly changing the course of an investigation. Therefore it is necessary to frequently update the information, making it impossible to provide accurate and complete information in a single presentation. Rather, a format that allows one to revisit a topic numerous times is essential."

What we're trying to do at *Earth and Sky* is difficult, but certainly not impossible. We've had to add more producers and more writers and spend more time on each individual show than ever before. We've had to make changes to every step of our process, from topic selection to interviews to shaping the final shows. But I think we're doing the right kinds of things to accomplish the NSF's goal of making the public more aware of how scientific research is conducted.

23

Crossing the Public and Commercial Broadcasting Barriers: ScienCentral's Two Public Understanding of Research Projects

Eliene Augenbraun

ScienCentral's mission is to make sense of science for the broadest possible audience. Our two public understanding of research (PUR) projects attack the problem of informing the general public of current findings in hot science fields in different ways. "NOVA News Minutes" exposes a new audience to *Nova* by repackaging the documentary material into two-minute news pieces appropriate for ABC local newscasts. The programs will encourage people who might otherwise ignore a PBS science documentary to tune into *Nova's* high-quality, in-depth explorations of important science topics. Our other PUR project, "Science Stories for ABC and NBC Newscasts," follows five significant fields in science and technology, reporting on developments as they happen for broadcast on NBC and ABC local television newscasts. Both PUR programs take advantage of a novel distribution system for science content that ScienCentral pioneered.

SCIENCENTRAL'S UNIQUE DISTRIBUTION SYSTEM FOR SCIENCE CONTENT

Local television network affiliates receive stories from their network parents every day. Local newsrooms combine their own local reporting with the international, national, sports, and feature stories that the parent network is obligated to provide. No U.S. television newsroom could run without outside content. ScienCentral's stories are distributed by the network in exactly the same way they distribute their own stories. Because ScienCentral's stories are accessible, user friendly, and have the network's assurance of high quality, local producers value them.

All local newscasts are composed of several segments. The beginning of the hour is devoted to leading local, national, and international stories. In the middle of the newscast are features such as health reports. After that come the weather and sports. An hour-long newscast is similar to two news half hours back to back, with more time in the second half hour for feature stories. The show ends with a "kicker," which is intended to be so interesting that it holds the viewer for the next show. ScienCentral news stories tend to run in the middle of the newscast, or occasionally as a kicker.

But television news is extremely expensive to produce. So why do it? Local newscasts reach more Americans than any other information distribution system. According to the Pew Research Center for the People and the Press, 56 percent of Americans watch local television newscasts. Only 46 percent read newspapers regularly. and only 30 percent watch network news shows.[1] When researching a particular topic, they turn to the Internet. Local television newscasters understand the importance of the Internet in informing their viewers—local newsroom Web sites are still increasing their audiences.

The pattern is the same for Americans seeking information about science. The 2002 Science and Engineering Indicators found that 44 percent of Americans turn to television for most of their science information, and far fewer turn to print resources.[2]

Over the past three years, ScienCentral news pieces supported by the National Science Foundation (NSF) have reached over 400 million viewers in aggregate with a budget of about $4 million. That means ScienCentral reached 100 viewers for every dollar invested by the NSF. Over that period, ScienCentral distributed approximately 200 stories, exposing millions of people to dozens of scientific research topics they might never have encountered otherwise (see figure 23.1).

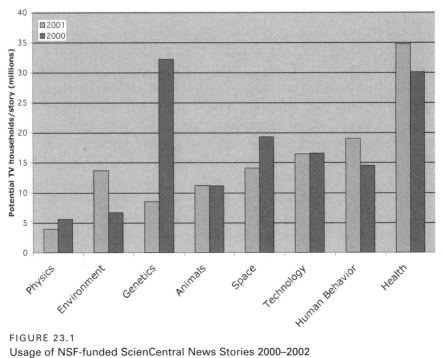

FIGURE 23.1
Usage of NSF-funded ScienCentral News Stories 2000–2002

WHY THIS IS A KEY PART OF THE PUR PROGRAM CONTINUUM

When does research become PUR news? The two-minute news format allows us to bring viewers short science features and rapid updates in a way that documentaries and museum exhibits can't. But local television news does not provide in-depth storytelling opportunities and isn't very effective for educating or instructing. For these needs, audiences should turn to museums or long-format documentaries. We consider commercial television news to be one part of a continuum of PUR education, generating interest that encourages people to explore science more deeply in an appropriate medium.

INSTITUTIONAL CHALLENGES

We encountered several major institutional challenges.

Financial Support

Short-format news production requires a complex business model since we have yet to identify a single source of funding that covers more than half the costs. ScienCentral News is an independent news organization supported mostly by NSF grants, ABC, NBC, archive sales, the Alfred P. Sloan Foundation, and other supporters over the years. About 10 percent of the news production costs are covered by universities and small contributors. Some of our operating budget comes from ScienCentral Productions—the profit-making television and Web production department of the company. The networks trust us in part because we are extremely selective about funding sources. That selectivity gives us greater access to the networks' resources and distribution systems, but restricts our fund-raising options.

Commercial versus Public Broadcasting

ScienCentral routinely works with three U.S. networks: ABC, NBC, and PBS. PBS is markedly different than the commercial broadcasting systems. They differ as much as an apple and a giraffe. Consequently, negotiating contracts, rights, approvals, trademark licensing, technical specifications, and every other part of the project become enormously challenging. It took many reasonable lawyers many, many months to work out the "NOVA News Minutes" deal:

- The two commercial networks required that we set up a "kosher video/ talent kitchen" to prevent ABC footage and talent from appearing on NBC and vice versa. Neither ABC nor NBC wants stories or talent from one network appearing on the other network.
- Technical standards for the two commercial networks are surprisingly different, and both are extremely different from public broadcasting standards. For example, commercial television newsrooms use two tracks of audio, while PBS stations use at least four. Commercial news still broadcasts in the older television format with a 4:3 aspect ratio, while all new PBS shows use the high-definition wide-screen format of 16:9.
- The rules change frequently and sometimes dramatically. ABC's video delivery costs shifted suddenly when they abandoned analog distribution and switched to a proprietary, video-on-demand, digital satellite delivery system. This shift required NSF and other funders to be flexible in the terms of the grant.

Legal

Though issues of indemnity (security against damage or loss), rights, and editorial approvals exist for news material, commercial broadcasting has evolved a series of routine approaches that translate into a widely accepted infrastructure. In our experience, documentary makers and distributors do not seem to have such a routine infrastructure. Thus, the contract negotiations were lengthy and detailed. For example, if ScienCentral provides a story to the ABC News network and one local affiliate alters the story and makes it inaccurate, someone involved with the story could sue the local affiliate, ABC News, and ScienCentral. To protect ourselves, we require the ABC News network to indemnify us and hold us harmless. Since ABC does not have control over the affiliate's news producers either, ABC requires the local affiliate to indemnify and hold it harmless. Thus, it is the erring affiliate responsible for defending itself in a lawsuit, not ABC or ScienCentral.

Branding/Trademark

WGBH had never licensed the *Nova* brand before, so a great deal of time was spent developing a licensing agreement for use of the public broadcasting brand on commercial television.

Indemnity

Because WGBH had never licensed their brand and ABC rarely uses other brands on its newscasts, both parties were concerned about indemnity.

Insurance

Since September 11, insurance rates of all types rose 40 to 100 percent. With the additional risk of the first-time use of a national brand in a new way, ScienCentral's media liability insurance rates increased even more. Next to personnel, rent, and sometimes legal fees, insurance is now our largest expense. We believe that this will be a significant expense to all parties who want to share material in the PUR network. Traditional interpretations of the U.S. Constitution give journalists protections in newscasts that may not apply to museum and other nonnews settings.

Approvals

Editorial and other approvals turn out to be extremely complex when multiple parties with many audiences are involved. Lengthy approval processes not only add to the expense of a production but, in some cases, prevent the production from occurring at all. The need for different institutions to approve content that will work for their own audiences conflicts with PUR's emphasis on rapid reporting of new findings and sharing content among many types of institutions.

Rights

In order to share material among different institutions, we are required to obtain more rights than we would to broadcast or display in a single medium. Acquiring expanded license rights can be extremely expensive. Going back and acquiring more rights later can be even more expensive.

Hiring and Training Reporters

There are no training programs for science television journalists aimed at local news. Many talented long-format documentarians find themselves frustrated at the rapid pace and strict constraints of the 90-second news feature. Others never "get" local news—they are either too highbrow in their approach, or too shallow or not culturally tuned to what makes Americans tune in. We have developed criteria to guess who will "get" it and what mix of talents in the newsroom will help them "get" it. We found that a mixture of local news-hounds, magazine writers, graduates of science-writing master's programs, and a smattering of Ph.D.s works best.

Once we hire them, we invest months of work in training them. Like any national or international news company, we consider ourselves a technology company, as well as a news company. Everyone is trained on the core technical functions of our newsroom and on key issues for science journalists, such as peer review, working with embargoes, and so forth.

Culture

We have cultivated a culture of news-junkie, fact-checking, skeptical people who enjoy watching *Survivor* and reading the latest *Nature* all in a day's work. We tried, but could not succeed in creating a consistently high-quality product with freelancers. Our corporate culture is a mix of news and documentary production that allows us to create high-quality "hard" news with a "soft" news shelf life. That is one reason our pieces make it to air in so many markets. Adding another layer of culture shock to our newsroom—say, to work with museums—might take a while.

"Techie-Feelies"

The network news business is a technology business. We either keep up, or we don't make it onto network television. That said, networks are enormously resistant to change since profit—not quality—is the reason for their existence. Like many aspects of our relationship with the networks, understanding the technology they use enhances our success. We meet regularly with the techies who handle our stories and pursue all avenues of improvement with them. It is very labor intensive, but if you have ever been a slave to a high-maintenance photocopier, you will understand why; the boss might order the machine, but the techies keep the world running.

Or not.

May the PUR be with you!

NOTES

I would like to thank some of our wonderful partners who make our programs possible. National Science Foundation/Public Understanding of Research, ABC News, NBC News, PBS, WGBH, Boston Museum of Science, the Franklin Institute, the Institute of Electrical and Electronics Engineers, the American Institute of Physics, *Nature*, Northwestern University, the Monterey Bay Aquarium Research Institute, and the Alfred P. Sloan Foundation.

This material is based on work supported by the National Science Foundation under grants ESI0206184 and ESI0201155. Any opinions, findings, and conclusions or recommendations expressed in this material are those of the author(s) and do not necessarily reflect the views of the National Science Foundation.

1. Investors now go online for quotes, advice: Internet sapping broadcast news audience, at http://people-press.org/reports/display.php3?PageID=203 (accessed March 30, 2003).

2. National Science Foundation Division of Science Resources Statistics, at www.nsf.gov/sbe/srs/seind02/c7/fig07-19.htm (accessed March 30, 2003).

Afterword

Not So Fast: Some Thoughts on Re-Visioning PUR

Don Pohlman

The field now taking shape in museums as the public understanding of research (PUR) is the latest expression of a concern nearly as old as scientific research itself: the desired relationship between the scientific community and those outside of it. Like the science literacy movement and other earlier responses to this concern, PUR promises to address perceived deficiencies in the understanding of science among nonscientists. This time around, the focus is on unfinished current research and on the nature of scientific inquiry. As a developer of several museum exhibitions focused on the workings of science, I welcome PUR's promised emphasis on the research process as a complement to the display of facts and objects that has been museums' stock-in-trade. However, I am concerned about the restrictiveness of the vision that appears to be emerging among museum practitioners of PUR. In what follows, I outline some questions I have about assumptions within the PUR effort that I see as limiting to its efficacy and sustainability.

A place to begin is with the rationale. I think the question of who is to be served by PUR demands more critical examination than it has received so far. In what seems a reprise of the arguments for science literacy, PUR advocates speak about what the public *needs* to know without demonstrating public affirmation of that need and without articulating how more information about

research will lead either to more understanding of science or to a greater public good. The case for PUR seems to rest on the hope that it will result in a citizenry that is more informed about and *therefore* more supportive of scientific
research. This wishful argument has been around for a while, but even if it
were believable, it would remain insufficient as a sustainable basis for PUR. It
suggests that the understanding in PUR be read as appreciation and the field
viewed an instrument of science boosterism. The value in that for the scientific community seems clear enough, if elusive, but the value for the public is
harder to discern. A sustainable PUR will require both, and I think it is the
creation of genuine value for the public that is most in question at this time.

So where might we seek the public value of PUR? As others have pointed
out in this volume and elsewhere, the public at large is not clamoring for an
understanding of scientific process. That observation does not in itself rule
out PUR initiatives, but it suggests that the field faces the challenge of creating demand for something its intended audiences don't yet know they need.
That may be unavoidable, but I think it is made more difficult by the way in
which PUR advocates have defined the field.

For example, it is worth asking whether either the scientific process or the
public is as unified and well bounded as the emerging PUR formulation
would have us believe. Recent scholarship across a variety of disciplines has
demonstrated repeatedly that science is complex, heterogeneous, and as culturally enmeshed as any other human activity. It cannot be understood fully
outside the specific histories, politics, and economies that have shaped and
sustained it. The *public* too is a problematic category that cannot be adequately defined along a simple axis of scientific understanding. As critics of
science literacy efforts have pointed out, even most working scientists would
have difficulty demonstrating literacy across the full range of what science
comprises today. If ignorance of some area of research is the criterion, it is unlikely that there is anyone who is not a member of the public for PUR. It suggests that we should think twice before designing PUR around a presumed
deficit of understanding and a hard distinction between those who know and
those who don't.

Expanding PUR's definitions of science and public is not just of theoretical
concern. The centrality of storytelling within almost all forms of museum
programs suggests that the availability of strong stories will prove crucial to
PUR as well. Opening up the definitions that underlie PUR will expand its

narrative possibilities and broaden its potential to attract and engage. Scientific research offers no shortage of plots and characters from which to draw, but if those elements are all subordinated to a standard narrative of *things you need to know*, their dramatic potential and breadth of appeal will be limited. Stories of individual curiosity, creativity, and persistence belong in the PUR catalogue, but so do stories of ethical uncertainty, political conflict, and indigenous knowledge—to name a few that don't end in the laboratory. A PUR that presumes richer and more complex notions of both science and public will be better positioned to engage nonscientists and scientists through stories that offer agency and authority to both.

A more useful and more approachable PUR would focus less on the distinctiveness of science and more on its very real continuity with other human practices, values, and problems. It would acknowledge that science operates within cultural contexts that affect and are affected by its findings. It would recognize the limitations of science as a means of fully describing or explaining the human experience. It would embrace the fact that science raises questions of meaning and value that are not answerable within science alone. It would include perspectives from outside of science that would illuminate the edges of science and the contexts in which it resides. In all of that it would provide both a fuller picture of science and a greater set of opportunities for nonscientists to connect it with their own experience.

Such an extended scope for PUR would in turn support more constructive roles for its participants. PUR needs not only a richer and more generous definition of its public but also more varied and active roles for that public—roles beyond those of ticket buyers, information consumers, and compliant taxpayers. A PUR worth wishing for will be one that involves and empowers all its participants to make meaningful connections between scientific research and the concerns of their own lives. This will require more shared authority in the design of PUR offerings and more opportunities for scientist and nonscientist alike to share how their values and experiences relate to the processes and findings of science.

Of course, sharing authority holds risks. But rather than assume that public understanding will result in public appreciation, PUR advocates need to embrace the possibility that at times the opposite may occur. European experiences with consensus conferences and other programs focused on science issues suggest that PUR efforts may lead to some greater public appreciation for science, but they may also lead to a more critical reception for what is done in its name. In my view, that would not be bad. It seems inappropriate to desire unquestioning public support for an enterprise that is itself so utterly dependent on critical thinking. I would argue that a more desirable outcome for PUR would be a citizenry that better understands what science is, what it isn't, how it works, and how it is used in everyday contexts that are never purely scientific. That is where science intersects the lives of those who are not directly involved in its investigations, and that is where we might find the kind of public understanding that would have truly public value. This approach might not lead directly to greater funding for research agencies or science museums, but it would be good for both science and society in the long run. And by tapping into issues of public concern, it might lead to PUR programs that really matter and that can attract long-term public support.

The need for greater understanding between the scientific community and those outside of it does not run just one way. I believe that PUR needs to be conceived as more of an exchange than it has been so far—more than the latest version of the voice of science telling the public what it ought to know. A PUR focused on communicating public needs and interests as well as scientific information offers a chance to build a community across the boundaries of science and public. In doing so, it will provide greater value to the public and the scientific community alike. It will require a greater emphasis on program experiments that pursue dialogue and position museums as facilitators and mediators rather than simply providers of information.

It is, of course, easier to propose dialogue than to make it happen. Although science museums are in some ways well positioned to facilitate discussion between scientists and members of the public, they face significant obstacles in transforming the idea of dialogue into viable programs. Face-to-face interactions between researchers and the public raise obvious difficulties of cost and scheduling to overcome, but the even greater challenge for these programs is shaping the expectations of both scientists and nonscientists to a point where dialogue is even possible. Even innovative and relatively well-funded efforts, such as the London Science Museum's Dana Center and La Cité's Forum des Sciences, suggest that it will not be easy to pull this off and that succeeding often enough to have an impact will be even harder.

I claim no special expertise in solving these challenges, but I do believe we are more likely to find solutions by defining the idea of dialogue within PUR as broadly as possible and by pursuing divergent lines of program experimentation. Real-time forums are one model of interaction and should be part of the PUR tool kit, but we need to look at other options as well. For example, asynchronous models, such as online discussion groups, comment books, and graffiti walls, could be options for more sustained discussions. I think it is important also to acknowledge that stimulating critical thinking and dialogue *within* the public audience is as important as direct or indirect communication between the public and researcher. Developers of other informal science programs have been working on that problem for some time. Some of the techniques we think we need to invent may already be incubating in the existing practices of museum program developers.

That brings us to issues of how PUR ought to be pursued. Much of the discussion within the field thus far has focused on large, capital-intensive projects, such as the London Science Museum's Wellcome Wing, the Current Science & Technology Center at the Boston Museum of Science, and the new Forum des Sciences program at La Cité in Paris. The most costly and ambitious ventures in any field will always command the lion's share of publicity, but I would question whether these projects, although in many ways excellent, offer templates for PUR that many other institutions can hope to use.

My particular concern is the emphasis and investment that all three have directed toward the presentation of science news. I am in no way questioning the decisions of those institutions to choose that path for themselves, but I do not think it should stand as the primary model for the rest of the PUR community. Let me explain why.

First, there is the matter of cost. Big-media science news production requires capital and operating resources that very few institutions can provide. The successful operation of the existing science museum news efforts has been impressive so far, but it is too early to say whether they are truly sustainable even for those institutions. Proposals to set up production partnerships and distribution networks may lower the price tag for individual museums but at the cost of fewer programs created and fewer opportunities for experimentation and innovation. I believe that it is crucial to find ways to involve a broader cross section of the informal science learning community in the effort to create successful PUR models. This will require funding and institutional support for small and medium-size efforts as well as the large projects that have attracted most of the attention so far. Projects that integrate PUR approaches within existing informal science efforts may prove as effective and *more* sustainable than larger projects dedicated solely to PUR.

Beyond the costs of production, there are other problems with defining science news as the primary path to PUR. One is the question of whether financially stretched science centers and museums can and should duplicate functions already performed by science journalists. Another is whether such efforts will achieve the desired results. If at least part of what is wished for from PUR is that nonscientists better understand the process of science, it must be asked whether greater access to science news would in fact lead to that understanding. More science news than most people can remember is already available through general media outlets, but its reporting often obscures rather than clarifies how science really works. Moreover, the portrayal of science as an ever-accelerating succession of events does not necessarily lead to an understanding of how those events are related to each other or to the lives of nonscientists. It may well be that fewer events presented in richer context are at least as good a path to the understanding desired for the public, and it may be that historical science lends itself more readily to the provision of that context than do the events of the day. There is undoubtedly value in depicting unfinished science, but that depiction alone will not furnish the perspective needed to understand how science works. Efforts to interpret new and still-unfolding scientific developments need to present those developments within science history and within other relevant social and political contexts if they are to lead to any real understanding of scientific process.

Yet another problem with the choice of science news as the preferred path to PUR is the limited role it leaves for its audiences. I have already suggested the need for more active public participation within PUR programs. The science news approach that I see emerging as the dominant flavor of PUR does not seem to support this participation, nor does it play to the strengths of the informal science learning community and its hard-won experience creating engaging and interactive learning experiences for its audiences. The defining of audiences as passive recipients of information has not worked for science center program developers and is not likely to work for PUR, either, but that deficit model of learning seems alive and well in these early days of PUR. I worry that PUR seems positioned to relearn what other forms of informal science learning already know.

The narrowing of the PUR vision around science news seems to be driving a corresponding narrowing in choices of suitable presentation media. PUR's emphasis on current events and the tight production schedules that result from that emphasis have tended to favor electronic media over the object-based and interactive approaches that have long been effective for science centers and museums. It may be that an approach to PUR that is less centered on science news will be more compatible with a fuller complement of presentation media and, again, more opportunities for active engagement by PUR audiences.

I do not want to suggest that the current high-profile science news projects are not worthwhile. They are important experiments in there own right, and all of us have much to learn from their efforts. But they do not represent the only possibilities for PUR, and we should not let their visibility obscure the other experiments we need to do.

Finally, we need to ask to what extent PUR should be defined and pursued separately from other informal science learning efforts and whether such a separation truly serves the goal of improving the public's understanding of research. I believe that coverage of recent developments in science and the explication of scientific processes are useful and even necessary components of the public understanding of science. They belong within the repertoire of all science centers and museums. I do not think, however, that PUR has yet been demonstrated to be a wholly new undertaking that should be funded and implemented apart from other forms of informal science learning. As I have suggested, I think it is important that PUR efforts be pursued in ways that provide more opportunities for dialogue, fuller historical context for unfolding scientific developments, and maximum use of existing assets and expertise within museums and other informal science centers. All these goals are compatible with flexible and smaller-scale approaches to PUR that can be integrated with existing galleries, programs, and collections and can involve many more informal science centers. I believe that this approach of embedding PUR efforts within other informal science learning programs, although less dramatic than the creation of large dedicated centers and initiatives, will turn out to be as much or more effective. I suspect it will result in more experimentation and be more sustainable as well. But unless it too receives support from funders and institutions, we will not get a chance to find out.

So let me conclude. As an emerging field (within museums anyway), the PUR community still has work to do on its goals, rationale, methods, and even measures of success. I have my own ideas about which directions to explore, but I am most concerned that we investigate many paths before we settle on the ones to pave.

In recent discussions about PUR, I've sensed an urgency to get beyond definitions and to get on with the doing of it. I agree, not because all the definitions are in place but because I believe that a more durable foundation for PUR will result from divergent experimentation than from a hasty focusing of our efforts around the relatively few existing program models. I think that the biggest risk to the field at this time is not that it is insufficiently defined but that prematurely narrow definitions of its ends and practices will prevent it from reaching its full potential. Perhaps when successful PUR outcomes become commonplace, a tested orthodoxy will emerge, but for now we need to remain both experimental and ecumenical for at least a while more.

BIBLIOGRAPHY

Bauer, Henry H. 1994. *Scientific literacy and the myth of the scientific method.* Urbana: University of Illinois Press.

Biagioli, Mario, ed. 1999. *The science studies reader.* New York: Routledge.

Downey, Gary Lee, and Joe Dumit. 1997. *Cyborgs and citadels: Anthropological interventions in emerging sciences and technologies.* Santa Fe, N.M.: School of American Research Press.

Gregory, Jane, and Steven Miller. 1998. *Science in public: Communication, culture, and credibility.* New York: Plenum.

Wynne, Brian. 1995. Public understanding of science. In *Handbook of science and technology studies,* ed. S. Jasanoff et al., 361–88.

Appendix

Background and Thoughts on Museums, Media, and the Public Understanding of Research: An International Working Conference

David Chittenden

As I looked out at the group of participants who had gathered for the opening session of "Museums, Media, and the Public Understanding of Research—An International Working Conference," I was struck with both feelings of awe and relief (typical feelings among conference planners?). Before me was a select group of professionals variously engaged in efforts to improve the public's understanding of contemporary science and research. This was a group of early adopters, science proselytizers, and committed practitioners in the emerging field of the public understanding of research (PUR). The 76 participants included 40 science museum directors and veteran exhibit developers/programmers, 14 producers of acclaimed science Web sites, television programs, or radio shows, 3 award-winning science journalists or science public affairs staff, 12 scientists and researchers committed to the communication of current research, and 7 others vested in the development and success of PUR efforts. We had selected them from among several hundred applicants from the United States and Europe, and here they were in St. Paul for an extended weekend in late September 2002. The agenda was to discuss and pick apart the issues, challenges, and early models associated with the emerging PUR movement and to explore how we might do PUR better in the future. As I welcomed them to the Science Museum of Minnesota, I began to appreciate what a creative, talkative, talented, opinionated, industrious, tenacious, challenging, and assertive group of leaders we had assembled for this conference. Our conference moderator, Graham Farmelo, then head of science communication at the Science Museum of London, was quick to set a tone of congeniality while acknowledging the challenges before us and supporting our serious responsibility to finish up the four days with concrete ideas and recommendations to increase effective PUR efforts. He shared his personal aspirations for the conference and a warning to avoid at all cost his "nightmare scenario" of ending the conference with a banal, self-serving, and bromidic report. As one participant characterized later, our moderator strode to the podium like St. George aiming to slay the Dragon of Pablum. To a great degree, he succeeded.

For over a year, the conference planning team had wrestled with competing ideas about how this conference should be organized, what process would be most supportive of our intended outcomes, and who should occupy the speaker's podium. But there was never any disagreement that the "stars" of this conference were to be the gathered participants. We did not want the typical "talking heads" conference. Rather, it was to be a working discussion facilitated across the several strategic PUR issue domains of "audience," "content," "production," and "funding/institutional issues." The presentations included in the program were intended to provide clear case study examples that focused on one of these key domains. We sought presentations that would emphasize PUR challenges and problems (the seamy underbelly, if you will) and future ideas and solutions. We stressed the obvious fact that PUR is in its earliest stages of implementation; thus, virtually all program efforts were prototypes, and key models were experiments. Our instructions were emphatic: please, no self-congratulatory presentations. We wanted presenters to share their program warts under the theory that we could learn most from mistakes, problems, and difficulties.

Photo courtesy of the Science
Museum of Minnesota

Did we succeed? Yes, mostly. Many case study presentations hit the mark, were stimulating and provocative, and launched vigorous discussions among the participant work teams. Because the overall participant group represented such an eclectic array of the most significant PUR programs and efforts in both the United States and Europe, we were able to organize diverse work teams that crossed cultures, institutions, and professional lines. Participants were assigned to work teams of eight or nine members each. Discussion sessions lasting several hours followed each set of case study presentations covering the targeted PUR domains. These discussions formed the heart of the conference. Often stimulating, occasionally frustrating, but always interesting, these discussions yielded significant ideas and strategies around each domain. For a detailed summary of these discussions as well as all case study presentations and participant poster case studies, readers may wish to visit the conference Web site at http://pie.smm.org/pur.

Photo courtesy of the Science Museum of Minnesota

Photo courtesy of the Science Museum of Minnesota

While this volume attempts to provide an overall synthesis of the major themes, strategies, and issues associated with the fledgling PUR movement, the following conclusions were summarized immediately following the conference by the conference planning team and have guided our thinking as we proceeded to develop the contributed chapters found in this volume.

PUR IS AN EMERGING EFFORT WITHIN THE INFORMAL SCIENCE EDUCATION COMMUNITY, BUT IT'S TOO EARLY TO CALL IT A TREND

The interest in this conference and the enthusiasm for continuing the dialogue beyond this event are signals from the field that PUR is finding a voice in our institutions' program priorities. There was a clear sense from this conference that a threshold of PUR activity was beginning to happen in the informal sector, but we need more time, support, and experimentation to produce a confident and workable set of model strategies. There was general consensus that a PUR initiative could have a profound impact not only on the institutional sector that would drive it, but also on the public audience sector that would benefit from it.

THE "WHAT" QUESTION REGARDING PUR NEEDS MORE ATTENTION

What does "understanding" mean in the context of contemporary research? Can we truly expect the public to "understand" the content and process of research? What are the elements of research that are most important to convey to the public, and are we striving more for "awareness of," "appreciation of," "engagement in," or "interest in" research than "understanding of" research? Should PUR focus on contemporary or current research stories only, or do historical research stories have an important role? Participants at the conference felt that answers to these questions will make a significant difference in how PUR programs are structured, conducted, and pursued in the future. As one participant expressed it, "While I'm not sure I have a clear definition of PUR that cleanly separates 'research' from 'science,' I think I'll know it when I see it." Another participant expressed similar sentiments: "I have still come away confused by the difference between understanding of the process of 'science' versus 'research.' Perhaps there is none, but maybe there is."

Ken Keller, professor of science, technology and public policy at the Humphrey Institute of Public Affairs at the University of Minnesota and one of the conference's designated commentators, was more expansive about this question of how to define PUR in relation to or separate from current science:

> Although the nagging question of how to define PUR as an issue separate from current science continued throughout the meeting, . . . I came to the conclusion that PUR is a necessary part of explaining current science, but that already completed science provides us with a very valuable opportunity to help the public to understand the research process. Necessity and opportunity are the two words that describe the difference in the role of PUR for new science and old science. To really make clear where current science is, we need to convey how scientific questions are asked and answered, what kinds of questions can be asked and answered through science and what kinds cannot. . . . The very complexity and uncertainty of unfolding science makes the job of explaining the research process pretty difficult (try it on particle physics or determining genetic function, or explaining the experimental difficulties in being certain about stem cell transformation). However, when the whole story is complete, it is a good deal easier to explain the process in a historical framework—hence the opportunity provided by completed science to increase PUR.

A CANDID AND HONEST LEARNING COMMUNITY NEEDS TO BE ENCOURAGED AROUND PUR

Rather than a group trumpeting their successes and congratulating themselves for their efforts, there needs to be more a forthright exchange of the problems, mistakes, and occasional failures that will undoubtedly emerge during the formative stages of PUR development within the informal science institution sector. This needs to be encouraged now while the PUR movement is being formed. As a conference participant noted, "I learned a tremendous amount about the different perspectives of communicating science and research. I don't pretend to understand how a museum exhibit is put together, but it was fascinating to listen to various participants describe how they approached problems." Another added, "The media participants (I'm a museum person) were particularly helpful in expanding my perspective and gaining appreciation of each other's assets/strengths. I learned a lot about where others are placing their emphasis in PUR. I heard of some barriers to collaboration with the media that I have not envisioned. I came away feeling like we can contribute to PUR in some very tangible ways." Another participant suggested the creation of an informal "online PUR veranda" where practitioners could upload their PUR activities and ideas, add comments, and exchange ideas in a more user-driven fashion than a more formal edited Web site or listserv model. The essential point is to create some friendly social venues and accessible means for the emergent PUR practitioner community to share their experiences as they move forward.

MORE AUDIENCE RESEARCH NEEDS TO BE CONDUCTED TO DETERMINE THE BEST WAYS OF ALIGNING PUR WITH KEY PUBLIC AUDIENCE INTERESTS AND NEEDS

While there was general agreement about the importance of PUR, there was less agreement around the best ways to connect PUR with the various audiences served by the informal education sector. Undertaking some key audience research to better understand the "values proposition" for PUR audiences was deemed an important priority at the conference. A participant summed this need up nicely: "I still want to know what it is about research that we want the public to understand. And, I also didn't really get any clarity about how to focus the PUR programs for different publics." Another participant, Valerie Knight-Williams, a professional evaluator, remarked on the need to organize a front-end audience research project that would focus on the perceptions, attitudes, misconceptions, and life experiences of selected nontraditional audiences relating to current and ongoing scientific research. Some of the questions that could be explored include the following:

- What does the public perceive science research is?
- What questions does the public have about science research and the research process?
- What misconceptions about science research and the research process do they hold?
- What are some of the prevailing attitudes surrounding their understanding of science research?
- What aspects of current ongoing research is the public interested in?
- What examples from their own lives can they draw from in which they have engaged in the research process?

Another participant suggested a series of coordinated audience focus groups at several sites across the country to uncover public interests, attitudes, fears, and hopes concerning current science and research and to obtain reaction to our best PUR ideas.

THE ROLE OF THE "PUBLIC'S VOICE" IN PUR PROGRAMS HAS TREMENDOUS POTENTIAL

Exploring ways to engage the public in the telling of PUR stories and the associated social, political, and cultural issues created great interest at the conference. There was a sense among participants that PUR has significant potential to engage our institution's visitors and the general public in new ways. A dialogic model that has museums/media in a mediator role connecting scientists, the research issues, and the public was advanced but not fully developed at the conference. As Ken Keller further noted in his comments about the conference, "The role of museums as intermediaries between scientists and the public has a number of interpretations, all interesting and useful—honest brokers, convenors of dialogues that allow the public to weigh in on issues that go beyond the science itself (ethics, distributional justice, cost), interpreters, and even teachers of the scientists (helping them to understand public sensitivities and public reactions)."

REDUCING BARRIERS TO CROSS-INSTITUTION COLLABORATION WAS A HIGH PRIORITY

This conference was the first significant gathering of the larger community of practitioners involved in PUR. A key step for encouraging and supporting broader and more consistent collaboration will be to address the structural barriers and persistent institutional practices that prevent meaningful collaboration, including restrictive legal agreements, such as intellectual property rights and copyrights. Some excellent suggestions surfaced during the conference to begin addressing these issues systematically so that the entire PUR community could advance. One participant expressed the hope "that museums work more closely together, share material, and start simple. Waiting for surveys and large-scale efforts to get in place drains the momentum." He also hoped that "more perspectives from scientists themselves, as well as the science writing community, will be included in future PUR efforts. These clearly are different cultures that don't understand each other very well." Another participant was more specific. She suggested changing the way scientists are recognized by their employers and funders so that their involvement in science education and science communication is given as much kudos as publishing in the scientific journals. In the United Kingdom, this would involve changing the Research Assessment Exercise so that PUR is taken into account in judging the quality of each university department.

THE NATIONAL SCIENCE FOUNDATION, THE NATIONAL INSTITUTES OF HEALTH, AND OTHER GOVERNMENT FUNDERS OF SCIENTIFIC RESEARCH SHOULD ESTABLISH A MORE TRANSPARENT SYSTEM TO ENABLE PUR OUTLETS (MUSEUMS AND SCIENCE PRODUCERS) TO IDENTIFY AND LINK UP WITH RESEARCH GROUPS WITHIN UNIVERSITIES AND PRIVATE LABORATORIES TO PURSUE PUR PROGRAMS AND PROJECTS

Partnership and collaboration opportunities are left too much to chance and serendipity. Steps that would encourage greater collaboration include having PUR dollars attached to research grants as a percentage of the overall grant and creating a "matchmaker" clearinghouse for linking researchers needing to publicize and disseminate their research with PUR practitioners. We were often reminded during our discussions that the partnership opportunities between museums and media are rich with possibilities. As Ken Keller noted, "The partnership with media could be very productive in both directions— the media linking to the museums when people want more depth, and the museums having available some of the sophisticated products produced by the media," hence the very significant value of a museum/media clearinghouse of resources, products, contacts, and materials.

PUR FUNDERS SHOULD CREATE A "BIGGER TENT" FOR PUR EFFORTS TO ENCOURAGE EXPERIMENTATION AND INNOVATION

Funding organizations should support a wider variety of PUR program efforts that attempt to test an extensive range of approaches and strategies. There was an undercurrent of feeling at the conference that the big PUR players, such as the London Science Museum's Wellcome Wing or the Boston Museum of Science's Current Science & Technology Center, were largely unrealistic models to export to the rest of the field. Large, expensive, and staff intensive, these models are beyond the means of most institutions. Participants at the conference were more in favor of encouraging and supporting a divergent playing field with lots of PUR experiments and ways to share the successes and failures that result.

A SUSTAINABILITY MODEL FOR PUR EFFORTS NEEDS TO BE THOUGHT THROUGH CAREFULLY

If an institution engages in long-term PUR programs and exhibits, there will certainly be increased financial and staffing consequences. How such additional costs are borne by the institution will require some novel and innovative strategies. Sustainability strategies are especially critical given the widely held assumption that PUR efforts will not be a robust attendance draw to our institutions or to our media programs. Of course, funders such as the National Science Foundation (NSF) have tools that could encourage development of a diverse array of PUR efforts of different scales and across different institutional types that could point the way toward sustainability or help minimize institutional operating costs. These tools include adjusting matching or cost-share requirements for PUR-based projects, increasing length of project periods, and providing additional avenues of support to add a PUR layer to ongoing program, research, or exhibit efforts.

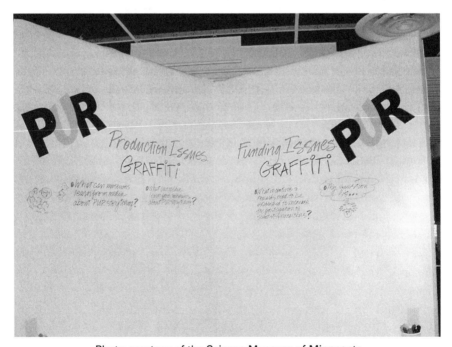

Photo courtesy of the Science Museum of Minnesota

INTERNATIONAL DISCUSSIONS AROUND PUR SHOULD BE CONTINUED

A unique and appreciated aspect of this conference was the involvement of a strong contingent of experienced PUR practitioners from Europe, especially the United Kingdom. Many participants commented that this international-ization did much to broaden and deepen the discussions and the range of ideas that found expression during the conference. There was strong consen-sus of the need to find ways to continue a substantive international dialogue around PUR models and strategies. The NSF is to be congratulated for sup-porting the international representation at this conference. It was clearly a much richer discussion because of it.

IT TAKES MANY DEDICATED PEOPLE TO SUCCESSFULLY CONDUCT AN INTERNATIONAL CONFERENCE

Of course, the final conclusion we derived from this conference was that it was an undertaking of great challenge, complexity, and, okay, fun. I am indebted to the NSF, which provided funds to conduct this conference, and to Hyman Field, who has been steadfastly committed to the effort to improve PUR within the sci-ence museum and science media communities. I am also deeply grateful to many staff from the Science Museum of Minnesota who were involved in the planning and implementation of the conference and who deserve more congratulations than I can possibly convey for a job well done. I would start with the core com-mittee that conceived, debated, and planned the program and the process un-derlying the conference. I have the greatest admiration for them all. They include my co-PIs for the project, Anne Hornickel, head of museum programs; Don Pohlman, director, Peoples and Cultures Program; and Ron Lawrenz, head of re-search and collections. We enjoyed spirited discussion, lots of homework, and numerous missed deadlines. Our staff discussions were enriched with a superb group of conference advisers who included Carol Lynn Alpert, manager, Current Science & Technology Program, Museum of Science, Boston; Graham Farmelo, director, Dana Centre Project, Museum of Science, London; Richard Hudson, di-rector of science, Twin Cities Public Television; Ken Keller, professor of science, technology, and policy, Hubert H. Humphrey Institute of Public Affairs, Univer-sity of Minnesota; Rob Semper, executive associate director, The Exploratorium; David A. Ucko, president, Museums + More, LLC; and Bonnie Van Dorn, exec-utive director, Association of Science-Technology Centers. A special thanks to Cynthia McArthur, who provided insightful counsel on the conference process.

Of course, the real coordination of the event fell disproportionately. The two staff who shouldered the greatest responsibility for implementing the conference details were Janelle Doyle, our overall conference coordinator, who kept us on track and maintained a lively repartee with our participants, and Valerie Lattery, who shined with a passion for detail and gracious hospitality. Unsung heroes included the ever-present Mark Rindfleisch, who handled the myriad audiovisual needs and challenges with calmness and skill, and Sylvia Crannell, who cast her wise view over the whole proceedings and offered timely advice to keep us on track. I would also thank Jackie Hoff, Rebecca Newberry, Deborah Schoenholz, and Kate Hintz, who spent many hours transforming our school entry and commons area into the PUR Café and exhibit area. They did a lot to make our space comfortable and welcoming. I also bow in tribute to Graham Farmelo, Bruce Lewenstein, and Ken Keller, who, as conference commentators, added positive value and articulate reflection to the entire conference. Their leadership, good humor, and intellectual acuity were key additives to the fuel empowering our conference discussions and outcomes. And finally, I need to thank and acknowledge the participants and lead presenters of the conference whose spirited discussion and engagement throughout was a testament to the importance of PUR and our collective efforts to develop it programmatically within our institutions. The participants included the following:

Ackerman, Steve, SSEC/CIMSS/AOS, University of Wisconsin, Madison

Airhart, Marc, lead producer, Edge of Discovery, Earth & Sky, Byrd & Block Communications, Inc.

Alpert, Carol Lynn (adviser), director, strategic projects, Museum of Science, Boston

Andorfer, Greg, executive director, chief executive officer, Maryland Science Center

Augenbraun, Eliene, president, chief executive officer, ScienCentral, Inc.

Bandelli, Andrea, international partnerships manager, Science Center, Amsterdam

Beck, L. Tony, program officer, SEPA, National Center for Research Resources

Bell, Larry, senior vice president for research development and production, Museum of Science, Boston

Birtzer, Carol, coordinator of distance learning, Bell Museum of Natural History, University of Minnesota

Bonney, Rick, director of education, Cornell Lab of Ornithology

Bossert, Carol, museum consultant, CB Services

Chittenden, David, vice president for education, Science Museum of Minnesota

Curry Rogers, Kristi, curator of paleontology, Science Museum of Minnesota

Dawson, Jim, senior news editor, *Physics Today* magazine

Dean, Cornelia, former science editor, *New York Times*

Devitt, Terry, director, research communication, editor and project coordinator, *The Why Files*, University of Wisconsin, Madison

Duensing, Sally, director, Center for Informal Learning and Schools, University of California, Santa Cruz

Durant, John, chief executive, At-Bristol, England

Farmelo, Graham (adviser), director, Dana Cenre Project Science Museum of London

Field, Hyman, senior advisor for public understanding of research, National Science Foundation

Fink, Laurie, project leader, Human Body Gallery, Science Museum of Minnesota

Finke, Coe Leta, graduate student researcher, Lawrence Hall of Science, University of California, Berkeley

Hamilton, Patrick, director of environmental sciences, Science Museum of Minnesota

Hauser, Walter, head, Center for New Technology, Deutsches Museum, Germany

Hellenga, Rachel, associate vice president of production and new ventures, Chicago Children's Museum

Hilke, D. D., executive director, Children's Museum of Utah

Hone, Bob, creative director, Red Hill Studios

Hoppe, Beth, director of science programs, Thirteen/WNET

Hornickle, Anne, head of museum programs, Science Museum of Minnesota

Hudson, Richard (adviser), director of science, Twin Cities Public Television (TCPT-TV)

Hurren, Caroline, head, consultation and education, The Wellcome Trust

Ivinson, Adrian, director, Harvard Center for Neurodegeneration and Repair, Harvard Medical School

Kanter, David, assistant professor, Northwestern University

Keller, Ken (adviser), Charles M. Denny, Jr., professor of science, technology, and public policy, Humphrey Institute of Public Affairs, University of Minnesota

Kern, Steven E., assistant professor of pharmaceutics, anesthesiology, and bioengineering, University of Utah

Knight-Williams, Valerie, Knight-Williams Research Communications

Kutner, Lawrence, codirector, Center for Mental Health and Media, Harvard Medical School

Lawrenz, Ron, head of research and collections, Science Museum of Minnesota

Leshner, Alan, chief executive officer, American Association for the Advancement of Science

Lewenstein, Bruce, associate professor, science communication, and former editor, *Public Understanding of Science*, Cornell University

Linde, Nancy, producer, *Nova*

Marshak, Marvin, professor of physics and astronomy, University of Minnesota

Martin, Laura, research director for the Center for Teaching and Learning, The Exploratorium

Mayfield, Heather, deputy head, Science Museum of London

McElroy, Tim, director of educational technologies, Liberty Science Center

Mendez, Flavio, director, SpaceLink Update Center, Maryland Science Center

Molinaro, Marco, chief education officer, Center for Biophotonic Science and Technology, University of California, Davis

Mouw, Michael, multimedia director, Minnesota Historical Society

Myllykoski, Mikko, head of exhibition planning, Heureka, Finnish Science Center

Nader, Richard, director, Institute for Pacific Asia, Texas A&M University

Naumann, Joerg, head of science unit, German Hygiene Museum

Newlin, J., director of physical sciences, Science Museum of Minnesota

Norton, Sue, head of production, Discovery Digital Networks (Science Channel)

Ogawa, Yoshikazu, science educator, Division of Science Education, National Science Museum, Tokyo

Paola, Chris, director, National Center for Earth-Surface Dynamics, University of Minnesota

Polman, Don, director of the people's and cultures gallery, Science Museum of Minnesota

Redline, Andy, director, paleontology program, Science Museum of Minnesota

Roberts, Doug, astronomer, Adler Planetarium (joint appointment with Northwestern University)

Roberts, Rebecca, technology reporter, *The World*, National Public Radio

Roman, Christine, associate director of science and galleries, St. Louis Science Center

Rosendahl, Jeffrey D., education and public outreach director, Office of Space Science, NASA

Rosenthal, Beryl, director of exhibitions and public programs, MIT Museum

Russell, Bob, principal, Learning Experience Design, LLC, and executive director, Self-Reliance Foundation/Acceso Hispano

Semper, Rob (adviser), executive associate director, The Exploratorium, San Francisco

Shane, Orrin, program director, informal science education, National Science Foundation

Shelley, Mark, chief executive officer, executive producer, Sea Studios Foundation

Storksdieck, Martin, senior research associate, Institute of Learning Innovation

Sucher, Walter, head, department of science and education, SWR TV, Germany

Tang, Carol, assistant chair, senior science educator, California Academy of Science

Terrill, Bronwyn, Dolan DNA Learning

Ucko, David (adviser), president, Museums + More, LLC

Van Dorn, Bonnie (adviser), executive director, Association of Science-Technology Centers

Vescia, François, Web chief editor, Cité des Sciences et de l'Industrie, Paris

Weiss, Martin, director of science, New York Hall of Science

Wolff, Tobias, manager, Exhibition Earth, Universum Science Center, Bremen, Germany

Zinnen, Tom, biotechnology policy and outreach specialist, University of Wisconsin Extension, Biotechnology Center

Bibilography

Carol Bossert

The following bibliography cites resources from the available literature to inform further discussion, research, and practice in activities that address the public understanding of science and research. The cited literature has been orga-nized into four categories: research that assesses the public's attitudes toward contemporary science issues such as cloning, genetically modified foods, and medical technologies; research and commentary that address scientists' roles in communicating with the public, including a survey on the attitudes of scientists; teaching methods that attempt to bring contemporary science into the classroom; and research, commentary, and methods used in communicating contemporary science to broad audiences. This bibliography is not meant to be exhaustive; rather, it should be greeted as the basis of what can become a rich body of literature related to activities that strive to increase public understanding of research and its "best practices."

PUBLIC ATTITUDES ABOUT CONTEMPORARY SCIENCE

Brennan, M., L. Frewer, S. Kuznesof, S. Miles, M. Ness, and C. Ritson. 2002. Public preferences for informed choice under conditions of risk uncertainty. *Public Understanding of Science* 11, no. 4: 363–72.

Brossard, D., A. Kroepsch, and M. C. Nisbet. 2003. Framing science: The stem cell controversy in an age of press/politics. *Harvard International Journal of Press/Politics* 8, no. 2: 36–70.

Carlsson, H., J. Hagelin, and J. Hau. 2003. An overview of surveys on how people view animal experimentation: Some factors that may influence the outcome. *Public Understanding of Science* 12, no. 1: 67–81.

Consumers' Association. 2002. *GM dilemmas: Consumers and genetically modified foods.* London: Consumers' Association.

Einsiedel, E. F. 2002. Assessing a controversial medical technology: Canadian public consultations on xenotransplantation. *Public Understanding of Science* 11, no. 4: 315–31.

Emslie, C., K. Hunt, and G. Watt. 2003. A chip off the old block? Lay understandings of inheritance among men and women in mid-life. *Public Understanding of Science* 12, no. 1: 47–65.

Flagg, B. N. 2001. Gender differences in interest in contemporary science topics. Paper presented at The Leading Edge: Enhancing the Public Understanding of Research, Boston Museum of Science, Boston.

Hines, P. J. T. 2001. The dynamics of scientific controversies. *AgBioForum* 4, nos. 3–4.

Hornig Priest, S. 2002. Issues emerging through the 2002 AAAS Roundtable on Biotechnology Policy Formation in Europe and North America. *Science Communication* 24, no. 2: 222–28.

Irwin, Alan, and Brian Wynne, eds. 1996. *Misunderstanding science: The public reconstruction of science and technology.* New York: Cambridge University Press.

Jones, I. 2002. Going public: Public attitudes to science and research. *Wellcome News* 32, nos. 8–9. www.wellcome.ac.uk.

Lynch, M., and R. McNally. 2003. Science, common sense, and DNA evidence: A legal controversy about the public understanding of science. *Public Understanding of Science* 12, no. 1: 83–103.

Nelkin, Dorothy. 1984. *Science in the streets: Report of the Twentieth Century Fund Task Force on the Communication of Scientific Risk.* New York: Priority Press.

Office of Science and Technology and the Wellcome Trust. 2002. Science and the public: A review of science communication and public attitudes to science in Britain. www.wellcome.ac.uk.

Palmer, C. 2003. Risk perception: Another look at the "white male" effect. *Health, Risk and Society* 5, no. 1: 71–83.

Roth, W., and S. Lee. 2002. Scientific literacy as collective practice. *Public Understanding of Science* 11, no. 1: 33–56.

Sublet, Virginia H., V. T. Covello, and T. L. Tinker, eds. 1996. *Scientific uncertainty and its influence on the public communication process.* Dordrecht: Kluwer Academic Publishers.

Waiting for a signal: Public attitudes toward global warming, the environment, and geophysical research. www.agu.org/sci_soc/attitude_study.html.

Wellcome Trust. 1988. Public perspectives on human cloning. www.wellcome.ac.uk.

Wynne, B. 2001. Creating public alienation: Expert cultures of risk and ethics on GMOs. *Science as Culture* 10, no. 4: 445–82.

RESEARCH SCIENTISTS AND PUBLIC UNDERSTANDING

Byrand, Sherri L. 1997. Venturing from researcher to reporter. *Science* 276: 2063.

Hughes, Catherine. 2001. Shackled to stereotypes. *Science and Public Affairs,* February.

Pollock, John, and D. Steven. 1997. Don't patronize the public. *New Scientist* 155, no. 2101: 49.

Riley, D. M. 1996. The representation and interpretation of the image of science and scientists at a museum of natural history. Ph.D. diss., Miami University, Oxford, Ohio.

Wellcome Trust. 2002. Survey of scientists. www.wellcome.ac.uk.

TEACHING AND CONTEMPORARY SCIENCE

Bruce, M. C., and M. DiGennaro King. 2003. Inspired by real science. *Science and Children NSTA Journal* 40, no. 5: 30–34.

Chambers, D. W. 1983. Stereotypic images of the scientists: The draw-a-scientist test. *Science Education* 67: 255–65.

Far more than required high school coursework. 1998. *Science* 279, no. 5358: 1858–60.

Finson, K. D. 1985. A study of student attitudes toward science-technology-society resulting from visitation to a science-technology museum. Ph.D. diss., Kansas State University, Manhattan.

Gross, Paul R. 1997. Science without scientists. *New York Times*, December 1.

Kahle, J. B. 1987. Images of scientists: Gender issues in science classrooms. In *Key Centre for School Science and Mathematics: What research says to the science and mathematics teachers*. Perth: Key Centre, Curtin University of Technology.

Levinson, Ralph, ed. 1994. *Teaching science*. New York: Routledge.

Mason, C. L., J. B. Kahle, and A. L. Gardner. 1991. Draw-a-scientist test: Future implications. *School Science and Mathematics* 91: 193–98.

Schauble, L., L. E. Klopfer, and K. Raghaven. 1991. Students' transition from an engineering model to a science model of experimentation. *Journal of Research in Science Teaching* 28, no. 9: 859–82.

COMMUNICATING CONTEMPORARY SCIENCE

Allen, S. 1997. Using scientific inquiry activities in exhibit explanations. *Informal Science Education* 81, special issue, no. 6: 715–34.

Anholt, Robert R. H. 1994. *Dazzle 'em with style: The art of oral scientific presentation*. New York: W. H. Freeman.

Augustine, Norman R. 1998. What we don't know does hurt us: How scientific illiteracy hobbles society. *Science* 279, no. 5357: 1640–41.

Back to bases. 2003. *Economist* 81.

Blum, Deborah, and Mary Knudson, eds. 1997. *A field guide for science writers: The official guide of the National Association of Science Writers*. New York: Oxford University Press.

Burge, J. 2002. In search of science on the big screen. *Science Reviews* 27, no. 3: 165–68.

Burkett, Warren. 1986. News reporting, science, medicine, and high technology. Ph.D. diss., Iowa State University, Ames.

Chen, Milton. 1994. Television and informal science education: Assessing the past, present and future of research. In *Informal science learning: What research says about television, science museums and community-based projects*, ed. V. Crane, H. Nicholson, M. Chen, and S. Bitgood. Dedham, Mass.: Research Communications, Ltd.

Cooper, Will. 1998. Science in the public eye. *The Skeptical Inquirer* 22, no. 2: 25.

Crawford, Susan Y., J. M. Hurd, and A. C. Weller. 1996. *From print to electronic: The transformation of scientific communication.* Medford, N.J.: Published for the American Society for Information Science by Information Today.

Cribb, J., and T. S. Hartomo. 2002. *Sharing knowledge: A guide to effective science communication.* Collingwood: Csiro Publishing.

Dangers of publication by press conference. 1998. [Editorial] *Nature* 397.

Day, Robert A. 1994. *How to write and publish a scientific paper.* Phoenix: Oryx Press.

Delacote, Goery. 1998. Putting science in the hands of the public. *Science* 280, no. 5372: 2054–55.

Durant, J. 1992. *Museums and the public understanding of science.* London: Science Museum.

Flagg, B. N., and V. Knight-Williams. 2002. Marketing science media to the public. *The Informal Learning Review* 57 (November–December).

Gastel, Barbara. 1983. *Presenting science to the public.* Philadelphia: ISI Press.

Goldsmith, Maurice. 1986. *The science critic: A critical analysis of the popular presentation of science.* London: Routledge and Kegan Paul.

Hoffstadt, R. M. 2002. Learning theory and current science. *The Informal Science Review* 57, no. 14.

———. 2002. Presenting the uncertain: Incorporating current science into science centers. Master's thesis, Bank Street College, New York.

———. 2002. Tensions to consider when presenting current science. *The Informal Learning Review* 56, no. 1.

———. 2003. Current science and nontraditional science presentations in science museums. *Informal Science Review* 59, no. 2.

Holton, G., and W. A. Blanpied, eds. 1976. *Science and its public: The changing relationship.* Boston: D. Reidel.

Kenny, Peter. 1982. *A handbook of public speaking for scientists and engineers.* Bristol: Adam Hilger Ltd.

Lewenstein, B. 2000. Why the "public understanding of science" field is beginning to listen to the audience. In *Transforming practice: Selections from the Journal of*

Museum Education 1992–1999, ed. H. L. Silverman. Washington, D.C.: Museum Education Roundtable.

Locke, David. 1998. Voices of science. *The American Scholar* 67, no. 3: 103.

Meadows, A. J. 1998. *Communicating research.* San Diego: Academic Press.

Nelkin, Dorothy, ed. 1995. *Selling science: How the press covers science and technology.* New York: W. H. Freeman.

Nicholson, H. J., F. L. Weiss, and P. B. Campbell. 1994. Evaluation in informal science education: Community-based programs. In *Informal science learning: What research says about television, science museums and community-based projects,* ed. V. Crane, H. Nicholson, M. Chen, and S. Bitgood. Dedham, Mass.: Research Communications, Ltd.

Paradis, James G., and M. L. Zimmerman. 1997. *The MIT guide to science and engineering communication.* Cambridge, Mass.: MIT Press.

Public engagement with science. 2003. [Editorial] *Science,* 977.

Rees, M. 2002. Science, communication, and the media. *Interdisciplinary Science Reviews* 27, no. 1: 10–12.

Rogers, C. L. 2000. Making the audience a key participant in the science communication process. *Science and Engineering Ethics* 6, no. 4: 553–57.

Treise, D. 2002. Advancing science communication: A survey of science communicators. *Science Communication* 23, no. 3: 310–22.

Venables, J. Rugby, ed. 2002. *Communication skills for engineers and scientists.* Warwickshire: Institution of Chemical Engineers.

White, Fred D. 1996. *Communicating technology: Dynamic processes and models for writers.* New York: HarperCollins.

Willems, J. 2003. Bringing down barriers: Public communication should be part of common scientific practice. *Nature* 422, no. 3: 470.

Readers interested in following the emerging literature of public understanding of research may consult two resources: 1) A regular bibliography of new scholarly work is published in each issue of the journal *Public Understanding of Science,* published by Sage (www.sagepub.com/journal.aspx?pid=9675), 2) A bibliography of new publications, including commentaries, reviews, reports, and scholarly work, is compiled monthly by the WellcomeTrust Library and made available through its psci-comlit service, available through its general science communication Web site at http://psci-com.org.uk/.

Index

MUSEUMS AND SCIENCE CENTERS

EXHIBITIONS, PROGRAMS, AND PROJECTS

PARTNER, PROFESSIONAL, AND RESEARCH ORGANIZATIONS

GENERAL
(includes historic exhibits and institutions)

About the Contributors

Marc Airhart is a producer for the Earth and Sky Radio Series based in Austin, Texas. He works to promote PUR through the Edge of Discovery radio shows and online scientist profiles. He can be reached at mairhart@earthsky.org.

Carol Lynn Alpert serves as director, Strategic Projects, for the Museum of Science, Boston. She led the team that created the museum's innovative, award-winning Current Science & Technology Center. Alpert is principal investigator for the Museum's NIH-NCRR-SEPA-funded Health Science Education Partnership with Harvard Medical School, the Harvard School of Public Health, Whitehead Institute for Biomedical Research, and other associated Boston health research institutions. She also serves as senior investigator for educational outreach for the NSF-funded Nanoscale Science and Engineering Center collaboration between Harvard, Massachusetts Institute of Technology, University of California, Santa Barbara, and the Museum of Science. She can be reached at calpert@mos.org.

Eliene Augenbraun, D.O., Ph.D., is president and CEO, ScienCentral, Inc., a company she cofounded in 1996. The company produces television, Web, and educational science programs. From 1995 to 1997, Dr. Augenbraun served as an AAAS Diplomacy Fellow at the U.S. Agency for International Development, studying media and political conflict. There she initiated a study of how mass media affects political conflict and reconciliation. She obtained her Ph.D. in biology from Columbia University in 1992, was a medical illustrator with a D.O. from the New York College of Osteopathic Medicine in 1986, and was a National Institutes of Health Postdoctoral Research Fellow at The Johns Hopkins School of Medicine. She can be reached at ea@sciencentral.com.

Larry Bell has worked at the Museum of Science, Boston, since 1971 in a variety of roles in the Education and Exhibit Divisions and is currently senior vice president for Research, Development, and Production. He received a B.S. in physics and an M.S. in earth and planetary science from the Massachusetts Institute of Technology in 1971. He can be reached at lbell@mos.org.

Rick Bonney is director of the education program at the Cornell Lab of Ornithology, where he has worked since 1983. He is the founder of the Lab's Citizen Science Program, and his research focuses on best methods of incorporating inquiry-based science education into classrooms and community programs nationwide, as well as on the social and educational impacts of citizen science participation. He is also a correspondent for *Wild Earth*, journal of the Wildlands Project, and a member of the advisory board of the Vitamin L Children's Chorus, which teaches character education through performances in schools throughout North America. He can be reached at reb5@cornell.edu.

Rick Borchelt is director of communications and public affairs at the Whitehead Institute for Biomedical Research in Cambridge, Massachusetts. A biologist by training, he has held science communication posts in academia, industry, and government, including special assistant for public affairs in the Clinton White House. His special research interest is communication about science public policy. He can be reached at rick_borchelt@wi.mit.edu.

Carol Bossert is an independent museum consultant based in Maryland and a member of the Museum Group. She can be reached at bossert@erols.com.

Peter J. Bruns is vice president for Grants and Special Programs at the Howard Hughes Medical Institute. He taught genetics at Cornell University for more than 30 years, where he also served as chairman of the Section of Genetics and

Development, associate director of the Cornell Biotechnology Program, director of the Division of Biological Sciences, and director of the Cornell Presidential Research Scholars. He helped develop the Cornell Institute for Biology Teachers and serves on the boards of directors of the Cornell Laboratory of Ornithology and the Boyce Thompson Institute for Plant Research. He can be reached at grantvpr@hhmi.org.

Christine Cansfield-Smith is the manager of the CSIRO *Discovery Center* in Canberra, Australia. From 1990 she was the science communication manager at the Australian Institute of Marine Science and then, from 1997, was responsible for the establishment of *Discovery*, a public showcase for CSIRO, Australia's largest research organization. She can be reached at Christine.Cansfield-Smith@csiro.au.

David Chittenden is the vice president of education at the Science Museum of Minnesota, where he initiated and oversees one of the largest museum-based education programs in the country. He has extensive experience developing and managing national and international science education, exhibit, and exchange projects. He can be reached at davec@smm.org.

Sir Neil Chalmers served for sixteen years as the director of the Natural History Museum in London and is currently the Warden of Wadham College, Oxford. Sir Neil trained at Oxford and Cambridge Universities as a zoologist, specializing in behavioral ecology based on studies of primates.

Cornelia Dean is the former science editor of the *New York Times* and currently a fellow at the Shorenstein Center at Harvard University's Kennedy School of Government.

Sally Duensing, Ph.D., is the project director for the Center for Informal Learning and School at the University of California, Santa Cruz. She previously worked at the Exploratorium developing exhibits and programs. She can be reached at sallyd@cats.ucsc.edu.

John Durant is chief executive of At-Bristol, an independent science and natural history center in the west of England. He is the founder and editor of the quarterly journal *Public Understanding of Science*, and has published widely on the history and public understanding of science and technology. He can be reached at john.durant@at-bristol.org.uk.

Albert A. Einsiedel Jr. is professor and executive director of the Institute for Professional Development, Faculty of Extension, University of Alberta. His research interests include the social and organizational issues surrounding e-learning systems in the context of continuing professional development. As an adult educator, he has been involved in the design, development, implementation, and evaluation of professional development programs of study as well as capacity building programs in the international development context. He can be reached at bert.einsiedel@ualberta.ca.

Edna F. Einsiedel is professor of communication studies at the University of Calgary and editor of the journal *Public Understanding of Science*. Her research interests include the social assessment of technology, with a particular focus on public participation in this process. Her research studies include the use of deliberative models such as citizen consensus conferences and citizen juries for policy questions on genomics and biotechnology. She can be reached at einsiede@ucalgary.ca.

John H. Falk, Ph.D., is founder and director of the Institute for Learning Innovation, an Annapolis, Maryland-based nonprofit learning research and development organization. He is known internationally for his research on free-choice learning, in particular for his efforts to understand why people visit museums, how they behave in these settings, and what the long-term impact of these experiences are on people's lives. He has published widely in the areas of education, biology, and psychology. Recent books include *Learning from Museums: Visitor Experiences and the Making of Meaning* (2000, AltaMira Press, with Lynn Dierking), *Free-Choice Science Education: How We Learn Science Outside of School* (2001, Teachers College Press), and *Lessons without Limit: How Free-Choice Learning Is Rransforming Education* (2002, AltaMira Press, with Lynn Dierking). He can be reached at falk@ilinet.org.

Graham Farmelo is director of the Dana Centre Project at the Science Museum, London, and associate professor of Physics at Northeastern University,

Boston. He was formerly head of exhibitions for the Museum's Wellcome Wing. He can be reached at g.farmelo@nmsi.ac.uk.

Mark D. Hertle is a former senior program officer at the Howard Hughes Medical Institute, where he managed grants to research institutions and informal science education institutions for pre-K–12 outreach in science education. His background includes a Ph.D. in developmental biology and management of an outreach program for teachers in Seattle.

Bruce V. Lewenstein is associate professor of science communication at Cornell University, former editor of the journal *Public Understanding of Science*, and editor of the book *When Science Meets the Public* (1992), translated into Korean in 2003. Trained as a science journalist and as a historian of science, he is coauthor of *The Establishment of Science in America: 150 Years of the American Association for the Advancement of Science*. He has taught science communication in Spain, South Africa, Australia, and Singapore, and presented scholarly papers on five continents. He is a member of the advisory board of Cornell Plantations, Cornell's botanical gardens, arboretum, and natural areas, and a member of the advisory board of the ScienCenter, a hands-on science center in Ithaca, New York. He can be reached at b.lewenstein@cornell.edu.

Nancy Linde is a television producer, writer, and director who specializes in science and technology documentaries. After spending more than twenty years at *Nova*, including a year-long attachment to the BBC's Science and Features Unit, she recently decided to try life as a freelancer. Currently, she is working on the development of a series about energy with David Grubin Productions and WETA. She can be reached at nlinde@tiac.net.

Laura Martin, Ph.D., is the research director for the Center for Teaching and Learning at the Exploratorium. She was previously the vice president for Education and Research at the Arizona Science Center.

Heather Mayfield is deputy head of the Science Museum, London, and head of Science Museum Live. She managed the "Who Am I?" and "Digitopolis" exhibitions in the Wellcome Wing. She can be reached at h.mayfield@nmsi.ac.uk.

Xerxes Mazda is manager of collections access at the Science Museum, London. He previously worked for seven years on the public engagement in controversy, and was responsible for the visitor feedback strategy and exhibits in the Wellcome Wing. He can be reached at x.mazda@nmsi.ac.uk.

Bill Nye is a licensed mechanical engineer in the State of Washington—really! He is better known as "Bill Nye, the Science Guy," writer, producer, and on-air host for the eponymously named nationally broadcast show that won an Emmy as best show; Nye won Emmys for best performer, best writing, and best producing. He now works with Noggin Television on MTV Networks. He can be reached at www.nyelabs.com.

Chris Paola teaches in the Department of Geology and Geophysics, University of Minnesota, Minneapolis. His research home is the S. Anthony Falls Laboratory in Minneapolis, where he is also director of the National Center for Earth-Surface Dynamics. He works on rivers and sedimentation, with emphasis on river dynamics over geologic time scales. He can be reached at cpaola@visi.com.

Don Pohlman is director of the Peoples and Cultures Gallery at the Science Museum of Minnesota. He has more than 25 years of exhibit design and development experience. He can be reached at dpohlman@smm.org.

Tim Radford is science editor of *The Guardian* newspaper, based in London. He can be reached at tim.radford@guardian.co.uk.

Rob Semper, Ph.D., a physicist and science educator, is executive associate director of the Exploratorium, and is responsible for leading the institution's work in developing programs of teaching and learning using exhibits, media, and Internet resources. Dr. Semper is the principle investigator on numerous science education, media, and research projects including leading the National Science Foundation–sponsored Center for Informal Learning and Schools, a research collaboration between the Exploratorium, the University of California, Santa Cruz, and King's College, London. Over the past ten years Dr. Semper has guided the development of the Exploratorium Web site program that has explored the role of museums in the online world. He can be reached at robs@exploratorium.edu.

Larry Stewart is professor and head of the Department of History, University of Saskatchewan, Saskatoon, Canada. He has published widely in the field of the history of science. He can be reached at stewartl@sask.usask.ca.

Martin Storksdieck, M.S., M.P.A., is a senior research associate at the Institute for Learning Innovation. His research interests include alternative measures for the public's understanding of science and research, factors that influence cognitive gains in free-choice learning environments, long-term and alternative outcomes of museum visits, and determinants of behavioral and attitudinal change. He can be reached at storksdieck@ilinet.org.

David A. Ucko, Ph.D., is president of Museums + More, LLC, a consulting practice focusing on creating competitive advantage through innovation, developing recreational learning experiences, and leadership counsel. Formerly, he was executive director for the Koshland Science Museum (National Academy of Sciences), president of Science City at Union Station and the Kansas City Museum, deputy director of the California Museum of Science and Industry, and vice president of Chicago's Museum of Science and Industry, in addition to serving as a presidential appointee to the National Museum Services Board. Ucko is an AAAS Fellow and was a chemistry professor at Antioch College and CUNY prior to entering the science museum field. He can be reached at ucko@museumsplusmore.com.